LAW IN THE SERVICE OF LEGITIMACY

Law in the Service of Legitimacy
Gender and Politics in Jordan

CATHERINE WARRICK
Villanova University, USA

ASHGATE

Published by
Ashgate Publishing Limited
Wey Court East
Union Road
Farnham
Surrey, GU9 7PT
England

Ashgate Publishing Company
Suite 420
101 Cherry Street
Burlington
VT 05401-4405
USA

www.ashgate.com

British Library Cataloguing in Publication Data
Warrick, Catherine.
Law in the service of legitimacy : gender and politics in Jordan.
1. Sociological jurisprudence--Jordan. 2. Women--Legal status, laws, etc.--Jordan. 3. Jordan--Politics and government.
I. Title
346.5'6950134-dc22

Library of Congress Cataloging-in-Publication Data
Warrick, Catherine.
Law in the service of legitimacy : gender and politics in Jordan / by Catherine Warrick.
p. cm.
Includes bibliographical references and index.
ISBN 978-0-7546-7587-7 (hardback) 1. Women--Legal status, laws, etc.--Jordan. 2. Women's rights--Jordan. 3. Law--Political aspects--Jordan. 4. Culture and law. I. Title.
KMM52.3.W37 2009
342.569508'78--dc22

2009015704

ISBN 978 0 7546 7587 7

Mixed Sources
Product group from well-managed forests and other controlled sources
www.fsc.org Cert no. SA-COC-1565
© 1996 Forest Stewardship Council
FSC

Printed and bound in Great Britain by
MPG Books Ltd, Bodmin, Cornwall.

Contents

Acknowledgements

I am indebted to a long line of scholars and friends for the existence of this book. The last few decades have seen the development of a large body of wonderful scholarship on gender issues in the Arab world, and this work has sparked my own interest and that of many others and formed the core of my understanding of the field. One of the pleasures of working in this field is its inherent interdisciplinarity, which allows the researcher to partake of the work of historians, anthropologists, political scientists, legal scholars, and many others. I therefore owe a debt of gratitude to many people I've never met, and I hope that they will approve of the way I have built on their earlier work.

The earliest incarnation of this study was my doctoral dissertation, for which Michael Hudson, Judith Tucker, and Mark Warren served as committee members, and Nathan Brown served as an external reader for part of the work. I am grateful for their assistance and guidance. Chapter 4 of this book was published in an earlier version in *Law and Society Review*; I thank the editor at the time, Herbert Kritzer, and several anonymous reviewers, all of whose suggestions greatly improved the article.

Grant support that allowed me to conduct the initial field research for this project was provided by the U.S. Department of Education's Fulbright-Hays Doctoral Dissertation Research Abroad program as well as the (no longer existing) U.S. Information Agency and the American Center of Oriental Research in Amman. A sabbatical semester at Villanova University allowed me to finish the writing and revision of the manuscript.

Among the many people in Jordan who gave generously of their time in interviews, conversations, and general helpfulness, I especially wish to thank Rana Taha, Theresa Phillips and Lo'ay Kreishan, Alain McNamara, Eman Nimri, Col. Walter Heidmous, the officers of the Family Protection Unit (later Directorate) and the military's Directorate of Military Women's Affairs, Judge Mohammad Tarawneh, Dr. Omar Aljazy, Ra'eada Freahat, Asma Khader, and Dr. Salah Bashir. I also thank Nihad Khdeir in Jordan and Laura Butterfield Linder in the United States for their able research assistance.

My editor at Ashgate, Eric Levy, has been kind and accommodating at every point of the process, and I thank him for his interest in the work and his efforts to make the process a smooth one. It was truly a pleasure to work with him.

I am especially grateful for the support and encouragement of my colleagues and friends, notably Bob Maranto, who thought there should be a book, Kimberly Cowell-Meyers, Borden Flanagan, Maria Toyoda, and everyone else who provides camaraderie in the academic trenches.

In a conversation years ago with a Jordanian colleague, we discovered that we both attributed our educations and our opportunities in life to the unswerving support of our fathers. No matter where a girl grows up, or what her circumstances, it seems that a good dad is one of the most important things she can have. I thank my own, Col. (ret.) Robert P. Warrick, Jr., for making sure I got every educational opportunity I wanted.

Finally, and most importantly, I would like to thank my patient spouse, Matthew DeBell, for his constructive criticism, his heroic service in reading nearly endless versions of the material for this book, and most of all for his constant encouragement and friendship.

PART I
The Pursuit of Legitimacy in Jordan

Chapter 1
Introduction

Introduction and Thesis

This book is a study of the relationship between culture and political legitimacy. Based on an analysis of issues of gender and law in the political system of Jordan, I argue that legitimacy, a crucial component of successful democratic systems, is significantly dependent upon cultural factors that affect the political system. This does not mean that a particular cultural basis is necessary for a political system to be legitimate but, rather, that the politicization of elements of culture contributes to the ability of the regime and other political actors to claim sociocultural legitimacy. Several factors contribute to legitimacy (see below), but the sociocultural strand of legitimation is the most fundamental, a sine qua non for state legitimation. States and particular regimes may gain or lose support on the basis of their functional administrative competence, but the issue of substantive sociocultural legitimacy is fundamental to the state's stability and, in the end, to the prospects for the development of democratic characteristics such as free contestation, equal rights and social tolerance.

Jordan, as a developing country, is particularly suited to this study because both the nature of the political system and the proper character of national culture are topics of intense and public debate. The state's pursuit of legitimacy is readily traced in its approach to gender issues and the law, an arena where the state seeks to entrench its legitimacy by engaging various social actors and appealing to more than one basis of governing authority. The debate over gender roles, particularly women's rights, has been a major contributor to the tendency of actors and scholars alike to see Jordanian society as characterized by "modern" and "traditional" forces locked into a zero-sum competition. This perception is flawed, however, because it rests upon a concept of tradition that, although often tactically useful in politics, is inadequate and misleading.

In the Jordanian case, the state is by far the most dominant actor in and shaper of the political system, and it is the question of the state's own legitimacy that brings the issue into the realm of political contestation. However, once the issue is politically salient, other actors can enter the legitimacy debate and seek to affect either the state's political position or their own by the mobilization of legitimacy issues. The sociocultural aspect of legitimacy has to do with appropriateness of the regime and the state within their social context, and thus the state finds it necessary to make and respond to claims about cultural authenticity. This is often accomplished through the creation, enforcement and reform of laws; the Jordanian system utilizes both state-created law derived from European models and *shari'a*-based (Islamic) law, the latter mostly in the area of family law (see Chapter 3). Both sources of law are deployed by the state, and challenged or defended by other actors, with an eye to claims about gender roles, rights and national culture.

I argue throughout this work that the legitimacy of the Jordanian state is woven from two sometimes contradictory, sometimes complementary strands, one traditionalist and the other liberal. I have also pointed out that the state legal system incorporates both Islamic and non-Islamic law. It might be tempting to draw a parallel between these pairs and view traditionalism and Islamic law as forces opposing women's rights, with liberalism and non-Islamic law serving to improve women's rights. Such a parallel, however, would be unwarranted; it is at best an oversimplification of the effects and uses of law with regard to women's rights. Some legal disadvantages for women are certainly located within the Islamically-constructed sphere of personal status law, but other uses of this law, such as the recent recognition of *khul'* divorce (Chapter 6), have served to improve the legal position of women. Likewise, the non-Islamic body of law contains provisions that are gender egalitarian (such as voting rights), or that improve the position of women (such as the parliamentary quota; see Chapter 7), but at the same time, non-Islamic law also does some of the most serious legal harm to women, as in the laws regarding nationality (Chapter 5) and honor crimes (Chapter 4). Therefore, it is important not to approach the issue of women's rights as a matter of *shari'a* burdens and liberal triumphs; the reality of the legal position of women is shaped for both good and ill by both types of law, as the state mobilizes them both in pursuit of its partly-traditionalist, partly-liberal legitimacy.

Legitimacy is a concept integral to political authority; it is that which provides the distinction between the power to rule and the right to rule. A government, or more broadly a state, that enjoys legitimacy is regarded by its citizens as an appropriate governing power. This is different, of course, from popularity; people may dislike the government (or its policies, or other aspects of the state) but still regard it as having the right to rule. Legitimacy is invaluable to states, not only because it reduces the extent to which coercive methods must be employed (as Gramsci argues with regard to hegemony), but also because it provides a positive justification for authority that creates a bond of duty between citizens and state. Several factors may contribute to the state's legitimacy among its citizens, including its policy successes, its administrative competence and its moral standing, but the most fundamental element of legitimacy, particularly in developing countries, is the aspect of cultural appropriateness. A state structure that, in its policies or its founding principles, is culturally disconnected from its society will find it difficult to justify its political power.

Not only the presence and degree but the *quality* of state legitimacy is a key determinant of the course of political development. Democratic development, specifically, requires that the state not only enjoy legitimacy but that its legitimacy be of a particular character favorable to the protection of important citizen rights and political processes. States, particularly in developing countries, may find it prudent or convenient to seek legitimacy on the basis of cultural authenticity; to the extent that this "authenticity" preserves (or creates) undemocratic social elements, the state's legitimacy and the path of democratization may well diverge. However, as states may appeal simultaneously to more than one source of legitimation, both democratic and antidemocratic elements may coexist in the political order, as is the case in Jordan. This phenomenon is an important influence on the character of political contestation in such systems and is particularly apparent with regard to gender issues.

An extensive literature exists on the importance of gender issues in political systems; most work has focused on such issues as they pertain to participation and contestation (the political participation of women; inclusion of often-marginalized interests into political life). In addition to these more apparent elements, gender issues, and particularly the social roles and rights of women, are connected to political legitimacy because they serve as an arena for contestation over authentic culture. This is because gender issues pervade many aspects of social life and are relevant far beyond the bounds of formal politics. It is common everywhere for women's roles to be considered most connected to the transmission of culture and the reproduction of social values through generations, and thus women become a symbol of cultural authenticity.[1] This does not mean that women themselves have no agency; women both participate in the maintenance of cultural norms regarding gender roles and, in other instances, challenge these roles. But it is important to recognize that women's social roles are politicized as *women's* roles, in a way that men's are not politicized as *men's* roles.

Both culture and legitimacy are generally recognized as important to understanding political systems, although they go in and out of fashion as subjects of research. The extent to which, and the means by which, political systems and governing regimes enjoy legitimacy in their societies is an important factor in democracy, democratization and political stability. Cultural variables are likewise important to political systems in a number of ways, having an effect on civil society, law, political behavior, the issues considered important in political life and, indeed, upon the nature of legitimacy and the foundation of the system. However, while

1 See Marie-Aimée Hélie-Lucas, "The Preferential Symbol for Islamic Identity: Women in Muslim Personal Laws," in Valentine Moghadam (ed.), *Identity Politics and Women: Cultural Reassertions and Feminisms in International Perspective* (Boulder: Westview Press, 1994) and Joseph Massad, *Colonial Effects: the Making of National Identity in Jordan* (New York: Columbia University Press, 2001), 99. This view of women's cultural role is not unique to Islam, of course, but found across cultures. Orit Avishai quotes an Orthodox rabbi's comment that "a society's cultural and moral hollowness is reflected in its women, and vice versa." ("'Doing Religion' in a Secular World: Women in Conservative Religions and the Question of Agency," *Gender and Society* 22:4 (2008): 409–433.) Helen Hardacre notes that religious fundamentalisms of all types share the "striking" characteristic that "women are called upon to embody and represent tradition." ("The Impact of Fundamentalisms on Women, the Family, and Interpersonal Relations," in Marty and Appleby (eds), *Fundamentalisms and Society*, (Chicago: University of Chicago Press, 1993), 139).

each of these topics has received significant attention over the last few decades, the nexus between the two has yet to be fully investigated.

Assumptions about the role of culture in politics have a marked effect on the study of the politics of the Arab world, and yet these assumptions are neither always openly acknowledged nor fully explored and justified. Problems of political legitimacy are common throughout the developing world, and in Middle Eastern cases are considered by many to be a product of the cultural elements that have led some scholars to argue that the region is "exceptional," not fully explicable by the tools of regular political science. Likewise, the treatment of tradition and modernity as poles in a competitive dichotomy, an approach which long ago lost favor among many political scientists, is still practiced in studies of the Arab world, both by general comparativists and by some area specialists. It is therefore useful to investigate a Middle Eastern case in the hope of elucidating further a political phenomenon that, I believe, is significant in the politics of all regions and in so doing to challenge persistent assumptions about both the role of culture in politics and political science and the place of tradition in Arab political systems.

The Jordanian case is well-suited to this study because it is a system undergoing an extended process of change in which issues of legitimacy are prominent; furthermore, it has had in recent years a relatively open political sphere in which competing views and goals are publicly visible. This is not to imply, of course, that access to the political system is fully democratic or that all interests are represented in civil society, but particularly with regard to issues of cultural authenticity and gender, debate is lively and far from one-sided.

The specific focus of this project is on law and gender, in part because culture is far too broad and complex a reality to be usefully treated in its entirety in a study such as this. It was therefore necessary to conceptualize the relationship between culture and political legitimacy fairly narrowly in order to identify the issues most likely to be of explanatory utility. Gender is a cultural characteristic[2] that is both universal and well-articulated locally; it permeates many areas of society and politics and forms a basis for both social organization and political action. Law, likewise, is a phenomenon of universal relevance which takes on specific local forms as a joint product of cultural forces and political demands. The relationship between these two spheres highlights important issues for the development of political legitimacy and the role of culture in political systems. These and other methodological issues are explained more fully below.

In the view of George Washington, "the true administration of justice is the firmest pillar of good government." The relevance of law to the quality of government extends well beyond its readily apparent effects in behavior regulation

2 Gender, as distinct from biological sex, is the social construction of sex-specific roles, virtues, restrictions and expectations for men and women. Gender is an element of society in itself, and other elements of society are "gendered;" politics, law, religion, economics, family structure, etc. are elements of sociocultural systems in which gender roles and associated values are reflected and carried out.

and dispute resolution. Law is a means by which shared norms and values are given formal recognition and political reality. It is also an area in which state power tends to predominate over other social systems, in that it is the state that formally defines and enforces the law. Law is both reflective and constitutive of cultural norms and thus becomes an arena in which contesting legitimacy claims can be reconciled or disputed.

The incorporation into legal codes of social values and practices with regard to gender serves cultural as well as governmental purposes; such laws preserve particular social practices and structures as a means of regulating social order, and in so doing, they contribute to the state's ability to present itself as culturally authentic, and thus legitimate. States facing significant legitimation concerns, such as the authoritarian regimes of the Arab world, incorporate "cultural legitimacy" claims into their official political discourses and programs, just as their chief opponents mobilize such claims in criticism of the state and its authenticity. Thus elements of culture become important determinants of the development of political systems, particularly in regard to issues of rights and freedoms.

It has been noted that the Third World state is often characterized by a political system that is neopatrimonial in nature.[3] In such states, political authority is derived in one sphere from rational-legal sources, such as legislatures and electoral processes, and in another sphere from the maintenance of traditional social relationships and practices. Christopher Clapham identifies this as a weakness of the Third World state, and he may be correct in the long term. It seems clear, though, that states and other political actors are able to use these two sources of authority in constructing political discourses that can claim the loyalty of different sectors of society as well as form a highly flexible framework for the presentation and justification of political choices. The Jordanian state, for example, is quite adept at presenting its "rational-legal" face to certain audiences (educated elites, liberal reformists, foreign observers) and its "traditional" face to others (tribal sectors, Islamists, etc.) in order to appeal to these different audiences on different grounds. Conversely, it can also make use of each authority type in denying the demands of particular sectors; feminists can be told that certain legal changes are impossible because they conflict with (or would be perceived as an assault on)

3 This term is most common in scholarship on African politics. See, for example, Jason Brownlee, "…And Yet They Persist: Explaining Survival and Transition in Neopatrimonial Regimes," *Studies in Comparative International Development*, 37:3 (2002): 35–64; Michael Bratton and Nicolas van de Walle, "Neopatrimonial Regimes and Political Transitions in Africa," *World Politics* 46:4 (1994): 453–489; Christopher Clapham, *Third World Politics: an Introduction* (Madison: University of Wisconsin Press, 1985) and Linda Kirschke, "Semipresidentialism and the Perils of Power-Sharing in Neopatrimonial States," *Comparative Political Studies* 40:11 (2007): 1372–1394. Work on neopatrimonialism in the Middle East includes Rex Brynen, "The Neopatrimonial Dimension of Palestinian Politics," *Journal of Palestine Studies* 25:1 (1995): 23–36.

valued traditional cultural forms, and Islamists can be told that certain policies are just because they were achieved through the proper legislative process.

The legal systems of Arab states reflect this duality, combining laws and legal frameworks of both Western and Islamic origin. The existence of dual legal systems represents a strategic tool for states in their quest for legitimacy, and the research here demonstrates that regimes and other actors make deliberate use of the dual legal systems in pursuing political objectives regarding both the nature of the system and policy outcomes.

This project treats the incorporation of Islamic law in the Jordanian system as a means by which traditionalist demands are addressed, but this is not meant to suggest that Islam and tradition are conceptually interchangeable. Religion and tradition appeal to different sources of authority – the sacred divine versus the sacred past. However, religion, in terms of practices and the social meaning of beliefs, is certainly a component of tradition, both in the Arab world and elsewhere. This connection between the two is, for example, the source of annual disagreements in the United States about the acceptability of Christmas decorations in government buildings and in Jordan informs the debate over the cultural place of honor killings. As this study shows, the religious and traditionalist sources of legitimacy for the Jordanian state are closely intertwined and generally reinforce one another, but the definition of tradition – and its deployment for political purposes – is increasingly contested.

Organization of This Study

In the following chapters, I will explain the theoretical and methodological bases for this study and then examine some of the most prominent gender-related issues in Jordanian law and politics. This introductory chapter lays out my argument, provides background information for understanding the context of the Jordanian case, and situates the present study with regard to existing literature on the politics of the Middle East and of Jordan. Chapter 2 explains the theoretical foundations of the study, relying on a revision of Habermas's idea of legitimation crisis and, to a lesser extent, on Gramsci's concept of hegemony. Chapter 3 examines what I call the "dual legal system" of Jordan and its importance in politics. Chapters 4, 5, 6 and 7 address particular legal and policy issues that provide evidence of the complex role of gender issues in state legitimation and political contestation by actors outside the state. Chapter 4 investigates criminal law, focusing on the issues of rape and honor killings. I argue that in these areas, law and legal practice are constructed to endorse traditional social practices because in so doing, the state enhances its cultural legitimacy with some sectors of the population. Nationality law, addressed in Chapter 5, is another example of the state's endorsement of a view of women's public roles as different from, and subordinate to, those of men. Chapter 6 turns to the question of the regulation of private, rather than public, issues, focusing on the provisions for divorce in personal status law.

Chapter 7 addresses the state's creation and management of "protected space" within the parliament and the military as a means of both empowering women and constraining the effects of this empowerment. All of these issues reveal that the state does not have a single unified approach to women's rights; it both supports and constrains women's rights initiatives, while simultaneously expanding women's professional roles in the military and continuing to require women to have male intermediaries in much of their business with the state. This is not evidence of chaos or ideological confusion within the state; rather, the Jordanian state is, like other states, not a monolithic actor. There are diverse interests within the state, and these are further complicated by the state's reliance on two strands of political legitimation, discussed below in Chapter 2.

Society and Politics in Jordan

Jordan is a small country, less than a tenth the size of Egypt in both area and population. It is formally a constitutional monarchy, but since the creation of the independent state, the powers of the monarch have predominated over other constitutional actors in the political sphere and have been subject to very few constraints. Jordan achieved full independence in 1946; the area was under British mandate control in the post-World War I period, and the first unified national government of the country, then known as Transjordan, was established in 1921.[4] In the years immediately after full independence, Jordan enacted a constitution that defined the powers of the monarch, created legislative and judicial bodies and identified a set of citizens' rights. Despite early experiences with democratic structures and processes through the 1950s and 1960s, the system has never fully democratized, and all democratic life was suspended during nearly 30 years of martial law beginning in the late 1960s.

The exigencies of regional politics have long served as the justification for authoritarian measures such as martial law.[5] In 1989, parliamentary elections were held for the first time in over 20 years.[6] Political parties, banned since 1957, were

---

4 Transjordan became nominally independent in 1928, under Emir (later King) Abdullah. Although some institutions of domestic politics, such as legislative councils, were established, Britain retained control over foreign and some financial affairs.

5 King Abdullah's official website describes martial law as "imposed as a result of the tense security situation resulting from the 1967 War and Jordan's loss of the West Bank to Israel;" it was also clearly intended to facilitate the state's internal political control by eradicating contestation and dissent. See www.kingabdullah.gov.jo.

6 Jordan controlled the West Bank from 1948 until it was captured by Israel in 1967. During Jordanian administration of the territory, representatives from West Bank electoral districts were included in the Jordanian parliament. Israel's occupation of the territory was cited as the rationale for keeping Parliament in abeyance, as the West Bank representatives could no longer participate and thus the full parliament could not meet. Jordan renounced its claim to the West Bank in 1988 in favor of Palestinian self-rule of the territory.

allowed to operate beginning in 1992, the same year that martial law was formally lifted. Parliamentary elections were held as scheduled in 1993 and 1997; the 2001 elections were postponed due to unrest related to the Israeli-Palestinian conflict. These elections were held in 2003, and the four-year regular election schedule resumed with the 2007 elections.

Jordan is a fairly poor country but one that is undergoing somewhat successful economic development. Per capita income has risen from US$1,533 in 1997 to $2,766.4 in 2007 (although it has not always kept up with inflation).[7] King Abdullah has been active in economic development since his coronation, promising from the earliest days of his reign to expand the private sector and increase foreign investment. Jordan's economy faces difficulties ranging from the lack of natural resources to the loss of Iraq as a major trading partner after the 1990–1991 Gulf War. Structural adjustment programs represented the primary approach to economic development in the 1990s, but these have not always been popular with poorer sectors of society, as they have led to reductions in subsidies for basic necessities such as bread.[8]

The Jordanian economy also relies in part on its expatriate workers, most of whom have been employed in Gulf countries. After the 1990–1991 Gulf War, approximately half a million such workers were repatriated to Jordan, an additional strain on the economy in terms of both income and employment levels.[9] Remittances sent home by Jordanians working abroad continue to play an important role in national income; the Central Bank of Jordan reports that worker remittances in 2007 amounted to over US$2.5 billion, just over 15 percent of the GNP.[10]

Unemployment is an ongoing problem in the Jordanian economy. Government estimates of unemployment in 1997 were around 14 percent, while private estimates were as high as 28 percent; the government later conceded that the latter figures were probably more accurate.[11] After a decade of fairly good economic growth,

7 1997 figures from Tareq Ayyoub, "CBJ annual report details Jordan's '97 economic, financial performance," *Jordan Times*, November 16, 1998. 2007 figures are from Central Bank of Jordan, Annual Report 2007, at www.cbj.gov.jo.

8 One assessment of the political effects of economic problems of the 1990s is found in Rex Brynen, "Economic Crisis and Post-Rentier Democratization in the Arab World: the Case of Jordan," *Canadian Journal of Political Science* 25:1 (1992): 69–97.

9 Many Jordanian citizens working abroad are Palestinians, and Palestinians were expelled from Kuwait during and after the 1990–1991 war, in response to the perception that they had supported Saddam Hussein's attempt to annex part of the country.

10 Central Bank of Jordan, Annual Report, 2007. The Central Bank reports worker remittances for 2007 of JD 1,822.9 million, and a total GNP for the year of JD 11,817.4 million. Conversions were calculated using the Central Bank's exchange rate of US$0.709 to the dinar.

11 The 28 percent estimate was produced by the University of Jordan's Center for Strategic Studies and reportedly used a more accurate methodology (in terms of both question wording and the definition of unemployment) than the government study.

unemployment is still high; official figures are still around 14 percent,[12] while most unofficial sources continue to cite rates between 25 and 30 percent. The Jordanian economy has, however, improved by other measures, with an average annual GDP growth of 5.1 percent in the 1996–2006 period.[13] Jordan is classified as a "medium human development" country by the United Nations Development Programme; its Human Development Index score currently places the country 85th out of the 177 countries assessed.[14] When this score is adjusted for gender-related disparities, Jordan's ranking falls slightly, from 85/177 to 79/156.[15]

Two important demographic issues in Jordan are the high population growth rate and the proportion of residents of Palestinian origin. Approximately 40 percent of the population is under the age of 15,[16] and the annual growth rate is between two and three percent, although beginning in the 1990s there was a "rapid fertility decline affecting all strata of society."[17] The population, currently around 5.7 million,[18] may double in size by 2029.[19] Christians constitute between four and six percent of the population and have a protected quota of seats in the national parliament;[20] Muslim-Christian conflict is more or less nonexistent in Jordan. The

---

12 Department of Statistics (Jordan), *Jordan in Figures 2006*, at www.dos.gov.jo. Unemployment is much higher among women (25 percent) than men (11.9 percent).

13 World Bank figures at www.worldbank.org.

14 Human Development Reports for 2007/2008, at http://hdr.undp.org/en/statistics/. The Human Development Index is in many ways a better indicator of general development than economic measures alone as it is a composite measure of life expectancy, educational attainment and income.

15 This is the "gender-related development index," or GDI, an adjustment of HDI that has been in use since 1995. Another commonly-used indicator, the Gender Empowerment Measure (GEM), is not produced for Jordan, so no ranking is available. See www.undp.org for further explanation of these measures and their uses.

16 According to Jordanian government statistics at www.kinghussein.gov.jo, the under-15 figure is 42.2 percent, while the CIA's World Factbook 2008 puts it at 32.2 percent.

17 Sara Randall and Nawaf Khalaldeh, "The Population of Jordan," in Jon Hanssen-Bauer, Jon Pedersen and Age A. Tiltnes (eds), *Jordanian Society: Living Conditions in the Hashemite Kingdom of Jordan* (Oslo: Fafo Institute for Applied Social Science, 1998), 51.

18 Department of Statistics (Jordan), Jordan in Figures, 2006, at www.dos.gov.jo/jorfig/2006/jor_f_e.htm. News reports sometimes put the figure as high as 6.5 million (MSNBC report, March 21, 2002), but this figure is not substantiated elsewhere. One reason for variation in recent figures is the presence of Iraqi refugees; estimates of the number of Iraqis in Jordan vary from 460,000 to 750,000. See Fafo, "Iraqis in Jordan: their Number and Characteristics," 2007, available at www.fafo.no/ais/middeast/jordan/IJ.pdf and Dale Gavlak, "Jordan Appeals for Help in Dealing with Iraqi Refugees," *Washington Post*, July 27, 2007.

19 USAID in Jordan, "Health," June 2006, at www.jordan.usaid.gov/sectors.cfm?inSector=20.

20 Of 110 seats in the elected lower house (*Majlis al-Nuwwab*, or House of Delegates), seven are reserved for Christians, three for Circassians or Chechens and six for women. The

more salient social division is not religious, but between residents of Palestinian and (East Bank) Jordanian origin. The proportion of Palestinians in the Jordanian population may be as high as 65 percent, some of whom arrived as refugees after 1948 and 1967 and many of whom were born and raised in Jordan. The government does not release official estimates on this issue because of political sensitivities but does acknowledge that 1.4 million Palestinians are registered as refugees with the United Nations Relief and Works Agency (UNWRA);[21] this does not account for all Palestinians in the country, as many neither live in the refugee camps nor receive UNWRA services.

Jordan has approximately 30 political parties, but these tend to be largely irrelevant in both electoral politics and the mobilization of public opinion on issues. The clear exception to this is the Islamic Action Front, which will be discussed in later chapters. The status of political parties generally, however, is fairly low; a recent poll found that 80 percent of respondents felt that no party in Jordan is qualified to form a government.[22] Jordanian society is often described as a tribal one, wherein family loyalties provide the predominant basis for political identity and interest formation. The East Bank tribes are widely recognized as a major source of support for the monarchy, especially during the reign of King Hussein; the state has addressed their needs and promoted this special relationship by employing primarily East Bank Jordanians (as opposed to Palestinians) in the civil service and military.

A number of women's organizations exist in Jordan, ranging from policy-oriented organizations, such as the Jordanian National Committee for Women, that seek to advise the government on various issues to more independent groups such as the local chapter of the Sisterhood is Global Institute. The women's movement gets mixed reviews in Jordan and is regarded by some as the special province of the social elite. While this characterization is at least partially accurate, the movement has since the 1990s addressed itself to the interests of the "grassroots" of Jordanian women, and its effect on Jordanian political life is perceptible though not radical (see Chapter 8 for further discussion of this issue).

Although Jordan is a predominantly Muslim society, it does not have an Islamic government like Iran. Women are not required by law to wear *hijab* (Islamic dress) of any form. Many Muslim women in Jordan wear a long dress (*jilbab*) and headscarf, while others wear more Western-looking clothing and a scarf, and some women do not wear a scarf at all. Freedom of movement and access to education and employment are in large part a function of an individual woman's family situation; women from more liberal families (which tend to be wealthier) travel, attend university and graduate school, pursue careers and enjoy a great

---

"women's quota" is discussed further in Chapter 7.

21 See www.kingabdullah.gov.jo. The relevant agency is the United Nations Relief and Works Agency, which administers the several refugee camps in Jordan.

22 Faris Braizat, "Democracy in Jordan 2007," Public Opinion Poll Unit, Center for Strategic Studies, University of Jordan. See www.jcss.org/UploadPolling/258.pdf.

deal of autonomy, while women from more conservative families, especially in rural areas, are likely to be less educated, employed in the home and much more restricted in their movements. Poorer women are also likely to have more children; the average family now has around six members,[23] but in poorer areas, it is not uncommon to find women with as many as 11 children.

The official government and royal position on women's rights in Jordan usually focuses on the constitution's guarantee of equal rights to all Jordanians. However, this article specifies race, language and religion as prohibited grounds of discrimination and does not mention gender.[24] There is some consensus among lawyers and within the women's movement that this article could be a basis for gender equality. However, it is clear that at present this is neither the intention nor the effect of this article. A great deal of Jordanian legislation would be unconstitutional if this interpretation of Article 6 were used, as many laws mandate or allow for differential treatment of women and assign particular privileges to men. It is unlikely that a challenge would be brought on the basis of this article, as it would almost certainly not succeed. Also, it is of some doubt whether full legal equality, in the sense of gender-blind laws, is something that would be welcomed even by Jordanian feminists. The few provisions in law that discriminate in women's favor, such as labor law provisions about working conditions, are cherished as practical protections of women's rights and status, and women would not be likely to renounce these without a significant alteration in the entire social structure, of a degree that is extremely unlikely.

The State-Dominated Political Sphere

> Ankh-Morpork had dallied with many forms of government and had ended up with that form of democracy known as One Man, One Vote. The Patrician was the Man; he had the Vote.
>
> –Terry Pratchett, *Mort*

The most significant characteristic of Jordanian political life is its domination by the state. This domination is felt in several ways: the powers reserved to the king,

23 See "Human Resources: the Demographic Challenge," at www.kinghussein.gov.jo.

24 Article 6 (1). Citations are taken from the Constitution of the Hashemite Kingdom of Jordan, 1952. It is somewhat interesting that the constitution's official English translation suggests a more limited extension of equality than does the original Arabic. The official English version reads: "Jordanians shall be equal before the law. There shall be no discrimination between them as regards their rights and duties on the grounds of race, language or religion." The original Arabic actually says, "no discrimination between them *even should they differ* as to race, language, or religion" (emphasis added). This difference of language was discovered in a conversation with lawyer Dr. Salah Bashir, who agrees that the actual wording of the Arabic suggests that the three named categories are examples of protected categories rather than a limiting list.

including the selection of the prime minister and the upper house of the legislature; the presence and activities of the internal security service, the *mukhabarat*; the legal restrictions on the formation not only of political parties, but of charitable and social-service organizations; the strategically-designed elections law, which stocks the lower house with pro-government members much as a game warden might stock a trout pond; and the limitations on freedom of speech, felt especially by journalists, who face the prospect of arrest and detention for unwise commentary.

During the long reign of King Hussein from 1953 to 1999, the state's authoritarian controls (including the imposition of decades of martial law) could be somewhat balanced or softened, for certain sectors, by the perception of the king as a paternal figure, who possessed authority naturally and wielded power in the best interest of his children. This was certainly a perception encouraged by the king himself. There is little disagreement about Hussein's political skill in preserving not only his own power but the security of Jordan, and when he died in 1999, the public expressions of grief were, in many cases, sincere. Nonetheless, the authoritarian character of the system has been its most predominant feature. It is unlikely this will change substantially during the reign of King Abdullah. The new monarch has indicated his interest in improving judicial independence, increasing government responsiveness and efficiency and securing greater rights for women, but despite his sweeping formal powers, he, like his father, faces the challenge of maintaining the support of the so-called "traditional sector" of society, which will limit his political reach as a practical matter.

King Abdullah also faces two challenges that his father did not. The first is that, immediately after his unexpected coronation,[25] he had to work to be perceived as a "real" Jordanian. The legacy of his father was tempered, for some people at the time of his coronation, by his British mother and his foreign education. His lack of grooming for the role of monarch is apparently less of a liability and may even help him by providing an image of a practical professional (he was a military officer before his father's death) rather than a spoilt prince brought up to expect the throne. However, while much has been made of his military career, it was also said, *sotto voce*, that he was, like the sons of other kings and presidents, something of a dilettante soldier.[26] This may or may not be the case, but it represents the importance of various elements in the king's public persona, all of which contribute to the public's evaluation of his suitability as a monarch. King Abdullah has, by

---

25 For many years, the Crown Prince and heir to the throne was King Hussein's brother, Prince Hassan. The change in succession was announced only days before the king passed away in 1999. Then-Prince Abdullah was a much less well-known figure than his uncle had been, and any number of conspiracy theories circulated in the weeks after the announcement, but there have apparently been no public challenges to Abdullah's reign.

26 This was a comment I heard occasionally in conversation with Jordanians and which was also suggested to me by an American military officer who was familiar with the king's career. The king was trained at Sandhurst, a British military academy, and held the rank of general in the Jordanian military at the time of his succession to the throne.

most reports, managed these elements very well and emerged as a fairly popular and well-respected leader.

The second special challenge constraining Abdullah as monarch is the regional and international context after September 11, 2001. Many authoritarian leaders have taken advantage of the new focus on terrorism to secure support, or at least tolerance, for harsh measures against their domestic opponents, thus entrenching their regimes and reducing the prospects for democratization. Some of this may be happening in Jordan, but the especially important factors are the close relationship between Jordan and the United States, which Jordan cannot afford to lose, and the operation of transnational terrorists within Jordan. The Jordan-U.S. relationship is strategically useful and politically practical in the international context, but American foreign policy is deeply unpopular with the Jordanian public, as elsewhere in the region. The regime's choices with regard to domestic reform, among other things, are constrained by these circumstances. Both the aftermath of September 11 and the terrorist attacks within Jordan[27] have done much to reduce the prospects for real democratization by increasing the apparent justification for the national security state.

In addition to the importance of the monarch, much of Jordanian political life has revolved around the concept of national unity. While consensus on the basis of the political system is certainly a necessity in any conception of democracy, the Jordanian discourse on national unity has been more often a tool to support the stifling of unpopular or "dangerous" interests. "Harming national unity" is a criminal charge for which individuals can be arrested, tried and jailed;[28] it is used for example against journalists who criticize the government and public figures who advocate the return of Palestinians to Palestine, an issue of extreme sensitivity in Jordan, where more than half of the population are Palestinians. The idea of a unified nation is also supported by assertions that unrest or crime are instigated by external, foreign forces seeking to harm Jordan; this type of claim has featured in explanations of the 1998 Ma'an riots,[29] murders in Amman and the opposition to the honor crimes law (see Chapter 4).

27 In November 2005, bombs were detonated at three hotels in Amman, killing dozens of people.

28 "Harming national unity" has been criminalized in two codes, the Press and Publications Law and the Penal Code. The press-related crime was one of a long list of punishable offenses for journalists and publishers, which also included defaming the royal family. These prohibitions became especially controversial with their inclusion in the 1998 Press and Publications Law, which was consequently amended by Parliament in 1999. However, the same offense is prosecutable (and not only for journalists) in the Penal Code; since a royal decree in 2001, individuals charged with harming national unity or *lese majeste* are tried in the State Security Court, where they have few procedural protections.

29 Tareq Ayyoub, "Ma'an riots continue; King warns Jordan will not tolerate instigation of violence," *Jordan Times*, February 22, 1998. King Hussein suggested that the violence was the result of "conspiracies [against Jordan]" by "malicious or ungrateful persons [who do] not believe in this country and [do] not have any allegiance to this country."

British scholar Bernard Crick has written of the dangers of regarding politics as the pursuit of unanimity rather than the reconciling of competing interests.[30] For Crick, political claims about unanimity presage the death of politics, as they are the first step toward totalitarianism. Crick's formulation may be somewhat overstated; consensus has an important role in politics and is, at the level of fundamental principles, necessary for the legitimacy of any political system. However, his point about the authoritarian uses to which "consensus" can be put are well taken and borne out by the Jordanian case. The justification for the notorious restrictions on speech, assembly and political organization that the Jordanian state enforces is most often one of the "good of the nation," based on a concern for the danger posed by the divisiveness of political contestation. So long as the state (in its various guises) values internal security over public freedom, prospects for democratization are significantly limited.

It is worth noting that the state has not cornered the market on the "national unity" discourse; other groups, including the state's chief opponents, have made use of the concept for their own political ends. This is entirely to be expected, as efforts to benefit from the powerful effects of an established hegemony are a logical tactic in any system where openly counter-hegemonic activity carries severe penalties. To advocate something on the basis that it contributes to national unity (by reflecting shared and authentic values as opposed to foreign ones, for example) is a fairly safe approach to political contestation.

The Jordanian Legal System

Jordan's legal system falls predominantly within the civil law tradition (see Chapter 3 for an extensive discussion of the legal system). Its civil and criminal codes are heavily influenced by European codes, particularly the French codes as received via the Ottoman *majallah* and other laws. Aspects of Islamic law (*shari'a*) have been codified in the Personal Status Code for Muslims, which regulates issues such as marriage, divorce, inheritance and child custody. Tribal law, the traditional practices of dispute resolution among family groups, was formally abolished in 1976,[31] but it continues to operate informally alongside the system of state-created law. The constitution, which came into force in 1953, is broadly similar to several other Arab constitutions and was in fact based largely upon earlier Egyptian constitutions.[32]

---

30 Bernard Crick, *In Defense of Politics*, 4th edition (Chicago: University of Chicago Press, 1992).

31 For a discussion of the special legal status of Bedouin tribes, see Andrew Shryock, *Nationalism and the Geneaological Imagination: Oral History and Textual Authority in Tribal Jordan* (Berkeley: University of California Press, 1997), 69.

32 Judicial Inspector Adel Khasawneh and retired judge Farouk Kilani, interviews, March 1999. Khasawneh also traced the Jordanian constitution to the Lebanese and Iraqi constitutions, as well as European influences.

It defines the Jordanian state and nation[33] and enumerates the rights of Jordanians. The constitution divides political power among the usual three branches of government, legislative, executive and judicial, and gives the rules of monarchical succession.

The form of the constitution is unexceptionable, but several of its substantive contents merit comment. First, the constitutionally-protected rights of individuals, such as freedom of speech, are all qualified by a restriction limiting them to "the extent allowed by law," or some similar formulation.[34] This suggests that these rights are not in fact foundational in the system, but rather subject to the definition and regulation of statutory law. As the government's ability to make law is rather broad, encompassing emergency and "temporary" legislation that can be enacted by the executive without the participation of Parliament, the actual protection of rights in the Jordanian system has been much more a political than a constitutional question. The constitution is of little practical legal value in this area and is rarely used as a basis for challenge to such laws. In one case that did involve a constitutional challenge, the courts made it clear that statutory laws do indeed trump constitutional guarantees.[35]

Second, the constitution's provisions with regard to the separation of powers are regarded with derision in many quarters. While the constitution provides explicitly for the independence of the judiciary, it is widely recognized that judges are subject to the political authority of the Ministry of Justice and generally beholden to the politically powerful. Likewise, the assignment of legislative power to the two houses of parliament, the Lower House or House of Deputies (*majlis an-nawab*) and the Senate (*majlis al-'ayan*), is in practice undermined by the frequent use of "temporary laws" originating from the executive, as described above. Finally, the parliamentary system itself departs from the usual form of such institutions, in that the prime minister is not, as in Westminster-model parliaments, drawn from the majority party in the lower house, but is an appointee of the monarch. This gives the king direct influence in the legislative as well as the executive arena.

This description of Jordanian society and politics will, I hope, provide a context in which to assess the thesis and the substantive evidence of this project.

Review of Literature

Among the countries of the Arab world, Jordan has not received the most attention from scholars (a distinction that probably goes to Egypt), but neither has it been

33 Jordan is defined as "an independent sovereign Arab State," whose people "form part of the Arab nation" and whose official religion is Islam. (Articles 1 and 2).

34 See Chapter 2 of 1952 Constitution, "Rights and Duties."

35 The Court of Cassation (Criminal Division) upheld the conviction of a man charged with *lese majesté*, explicitly endorsing the executive's power to restrain "insulting" speech about the monarch despite constitutional provisions about freedom of expression. Decision No. 171/96, cited in *Yearbook of Islamic and Middle Eastern Law*, vol. 3, 1996, 216.

neglected. Several notable studies of Jordanian society and politics have been published, including the work of Linda Layne, Richard Antoun, Laurie Brand, Marc Lynch, Joseph Massad, Lisa Taraki, Glenn Robinson and others.[36] It will be helpful to discuss the relationship of the present project to the work that has already been done in this field, both in comparative politics of the Middle East generally and specifically on the Jordanian case.

A general consensus seems to exist among scholars that the most salient elements of the Jordanian political system are its tribalism, its authoritarianism, its economic woes and the Palestinian-Jordanian split. The present study does not take issue with the importance of any of these factors; indeed, each is considered significant not only by scholarly analysts but by participants (or would-be participants) in actual politics in Jordan. My hope is to add to these an additional aspect of politics that, I will argue throughout the coming chapters, is likely to be partially determinative of the course of Jordanian political development and the prospects for democratization. Cultural explanations of Jordanian politics have not been absent from the scholarly scene, but we are lacking a theoretically-grounded (post-modernization theory) analysis of the means by which cultural issues become politically salient and with what effect on the system itself. This project is intended to be an initial step toward an analysis of political development that considers culture not merely as a context or an explanation of last resort, but as a powerful, flexible and significantly determinative element of system stability and democracy.

---

36 For anthropological accounts of Jordanian society, particularly tribal structures and identities, see Linda Layne, *Home and Homeland: the Dialogics of National and Tribal Identity in Jordan* (Princeton: Princeton University Press, 1994); Richard Antoun, *Arab Village: a Social Structural Study of a Transjordanian Peasant Community* (Bloomington: Indiana University Press, 1972); Andrew Shryock, *Nationalism and the Genealogical Imagination: Oral History and Textual Authority in Tribal Jordan* (Berkeley: University of California Press, 1997). Recent political science on national identity includes Joseph Massad's *Colonial Effects: the Making of National Identity in Jordan* (New York: Columbia University Press, 2001); and Marc Lynch, *State Interests and Public Spheres: the International Politics of Jordan's Identity* (New York: Columbia University Press, 1999). Laurie Brand has made important contributions on political economy (*Jordan's Inter-Arab Relations: the Political Economy of Alliance Making* (New York: Columbia University Press, 1994)) and analyses of gender and the state (*Women, the State, and Political Liberalization: Middle Eastern and North African Experiences* (New York: Columbia University Press, 1998), as well as several articles), while Glenn Robinson and Lisa Taraki have written about the role of the Islamist movement in Jordan (see Glenn Robinson, "Can Islamists be Democrats? The Case of Jordan," *Middle East Journal* 51:3 (1997): 373–388, and "Defensive Democratization in Jordan," *International Journal of Middle East Studies* 30:3 (1998): 387–410; Lisa Taraki, "Jordanian Islamists and the Agenda for Women: Between Discourse and Practice," *Middle East Studies* 32:1 (1996): 140–158).

This is not, of course, to argue that culture, in the sense of a civilizational identifier along the lines suggested by Samuel Huntington,[37] determines the nature of political systems or the substance of political outcomes; rather, I suggest that cultural elements are relevant to stability and democracy in all political systems, through their effect on legitimacy. Jurgen Habermas offered a persuasive account of the importance of the sociocultural realm to the politics of advanced capitalist countries, and I argue in this study that similar forces operate in the developing world.

In coming to this conclusion, I have, of course, drawn on the existing scholarship on the comparative politics of the Middle East. Michael Hûdson's well-known work on legitimacy in Arab countries[38] offered an important contribution to the analysis of the phenomenon throughout the region. Hudson identifies political legitimacy as "the central problem of government in the Arab world" at the time of his writing; in my view, it continues to be so today, although under somewhat different domestic and regional circumstances. Hudson's work utilizes a generally Weberian conception of legitimacy and locates the political problem of legitimacy failure in the forces of modernization then considered to be sweeping the region. He accounts for both domestic and external factors in analyzing state legitimacy and identifies several key requirements for political legitimacy; a number of these, at least as regards the Jordanian case, have yet to be fulfilled and continue to contribute to the political failures of the state. These include the institutionalization of political participation throughout society, a consensus on national identity (and, I would add, its implications for citizenship in the fullest sense), and shared conceptions of authority. However, not all of his assessments are still equally useful in understanding legitimacy issues; for example, he argues that "Arab society is no longer traditional in the sense that any significant sectors can be swayed by appeals to custom, status, or superstition."[39] I hope to demonstrate that currently in Jordanian politics, appeals to custom are not only popular, but integral to dominant notions of the requirements for political legitimacy. This is not because notions of modernity and rational (in the Weberian sense, as opposed to traditional) politics have had no effect on the role of tradition in politics but because the divide between "traditional" and "rational" appeals to authority is not necessarily an absolute one.

One of the chief contributions of Hudson's work was its successful application of the tools of general political science to the study of the Arab world, a region usually (especially at that time) treated as an exceptional "special case." The most thorough recent challenge to the exceptionalist treatment of the Arab world in political science is perhaps Nazih Ayubi's *Over-stating the Arab State*, in which he

---

37 Samuel Huntington, *The Clash of Civilizations and the Remaking of World Order* (New York: Simon & Schuster, 1996).

38 Michael Hudson, *Arab Politics: the Search for Legitimacy* (New Haven: Yale University Press, 1977).

39 Hudson, 17.

argues that "Arab politics should no longer be perceived as being peculiarly and uniquely Arab."[40] To that end, Ayubi applies concepts developed in the study of other regions, particularly Latin America, to the analysis of Arab states.

While I am in sympathy with Ayubi's desire to eviscerate, once and for all, the thesis of Arab exceptionalism, I disagree with his position that culture must be rejected as an explanatory variable. This is not because Arab politics are somehow "more cultural" than politics in more developed systems. Rather, a great deal of politics, in both developing and developed systems, is about connecting the political order to society. Whether in choosing systems of representation, in defining basic rights or in selecting policies that produce desired outcomes, cultural issues from shared notions of justice to preferences about the use of public space are deeply embedded in the choices offered and made.

Ayubi's work is most relevant to the present study in his treatment of the state and hegemony, a term he prefers to legitimacy.[41] Ayubi, like many other observers, sees the state as central to Arab politics[42] but argues that it is not as strong as it is often portrayed. The state, in his view, has been weakened by a "crisis of hegemony," and this crisis is a key element in Arab political development. Ayubi draws an interesting distinction among strength, hardness and fierceness as characteristics of states; here again his work closely relates to general comparative politics, as these concepts relate to the work on strong versus weak states by Clapham, Migdal and others.[43] His argument about the fierceness, rather than the strength, of the Arab state is particularly useful in the analysis of Jordan presented in this study. The Jordanian state has many of the attributes of power, such as an extensive internal security system and harsh penalties for its political enemies, and its underlying weakness is located in exactly the place that Ayubi (and, in a slightly different sense, Habermas) would expect – the need for popular legitimation.

Another major work of direct relevance to this project is Hisham Sharabi's *Neopatriarchy*. In developing a systematic framework for studying Arab society,

---

40 Nazih Ayubi, *Over-stating the Arab State: Politics and Society in the Middle East* (New York: I.B. Tauris, 1995), xi.

41 Although, like Ayubi, I find Gramsci's hegemony concept to be very useful in analyzing the state, I do not consider the term to be an alternative to legitimacy. In my view, hegemony as described by Gramsci suggests a nearly irresistible force which usually affects individuals (and thus shapes society) without their full critical awareness of it. Legitimacy, on the other hand, while largely a cultural product, is something of which people tend to be quite conscious and able to consider critically, even if they do not choose to do so (as in systems in which legitimacy is regarded as a settled question). Challenges to legitimacy may also be counter-hegemonic, but the two are not synonymous.

42 Ayubi, 25.

43 Christopher Clapham, *Third World Politics, an Introduction* (Madison: University of Wisconsin Press, 1985), Joel Migdal, *Strong Societies and Weak States: State-Society Relations and State Capabilities in the Third World* (Princeton: Princeton University Press, 1988).

Sharabi offers an interesting refinement of, although not a challenge to, the idea of modernity as the end product of political development. Although Sharabi deliberately excludes "culture" from his approach, on the grounds of the term's misuse by Orientalists and modernization theorists,[44] his analysis is essentially an accounting of the effect of a dependent modernization process upon an existing patriarchal sociocultural system, a combination that results in a neither-fish-nor-fowl social form he calls neopatriarchy. In order for democratic political development and true "modernity" to become possible in Arab societies, this neopatriarchy must be overcome.

Sharabi identifies (as do many observers) Islamic fundamentalism and secularism as the two competing discourses shaping Arab society.[45] For Sharabi, these two discourses are dichotomous, with Islamism being an "absolutist, traditionalist position" characterized by "total hegemony" and secularism a "self-limiting, rationalizing position" offering "free pluralism."[46] I suggest that this dichotomy is more perceived than actual. Both discourses must, and do, address the issue of tradition in terms of its definition, its proper role in society and thus in political life. The Jordanian case demonstrates the propensity for Islamists and traditionalists to ally on particular social issues, but also for religious justifications and arguments to be put forward by feminists and others in opposition to traditional practices such as honor killings. These issues, discussed below, demonstrate the importance of "tradition" in political contestation on both sides of Sharabi's dichotomy.

The extent to which secular positions are necessarily more pluralistic than Islamist ones is likewise debatable. Certainly in theory secularism should offer space for a wider range of interests and views, but in practice, the pursuit of culturally-grounded legitimacy tends to constrain the range of politics for everyone in the system. In combination with the authoritarian practices of even the most secular states, this produces an environment in which "free pluralism" is nowhere to be found. It could be added that few political actors, whether Islamists, traditionalists or democrats, seem to be pursuing such pluralism outside the relatively safe bounds of rhetoric. Democrats are often quite suspicious of Islamists as a political force presumably dangerous to democracy, and at least in the Jordanian case, Islamists have become fairly adept at using pluralist language to secure their own position within the political system.

A great deal of recent scholarship has focused on the role of civil society in the development and maintenance of democracy, in both developed and developing countries.[47] The often-noted tribalism of Jordanian society is generally considered, both by scholars and by activists, to be a barrier to real democratization in Jordan;

44 Sharabi, ix–x.

45 Sharabi, 11–12.

46 Ibid.

47 See, for example, A.R. Norton (ed.), *Civil Society in the Middle East* (New York: Brill, 1995), Jillian Schwedler (ed.), *Toward Civil Society in the Middle East* (Boulder:

the argument holds that as long as family ties are the basis of social organization and interest formation, associational life cannot develop in a way that fosters democratic contestation.[48] I find this argument generally persuasive because of the hierarchical nature of this form of organization and interest-definition. However, tribalism does not preclude internal differences and even competition, family structures are not static but amenable to change over time, and not all citizens of Jordan have a tribal tie as their primary identity. For these reasons, the "functional" effect of tribalism is not, in my view, fully explanatory of current political outcomes nor predictive of future ones.

Perhaps as significant as the contestation-limiting patronage relationships in tribalism, in fact, is the role of tribes in people's images of what it means to be Jordanian. In Linda Layne's 1994 study of Jordanian identity, she argues that identity is based on several elements including a constructed dichotomy of "true Bedouin"/primordial past versus advancement and modernization.[49] Thus,

---

Lynne Rienner, 1995), Robert D. Putnam, *Making Democracy Work: Civic Traditions in Modern Italy* (Princeton: Princeton University Press, 1993).

48 Anthropologist Richard Antoun offers a counterargument to the position that traditional structures are a barrier to the development of civil society (see Richard T. Antoun, "Civil Society, Tribal Process, and Change in Jordan: an Anthropological View," *International Journal of Middle East Studies* 32:4 (2000): 441–463). In his view, informal mechanisms of association, such as tribal law and the practices surrounding it, should be regarded as potential elements of civil society. I agree that civil society need not be seen as constituted only by formal organizations that replace traditional forms, but while tribal conflict resolution practices may constitute part of civil society, they do not in my view contribute much to a democratic civil society because they are predicated upon (1) a type of authority not constituted on a democratic basis and (2) access to participation that is based upon possession of appropriate social status (e.g., usually not women). Thus, not everyone is equal before the law, and not everyone has equal access to the law (of course, nor do they in democratic legal systems because of economic, educational and other inequities, but they do both fully in theory and to a much greater degree in practice). Another commentator points out that the "emphasis on 'tribal process' might unintentionally reinforce reactionary trends" particularly with regard to those, such as Palestinians, who do not share in the tribal heritage. (See Jonathan Benthall, A Comment on Richard T. Antoun, 'Civil Society, Tribal Process, and Change in Jordan: an Anthropological View,' in *International Journal of Middle East Studies* 33:4 (2001): 668–670.) While the notion that traditional social structures can form part of civil society seems a valid one, it prompts the corollary reminder that not all civil societies are democratic ones.

49 Linda Layne, *Home and Homeland: a Dialogic of Tribal and National Identities in Jordan* (Princeton: Princeton University Press, 1994), 14. While not a work of academic scholarship, a monograph by Prince Ghazi bin Muhammad, a cousin of King Abdullah, offers an interesting example of the romantic image of the tribe as the pure and authentic essence of Jordanian society. (*The Tribes of Jordan at the Beginning of the Twenty-first Century* (Jordan: Jami'at turath al-urdun al-baqi, 1999)). He wrote the work in order "to reveal the essential nobility of the tribes of Jordan," and to present a philosophy of the

authenticity and modernization are seen to exist in tension, with one available only at the cost of the other. The tricky task is, therefore, to secure the benefits of both. King Hussein was adept at presenting himself as able to bridge the contradiction; Layne gives the example of the dinar bill, on which Hussein appears in two images, wearing in the first a business suit and tie, and in the facing image a traditional *kufiyyeh*.[50]

The issue of tribes and identity also relates to the Palestinian-Jordanian question,[51] a distinction which, as Layne points out, is "often considered the most significant in Jordanian society."[52] It is, according to Layne, difficult to define the two groups precisely, either by place of family origin[53] or social characteristics, and yet the distinction has enormous social meaning. In the absence of opinion polling as a basis for describing attitudes and beliefs about this distinction, this example may serve to illustrate the phenomenon: in trying to explain the differences between Palestinians and Jordanians, a friend (herself Palestinian) pointed out university students walking past us on the University of Jordan campus, and quietly identified each of them as either Palestinian or Jordanian. She could not explain to me precisely the characteristics that made her sure of her identifications in each case, but was adamant that her labels were correct. Shortly thereafter a group of her friends joined us, and upon hearing of her efforts, set out to help her show me the difference in the two groups. They were unanimous in every identification (although of course I have no way of knowing whether or not they were correct!). This exercise did not have the intended effect of enabling me reliably to identify physical or sartorial differences in Palestinian and Jordanian students, but it did impress upon me the importance that people place upon these identities. Jordanian friends, queried separately, were just as adamant about the existence, and salience, of the distinction.

---

importance of tribes in Jordanian society. The author's position corresponds neatly to the "Bedouin versus modern" dichotomy identified by Layne; he writes of modernization as leading to the corrosion of the tribal system and the "casting away [of] solutions worked out, with wisdom and patience, over thousands of years" (14). For Prince Ghazi, the "nobility" of the tribes must be preserved in the face of modern threats in order to ameliorate the flaws of the modern world (61–62). This view of the tribal system and its meaning in Jordanian society is often echoed by those who wish to preserve particular traditional practices challenged by liberal reformers.

50 Layne, 154.

51 For simplicity's sake, I use the terms "Palestinian" and "Jordanian" in discussing Jordanian citizens of those origins. While it would be more accurate to call them "Palestinian-Jordanians" and "Jordanian-Jordanians," this usage is cumbersome and does not reflect the standard practice in Jordan, where both groups simply use the terms "Palestinian" and "Jordanian."

52 Layne, 19. See also Laurie Brand, "Palestinians and Jordanians: a Crisis of Identity," *Journal of Palestine Studies* 24:4 (1995): 46–61.

53 Layne, 20. Some families currently considered "Jordanian" originated in the West Bank, for example.

In this context of the Jordanian-Palestinian difference, the power of the state is widely seen as connected to the maintenance of the (East Bank) tribes; the army and the civil service are largely drawn from the East Bank Jordanian segment of society, and the monarchy is considered to have a symbiotic relationship in which a certain degree of political power and privilege is provided to the "tribal sector" in exchange for their support. Palestinians, who constitute over half of the population of Jordan, are largely excluded from this special relationship with the state. Furthermore, the Jordanian parliament is, largely due to the purpose-built elections law mentioned above, considered by most to be a pro-tribal, or non-Palestinian Jordanian, body. On the other hand, Jordan was the only Arab country to grant citizenship to Palestinian refugees after the creation of Israel, and many Palestinian families have built secure middle-class or even wealthy existences in Jordan. This split in society is potentially destabilizing for Jordan, and so the government has partially controlled its effects by essentially forbidding the fomentation of inter-group conflict; those who openly question the make-up of society are potentially committing the crime of "harming national unity."

Another reason that this distinction is not, in my view, a sole determinant of politics is that the two groups are fairly internally diverse. Palestinians may be destitute residents of refugee camps or wealthy businesspeople; East Bank Jordanians may be illiterate rural villagers or powerful residents of the posh section of the capital. Attitudes, as well as socioeconomic class, vary within the groups. Honor killings, for example, occur in both groups, and opponents to the practice are likewise to be found among both Palestinians and Jordanians. I also found that among those who were opposed to the practice or wished to minimize its publicity, some Palestinians would attribute the practice to "backward (Jordanian) tribespeople," while some Jordanians told me that such things happened "only in the (Palestinian refugee) camps." The appeal of traditionalist claims seems to have more to do with education and income levels than with identity as a Palestinian or Jordanian, and so the split, while politically significant, is not a prime explanatory variable for the present project.

The question of what constitutes a "true" Jordanian identity and how it incorporates tribes, Palestinians, etc. is for the purposes of this study chiefly treated as another element to be contested in the politics of tradition. Of course, the importance of defining national identity is not unique to Jordan; it has figured in nation-building projects around the world, and not always with happy results, as any number of "ethnic cleansing" atrocities will attest. The point is that while people quite rightly expect in the era of self-determination that their government should have some meaningful connection to them and their society, the basis of the identity on which this link is to be established is itself constructed rather than a biological fact.[54] The contingent nature of identity itself is therefore an important element in the pursuit of legitimacy and often plays out as a debate over the content and place of tradition in the public sphere.

54 For an excellent extended treatment of the topic of national identity construction in Jordan, see Massad's *Colonial Effects: the Making of National Identity in Jordan* (2001).

Chapter 2

Theoretical and Conceptual Issues

The argument about culture and political legitimacy presented in this project is derived in part from Habermas's theory of legitimation crisis although it is not a direct application of that theory to the Jordanian case. Habermas intended his analysis to explain a problem specific to advanced capitalist states and the interaction of their political-administrative, economic and sociocultural aspects. However, the crux of the legitimacy issue lies in the relationship between the state and its sociocultural milieu, and in my view a very similar potential legitimation crisis faces states in developing countries. The study of legitimation issues in developing countries can perhaps contribute to the elucidation of the effects of culture on political development, an issue which has long been of interest in political science but which has also been the subject of some deeply flawed work. It is not the business of the present study to recreate these roundly-criticized arguments but rather to contribute to the rescue of terms like "tradition" and "political development" from their modernization-theory ghetto.

While the heyday of modernization theory has long since passed, some of its assumptions continue to permeate aspects of current political science. Modernization theory originally regarded political development as a teleological process with one possible outcome. During the process of political development, traditional beliefs and practices would die out, to be replaced with modern forms of social interaction, modern institutions and modern values. Modernity, in Gabriel Almond's structural-functionalist approach, was a matter of the degree of specialization and structural complexity of the sociopolitical system, but the concept often took on a Western character as well. In a well-known work on developing countries, Daniel Lerner characterized the problem of modernization in the Middle East as a question of having the right "state of mind" and asserted that "what the West is, the Middle East seeks to become."[1]

There were several problems with this approach to the politics of developing countries. First, "tradition" was never particularly well defined and seemed in many cases to mean merely "that which is not modern."[2] Many writers regarded tradition as static, a view which I believe underlies continuing misperceptions among some scholars that "culture" is not a useful analytical variable because it

---

1 Daniel Lerner, *The Passing of Traditional Society* (London: Collier-Macmillan Ltd, 1958), 47.

2 For a useful review of modernization theory, its flaws and revisions, see Vicky Randall and Robin Theobald, *Political Change and Underdevelopment: a Critical Introduction to Third World Politics*, 2nd edition (Durham: Duke University Press, 1998).

cannot explain social and political change. Max Weber's typology of authority, while intended to identify analytical "ideal types" rather than to describe attributes of existing systems, has also probably contributed to the understanding of tradition and modernity as mutually exclusive and as stages of development although Weber himself did not regard them that way.[3]

Over the decades following the end of the colonial era in the mid-twentieth century, it became increasingly clear that tradition was not going to die, or at least not quietly. Many have noted the apparent persistence or resurgence of various traditional values, structures or practices, from India's tenacious caste system to the "revival" of Islam in the Arab world. This led to revisions of modernization theory which took the view that some cultures may simply be unamenable to democratic politics. This is the basis, for example, of the thesis of "Islamic (or Arab) exceptionalism" decried by Ayubi and others, and of Samuel Huntington's famous (or infamous) "clash of civilizations."

The tradition/modernity dichotomy has long been the target of scholarly criticism,[4] but yet it persisted in some quarters despite its problems. For example, in a popular textbook on Middle Eastern politics, the authors begin by asserting that "the dialectical clash between the challenging forces of modernity and the persistent strength of tradition is a fundamental reality in the region."[5] They go on to identify a "growing trend to recapture important practices of the past," such as veiling, and characterize Middle Eastern social change as "marked by a bizarre blend of tradition and modernity."[6] In this view, tradition is a fixed and objectively identifiable reality, originating in the past rather than in contemporary political construction. Thus the appeal of different actors to the dictates of tradition or to the principles of democracy would, from this perspective, be an inevitable and natural result of the nature of Middle Eastern societies caught up in modernization.

---

3 Max Weber, "Politics as a Vocation," in H.H. Gerth and C. Wright Mills (eds and trans), *From Max Weber: Essays in Sociology* (New York: Oxford University Press, 1946).

4 For example, Dale F. Eickelman and James Piscatori, *Muslim Politics* (Princeton: Princeton University Press, 2004), especially 22–30.

5 James A. Bill and Robert Springborg, *Politics in the Middle East*, 4th edition (HarperCollins: New York, 1994). Notably, this book is part of a series whose general editors are Gabriel Almond and Lucian Pye, two major figures in the development of modernization theory. A more recent example is found in Michael G. Roskin and James J. Coyle's *Politics of the Middle East: Cultures and Conflicts*, 2nd edition (Saddle River, NJ: Prentice Hall, 2008), in which the authors write that modernization "is the difficult transition between traditional and modern, during which much can go wrong" (277). They describe modernization as "setting the stage" for democratization, but warn that "democratization in the Middle East, however, leads to the emergency of political Islam." The Middle East, in their view, must inevitably become modern "whether or not they wish to be" (288) but will "keep much of its traditional values." The modernity/tradition dichotomy, with all its modernization theory implications, is alive and well here.

6 Ibid., 2.

It is more useful and, I believe, more accurate to regard tradition as a basis for the construction of political appeals rather than a section of a development timeline falling before that labeled "modernity." The conscious use of tradition for political appeal and as an underpinning for political authority is very much a part of modern politics. Christian conservatives in the United States link their political goals to the characteristics of a past that, they argue, was more moral than current society; Hindu nationalists argue for an understanding of India as defined by its Hindu traditions; Scottish nationalists center their identity and political claims around civic traditions of education, religion, law, etc. that distinguish the Scots from their southern neighbors. Clearly, tradition has an important role to play in even the most modern and most democratic political systems.

The nature of tradition and its political role are of importance to this study not because people in Jordan are somehow trapped in tradition, or insufficiently modernized, or because tradition must necessarily oppose that which is modern. Rather, tradition is important because it has been made a subject for political contestation. Tradition as depicted by those who advocate it as a basis for political organization has the appeal of being familiar and comprehensible; it is valuable for its own sake, as a bulwark against the designs of foreign powers, and for the moral outcomes it is said to produce. For example, the practice of honor killings (see Chapter 4 below) is justified by those who endorse it as a link with the virtuous and authentic past, an aspect of local culture which foreign interests (such as human rights groups) seek to destroy and a practical means of promoting morality and public decency. The appeal to "cultural authenticity" is one that is made with great regularity in Jordanian politics, and the question of defining and giving political meaning to traditions is important to the process of political development.

I find it necessary to use the term "political development" in discussing these contestational issues in Jordan. In doing so, I do not mean to endorse the "developmentalist" view that characterized the work of modernization theorists because I do not believe that political development need follow a predetermined path or produce any particular outcome. "Political development" as used here means the ongoing process of construction, reform and entrenchment of the political system. States and people regard the building or modification of the political system as a process not merely of change, but of directed change, toward a goal and involving increasing improvements to the system (although what constitutes an improvement is, of course, a matter of debate).

Hegemony

An important concept in analyzing the factors that shape political development is that of hegemony. Antonio Gramsci, in perhaps the best-known work on hegemony, defined it as "the 'spontaneous' consent given by the great masses of the population to the general direction imposed on social life by the dominant fundamental group."[7]

For Gramsci, the state is partially dependent (in fact, as dependent as possible) on this mobilization of consent, so as to avoid costly coercion. The degree of spontaneity is perhaps questionable, as his quotation marks suggest, for two reasons. First, people everywhere are socialized by the cultural and political systems in which they live, so the degree of free choice in conforming to hegemonic norms is necessarily limited. The effects of socialization are particularly notable in gender roles; practices and beliefs that would be considered objectively harmful to women, such as clitoridectomy,[8] are often largely transmitted and enforced by women themselves. Jordanian and other feminists often cite the need to radically alter socialization of gender roles in the family, particularly among siblings, as a basis for broader societal changes.

Second, where conscious choice is possible, failure to endorse the hegemony can come at a fairly high social cost. For example, women who reject or depart from the hegemonic understanding of femininity may be taunted, punished by social exclusion, rejected as a potential mate, etc. The social cost of operating outside the hegemony varies by actor, issue and circumstance; an American woman of the early twenty-first century who does not wish to have children may attract only mild curiosity, whereas she would have faced social condemnation in earlier times, and a woman from another culture might face significantly higher costs for this departure from the feminine norm.

Gramsci's treatment of hegemony as an alternative to coercion does not suggest that states do not also engage in coercive actions where this is considered necessary or useful. Rather, it points to the importance of sociocultural factors in the maintenance of a political system. This understanding of the relationship of consent and coercion is especially usefully applied to developing countries, which Christopher Clapham suggests are characterized by a combination of power and fragility.[9] The power, that is to say the coercive capacity, of the state is the most evident element of the two, but the success of the state rests in the final analysis on its legitimacy. Problems of legitimacy, a lack of connection between the people and the state, are the basis for the state's fragility. Thus states, particularly in developing countries where the course and content of political development

7 Antonio Gramsci, *Selections from the Prison Notebooks of Antonio Gramsci*, Quentin Hoare and Geoffrey Nowell Smith (eds and trans) (New York: International Publishers, 1971), 12.

8 Clitoridectomy, sometimes called "female circumcision," is primarily an African practice; while it is widespread in Egypt, it is virtually unknown in Jordan.

9 Clapham, *Third World Politics*, Chapter 3. See also Nazih Ayubi, *Overstating the Arab State* (New York: I.B. Tauris, 1996), on the difference between "strong" states and "hard" or "fierce" states and Joel S. Migdal, *Strong Societies and Weak States: State-Society Relations and State Capabilities in the Third World* (Princeton: Princeton University Press, 1988).

is conscious and hotly contested, must concern themselves with sociocultural legitimacy based upon the hegemonic values of the society.

Gramsci's work on legitimacy has already been put to productive use in the study of culture and politics. One well-known example is David Laitin's *Hegemony and Culture*, which applied Gramsci's analysis to the issue of religion and politics among the Yoruba of Nigeria.[10] In this work, Laitin argued for the need to connect the study of culture to the study of the state. Departing from earlier treatments of culture and politics by structuralists such as Geertz, Laitin applied Gramsci's concept of hegemony to an analysis of the means by which particular cultural subsystems, like religion, are or are not brought into the political sphere. This useful approach demonstrates, among other things, that the effect of Islam on politics is not inevitable but rather a product of particular sociopolitical forces. This is a view now taken by many political scientists specializing in the Middle East.[11] I make a similar argument in this study, that while the contestation over cultural legitimacy and the role of "authentic tradition" is enormously significant for political development in Jordan, this is not because of any objectively necessary "clash" between tradition and modernity, Islam and democracy, or civilizations.

Hegemonies affect both state and non-state actors, and represent one means by which the latter are related to the former. In the past decade, a great deal of research has begun to investigate the ways in which feminist groups in the Middle East are challenging not only established cultural practices and beliefs but the autonomy of the state and the hegemony of state-dominated political discourses.[12] However, in the Jordanian case, we must begin by examining the premise underlying much of this research, that is, that women's rights movements necessarily represent a challenge to the state's ability to dominate the political sphere. In many cases, in the Middle East and elsewhere, the initial question should address not *how* the political hegemony is being challenged but *if* it is being challenged. Certainly most, if not all, women's movements exist to pursue social and political change, and that change is of a significant kind, usually requiring a restructuring of political and legal rights and implying expansion of both political participation and the nature of issues within the political arena. Yet these goals need not represent a cost to the state and, in fact, can serve one or more of the purposes of the state itself, particularly in cases where the state is addressing demands for greater political liberalization. This is the case in Jordan, and therefore the Jordanian women's movement is not, strictly speaking, counterhegemonic. Rather, it works within

---

10 David Laitin, *Hegemony and Culture: Politics and Religious Change among the Yoruba* (Chicago: University of Chicago Press, 1986).

11 See, for example, Jillian Schwedler, "Islamic Identity: Myth, Menace, or Mobilizer?" *SAIS Review*, 21:2 (2001): 1–17.

12 Notable recent examples of this extensive literature include Laurie Brand's *Women, the State, and Political Liberalization: Middle Eastern and North African Experiences* (New York: Columbia University Press, 1998) and Mai Yamani (ed.), *Feminism and Islam: Legal and Literary Perspectives* (New York: NYU Press, 1996).

the dominant discourse to promote improvements in the position of women, and it allies itself closely with the state and utilizes existing paths of institutional and personal power. This is, to a great extent, a result of the nature of sociopolitical hegemony and gender in Jordan and, in particular, the predominant role of the state.

In the Jordanian case, there is no feminist movement constituted as a direct opponent to a nationalist or traditionalist discourse. The movement and the dominant state discourse are both fairly moderate, as will be described below. The state itself is neither harshly oppressive of women nor an unswerving champion of their rights. Likewise, women's organizations are not outposts of radical feminism,[13] but neither are they completely docile servants of the state. In this context, finding the counterhegemonic actor among such apparent moderation requires careful sorting of agendas and legitimation sources. It would be an overstatement to claim that women's organizations are completely co-opted by the state, nor is it true that the state can always be understood as a force countering the goals of the women's rights movement. In some cases, we even find that elements of the state itself appear to challenging the hegemonic discourse.

Looking for counterhegemony in the Jordanian case requires first finding the hegemony, which involves distinguishing different strands of authority and legitimacy. Political discourse in Jordan is dominated by the state, but the state is neither isolated nor a monolithic entity. Thus the state-endorsed and state-wielded hegemony draws both on various state elements and on societal sources in shaping the dominant discourse.

I identify two strands of hegemonic discourse in Jordan, which operate together to form the dominant discourse.[14] These strands are hegemonic in the sense that they are each the dominant and determinant discourse within their areas of application. This is a key point: the dominant Jordanian political discourse is highly sensitive to issues of actor and audience; thus the discourse that claims

---

13 As used here, "radical" does not mean extremist but rather refers to the school of feminist thought by that name. Radical feminism generally holds that gender oppression is the most fundamental form of oppression, extending across history and societies and, consequently, that fundamental changes in the bases of social organization are needed to achieve equality for women. (For a useful discussion of the various schools of feminism, see Rosemary Tong, *Feminist Thought: a Comprehensive Introduction* (Westview Press: Boulder, 1989)). This would indeed be an extreme position in the Jordanian context, but it is not extremist in the sense of fringe lunacy.

14 Although she does not discuss them in terms of discourse and hegemony, Mary Ann Tétreault has noted a similar phenomenon in Kuwaiti politics, which she describes as the rulers' "impossible dream: that Kuwait can be simultaneously a 'developed' country and a 'traditional' tribally organized social formation run by autocratic rulers." ("A State of Two Minds: State Cultures, Women, and Politics in Kuwait," *International Journal of Middle East Studies*, 33:2 (May 2001): 203–220). As I argue in the case of Jordan, Tétreault points out that this combination of traditionalism and "developed" politics results in apparently contradictory policies on women's rights.

greatest authority depends to some extent on the topic in question. However, this is not to suggest that these should be understood as competing discourses. Rather, the hegemony that the state has constructed is one that claims the compatibility of these strands. Whether this compatibility is real or false is not the point; the *claim* of compatibility is what carries political force.

The two discourses that make up the general hegemony are the royal-liberal and the traditional. By royal-liberal, I mean the sphere of discourse that generally endorses liberal democratic ideals and has the support of the royal family. This is not identical to liberal discourses elsewhere, as a great deal of attention is given to constructing "locally appropriate" understandings of rights. In effect, these are liberal notions reconstructed to serve the state's needs for both domestic control and international legitimacy, and the probably sincere interest of members of the royal family in promoting more liberal notions of rights. The "traditional" sphere of discourse is that endorsed by what are considered the traditional sectors of Jordanian society, most importantly the tribal elements that are key supporters of the state and the monarchy. This discourse utilizes the appeal of tradition (as defined by its advocates) and has sufficient authority to hold other elements accountable to the claims of tradition; even those who are not themselves "traditionalists" find it necessary to adopt this language of authenticity. Thus, for example, plans to improve the status of women are often couched in terms of religious duty or cultural appropriateness, rather than feminist egalitarian rights. The success of this discourse in claiming cultural authenticity for itself serves to constrain other discourses; likewise, the royal power endorsing the more liberal discourse prevents its outright rejection by traditionalist actors. The result is a combining of the two strands into one hegemonic discourse, in which liberal and traditional elements both command authority. This makes for a highly flexible and politically adaptable hegemony, different elements of which are stressed according to audience and issue. That it is hegemonic is clear, however, as contestation outside this framework is not tolerated.

This discussion of hegemony in Jordan is a necessary basis for understanding the nature of Jordanian political discourse and the related legitimation strategies of the state and other actors. Liberal and traditional elements are combined rather than counterpoised in the dominant discourse, and thus we see them combined as well in state policy and the activities of other actors such as women's organizations.

Legitimacy

While these issues have important implications for democracy, this project is not a study of democratization; it is a study of political legitimacy in Jordan. Not just the fact but the type (or quality) of legitimacy has significant implications for the success of democratization processes and more broadly for the nature of the political system. The theory of legitimacy that undergirds the thesis of this project is based, as mentioned above, on the work of Jürgen Habermas.

Habermas's theory of legitimation crisis was created to explain a phenomenon specific to advanced capitalist states. According to Habermas, such a state contains inherent contradictions in its required functions; these contradictions both jeopardize the state's legitimacy and make the state unable to generate new legitimacy. This legitimation problem is inherent in the nature of the advanced capitalist state, rather than situational or contingent.

Habermas's theory was not intended to explain the legitimacy problems of developing countries, but I believe that its basic explanatory principles hold true in cases like Jordan, for reasons described below. In his description of types of system crisis, Habermas gives brief attention to system types or stages other than advanced capitalism, including primitive, traditional and liberal-capitalist systems; unfortunately, his analysis of "traditional" systems is not of use here, either descriptively or analytically. Habermas defined traditional systems as those in which the "principle of organization is class domination in political form,"[15] which does not describe the Jordanian system. Nor, as he suggested was the case for traditional systems, is the legitimation issue in Jordan one of reconciling internal norms with exploitation that produces class conflict. His analysis of liberal-capitalist systems does not fit our purposes either, as it describes a society in which the "bourgeois constitutional state finds its justification in the legitimate relations of production" and a "society that no longer recognizes political domination in personal form."[16] Of course, it was not Habermas's project to explain legitimacy in developing countries, and his typology was designed with the history of Europe in mind; its lack of direct application to the present case is not surprising. However, Habermas's analysis of the role of the modern state and the issue of legitimacy is, unlike the description of system stages or types, conceptually portable to systems beyond the advanced capitalist type and useful in examining the rise and operation of legitimacy issues.

Habermas (and others, like Claus Offe) sees advanced capitalist society as a system with three subsystems: sociocultural, economic and political-administrative. In advanced capitalism, the state has had to take on market-related functions that were earlier the province of the private sphere. However, while the state possesses autonomy as a decisive actor, it depends on the processes of advanced capitalism for its material content. The state can influence these economic processes, but cannot control them, and it must function so as to ensure their continuation.

At the same time, the state must maintain the loyalty and support of its citizens. However, the capitalist system works against the social integration necessary to produce legitimation because it brings formerly nonpolitical issues into the arena of political contestation and justice claims. The state cannot create legitimation in the sociocultural sphere because its attempts to do so result in the further politicization of cultural or traditional issues. This increases both the demands on the state and the probability of a crisis of legitimation.

15 Jürgen Habermas, *Legitimation Crisis* (Boston: Beacon Press, 1973) 18.

16 Ibid., 22.

The legitimacy problems theorized by Habermas grow out of a tension between the state's functional imperatives. While the concerns of the developing state are not identical to those of the advanced capitalist state, I argue that they are analogous; the economic processes for which the state bears responsibility are more securely established in advanced capitalist states, while the developing state must provide not merely for their continuation, but for their establishment, entrenchment and improvement, all the while subject to both internal and external demands and constraints. Additionally, the developing state must continually justify not only the regime, especially when not democratically elected, but often the framework of the state itself, even including its borders, its administrative powers and the identity of its citizenry.

Developing countries' states are faced with a nation-building project involving fundamental questions of political power, individual and group rights and administrative efficiency *in addition to* their responsibilities in the economic sphere. Thus the scope of issues that can be brought into political contestation is greater, while, as I hope to demonstrate in the following chapters, the sociocultural issues that directly provoke legitimacy questions are already more visible. This is the source of the politics of legitimation that are so fundamentally important in Jordan as it engages in a deliberate and highly public process of political development. While Jordan is not an advanced capitalist system of the type envisioned by Habermas, the state's functional responsibilities have, in a manner similar to what he described, led to the politicization of sociocultural elements that raise legitimacy issues that the state must address.

In the Jordanian case, the potential for legitimation crisis lies in the questionable stability of the very dualities the state has found so tactically useful. Its two-stranded hegemony has allowed it to appeal to various audiences and constituents with admirable flexibility, an approach at which the late King Hussein was adept. The dual legal system, discussed in Chapter 3 below, has served practical and political purposes by giving the state and the people access to both traditionally-valued elements of Islamic law and modern-style criminal, civil and administrative codes and courts. At the policy level, the state has both encouraged the promotion of women's rights and limited the extent to which such demands could challenge the state's policies (see Chapter 6). These dualities have, to a great degree, permitted the management of the Jordanian state in a way which safeguarded the monarchy's power by offering a way for nearly every subject to find something legitimate about it.

However, despite their tactical utility, these dualities are not necessarily stable in the long run. By offering more than one strand of hegemonic political discourse, the state has broadened the bases upon which claims and challenges must be taken seriously. If, for example, Islamic law is to have a role in the state, then why not a bigger role? If women's rights are to be protected, then why not to a greater extent? In addition to suggesting the forms of its own opposition, the state's approach to legitimacy has also made its legitimation task more complex. Not only are Islamists seeking a greater role for Islam in the system and women's rights activists seeking more rights for women, both using the state's own authority logic, but each also borrows from the authority of the "other side."

A notable example of this, discussed further in Chapter 3, arose in the 1999 municipal elections. Islamists used the logic of individual civil rights to argue that veiled women should not have to reveal their faces for identification at polling places. The government was caught unawares and had no suitable response; the issue garnered extensive public attention, and Islamists enhanced their own position as actors in a democratic system not by moderating their claims for religion in the public sphere but by casting the issue as one of civil rights instead of portraying it as an issue of public morality.

This example suggests a potential point at which legitimation crisis could occur. Crisis is likely to take place over sociocultural rather than political economy issues; the state is more adept at portraying economic problems as technical, externally-affected and an issue receiving the state's best efforts. The government's popularity may wax and wane with the variation of economic indicators, but legitimation crisis is likely to be oriented toward questions of values and principles that are at the foundation of the political system. In particular, crisis could occur over issues of the state's ability to combine, as it claims to do, respect for cultural (especially religious) values and practices with the principles and procedures of a democratizing state.

If a sociocultural legitimation crisis does develop, the state's responses are particularly likely to be felt in the areas of law and rights. Even in the absence of a full-blown crisis of legitimation that threatens to break down the political system, ongoing pursuit of legitimacy by the state and challenges from other actors will have a defining effect on the development of the Jordanian political system, again especially with regard to law and rights. Either democracy or renewed authoritarianism could result from the state's choices in seeking to resolve its legitimation dilemmas.

Choices made with regard to legitimacy will have a strong effect on the principles and practices that are necessary for democracy; if legitimacy continues to be drawn significantly from claims of cultural authenticity, and that authenticity is defined in a way that precludes political equality, then prospects for democracy are dim. This is not, in my view, a product of the salience of Islam in the political system. While I would agree that Islam generally values substantive ethical norms over norms of process,[17] this does not mean that process norms are not valued, and in fact they can be considered crucial to the ethical outcome itself. For example, there are some who justify the murder of an adulterous wife by her husband on the grounds that Islamic law provides for a death penalty in adultery cases, and so the correct outcome is achieved. Mainstream legal scholars in Islamic history, however, condemn this position, arguing that the law's procedural requirements

17 I thank Mark Warren for raising this question and pointing out the importance of the distinction between substantive and process norms although we differ as to its application in the current issue.

(of evidence, judgment and execution) are themselves essential to the ethical outcome;[18] the death of the adulterous woman is not just unless it was brought about through the correct procedures.

This would appear to be a potential basis for developing an ethics of procedure in support of democratic processes, separate from the substantive norms concerning outcomes. If this can occur, then there is no necessary contradiction between Islam and democracy, even where democracy is understood in its fullest sense as not only the implementation of the will of the people, but the safeguarding of norms of process that precede and produce political outcomes.

Therefore the risk to democracy posed in the Jordanian case does not come from Islam itself in terms of the absence of processual norms, but from the substantive ethical norms being contested by traditionalists (both Islamist and non-Islamist). If the political system incorporates an understanding of individual rights as being defined a priori by the individual's gender, and perpetuates a hierarchy in which women's rights are different from and subordinate to those of men, this is a serious compromise of the principle of equality before the law that is a fundamental element of democracy. Equality of representation, participation, rights to contest views and pursue interests in the public sphere, all are predicated upon an understanding that every individual in the system has those rights, and to the same degree. To compromise equality before the law, not merely in discrete policies but as a matter of principle, would undermine the very logic of democracy and doom it to a stunted and unstable existence at best and would create the potential for significant oppression and unrest.

The issue of legitimacy and its connection to a particular definition of cultural authenticity is thus poised to be a primary determinant of the character of the political system as Jordan continues its process of development and, perhaps, further liberalization. Other issues will certainly shape political outcomes, but none are as likely to determine the character of the system itself. The Palestinian-Jordanian split is, in my opinion, not likely to be a major factor in the character of sociocultural legitimacy in the political sphere because while that element of identity does have a great effect on individuals' and social sectors' relationships to the state, it is not a cleavage that is salient in the traditionalism/liberalism debate. Supporters of each of the two camps can be found among both Palestinian and East Bank Jordanians. Perhaps ironically, the cultural legitimacy question could be one that helps to defuse this cleavage even as it creates others.

The following chapters examine these issues and the contestation over legitimacy that is pursued by the state as well as other actors. The subject is a crucial one for understanding political development, since the power of the state, while most obvious in its coercive features, is ultimately dependent upon legitimation.

---

18 Several such examples are cited in Mohammad Fadel, "Islamic Law Sources Against Honor Crimes," written for the Islamic Supreme Council of America, 2000. www.islamicsupremecouncil.org.

Chapter 3

Dual Legal Systems and the Basis of Law in Jordan

> "You are charged with having washed your clothes in the canal!"
>
> "Your Honour – may God exalt your station – are you going to fine me just because I washed my clothes?"
>
> "It's for washing them in the canal."
>
> "Well, where else could I wash them?"
>
> The judge hesitated, deep in thought, and could give no answer. He knew very well that these poor wretches had no wash basins in their village, filled with fresh flowing water from the tap. They were left to live like cattle all their lives and were yet required to submit to a modern legal system imported from abroad.
>
> –Tawfik al-Hakim, *Maze of Justice*

In his novel *Maze of Justice*, Tawfik al-Hakim depicts with rather black humor the frustrations involved in subjecting a backwater Egyptian village to the new laws and procedures of the "modernizing" state. Because the new laws have no connection to local social reality, they are meaningless and incomprehensible to the people they are meant to regulate; the village prosecutor alone stands in both camps and recognizes the futility of his task. Law and administration are essential powers of the state, but their exercise outside of a meaningful social context is, Hakim suggests, worthless. It is notable that the problem is not one of the intractability of tradition but the disconnection between two different bases of authority; Hakim is as critical of the mindless bureaucracy of the new system as of the subjective and socially-variable justice of the old one. The novel points out a vital issue in the establishment of state legal systems: the manner and degree of their relevance to the sociocultural context. The law's basis of authority must, if the state is to enjoy legitimacy, be comprehensible to and respected by the people. To this end, states facing legitimacy issues take conscious steps to reconcile the nature of authority with perceived social demands.

The legal systems of many Arab states, including Jordan, are characterized by the combination of two conceptually different legal traditions. In most cases, criminal and civil codes are drawn from, or heavily influenced by, European codes created by legislatures,[1] while Islamic law is the predominant source of "personal

---

1 State law (as opposed to *shari'a*) should not, however, be seen as an entirely European development; temporal rulers in the Islamic world developed criminal codes distinct from *shari'a* well before the colonial era. Haim Gerber, citing Uriel Heyd, discusses the establishment of distinct spheres of *qanun* (state law) and *shari'a* in the core of the

status codes" that regulate issues such as marriage, divorce and inheritance. In the Jordanian case, the state even maintains separate court systems: one for dealing with cases based on the civil and criminal codes, and another for dealing with the *shari'a*-based personal status code. The two traditions have not, however, remained entirely separate, as Islamic principles have influenced civil and criminal law, and "Western" legal concepts have helped to shape the content and creation of the Personal Status Codes. But while they have not remained isolated from one another in practice, the conceptual distinction between the two types of law has remained intact and has, in fact, greatly informed the legitimacy struggle that these states have faced. This chapter investigates the phenomenon of these dual legal systems[2] and their political significance. Because dual legal systems exist throughout the Arab world, and because Arab legal systems draw on many of the same legal sources and sometimes borrow directly from one another, it is necessary to discuss legal dualism in Jordan in the broader context of the regional phenomenon.

By "legal system," I mean the "operating set of legal institutions, procedures and rules," as that of a state or other political entity.[3] A legal tradition, by contrast, has been well-defined by Merryman as

> not a set of rules of law. Rather, it is a set of deeply rooted, historically conditioned attitudes about the nature of law, about the role of law in the society and the polity, about the proper organization and operation of a legal system, and about the way law is or should be made, applied, studied, perfected and taught. The legal tradition relates the legal system to the culture of which it is a partial expression. It puts the legal system into cultural perspective.[4]

This is precisely the nature of the political issues of law which arise in the Jordanian case, and they go directly to the heart of the relationship between culture and politics. The two political traditions that are combined in the Jordanian legal system draw on different sources of authority, have somewhat differing orientations to the role of law in society and construct the relationship of individuals and society

---

Ottoman empire as early as the fifteenth century and points out that the original body of state penal law was in large part a wholesale adoption of *shari'a* penal law. The authority of temporal sovereigns in this area was furthermore not regarded as a usurpation of religious authority but a rightful power of political rulers. See Haim Gerber, *State, Society and Law in Islam: Ottoman Law in Comparative Perspective* (Albany: State University of New York Press, 1994), especially 61–63.

2 This term as used here applies to what are elsewhere sometimes called "plural" or "mixed" legal systems. I avoid the term "legal pluralism" for reasons discussed below and feel that "dual" more precisely describes the perception of a dichotomy between the two systems than would the term "mixed."

3 John Henry Merryman, *The Civil Law Tradition*, 2nd edition (Stanford: Stanford University Press, 1985), 1.

4 Ibid., 2.

in different ways. I argue below that this dualism within the system is, from the practical standpoint and that of state legitimation, both a strength and a liability.

The presence of two legal traditions is in large part a simple result of historical circumstance: Jordan, along with Egypt, Syria and Lebanon, once came under the authority of the Ottoman Empire, which instituted legal codes directly modeled upon the French Code Napoléon and relying in part upon Islamic principles. This circumstance has had important political consequences; the generally secular authoritarian states of the region have found that their legitimacy is particularly open to challenge on grounds of cultural authenticity, and so the "imported" legal systems must be made to appear appropriate to the societies they regulate. This has been accomplished in part by defining such systems as the norm for modern states and in part by managing national legal frameworks to allow the "preservation" of traditional social frameworks, as in the Personal Status Codes.[5]

This approach has been largely successful. The most credible opposition challenge to secular authoritarian regimes in recent years has come from Islamist movements. This is particularly the case in Jordan, where the Islamic Action Front (IAF) is the largest, best organized and most successful of the political parties. Throughout the region, only a few, fairly extreme opposition movements have advocated the complete destruction of the state and its institutions and their replacement with an Islamic system of governance, relying upon Islamic law. Other Islamist opponents of the state, such as the IAF and its parent Muslim Brotherhood, have exhibited varying degrees of willingness to operate within the existing structure, seeking to alter its policy output and some of its laws, in order to produce an acceptably "Islamic" political order. Thus it is generally accepted that such legal frameworks should exist, and the political question becomes one of how to arrange the content of the codes so that they are appropriate for Muslim society. By the demarcation of certain areas of life as appropriately regulated by Islamic law rather than the secular state, many of these demands for legitimacy can be met. The state can plausibly claim that it is properly respectful of its citizens' traditions and values and that it maintains the necessary framework to carry out the business of governing.

A caveat about the "Islamic-ness" of Arab legal systems is necessary here; although the presence of some elements of Islamic law in most Arab states may be well-known, it is not necessarily well-understood. Western views of law in the Arab world tend to emphasize the Islamic aspects, as though legal systems are primarily Islamic in their rules and/or principles. Lama Abu-Odeh has identified a "fantasy" in the teaching of Islamic law in American law schools "to the effect that Islamic law is a foundational category for anyone attempting to understand law

5 The political claim is that these traditional frameworks are "authentic" in that they pre-existed the state and its imported legal systems and have been left untouched, in their original form. In fact, the Islamic-law based Personal Status Codes are themselves creations of the state, rather than the simple adoption of a body of uncontested legal rules and practices. This is discussed more fully below.

in the Islamic world…Its modus operandi is a rhetorical slippage…that gradually and almost imperceptibly substitutes 'Islamic Law' for 'Law in the Islamic countries.'"[6] This has led, in her view, to the understudying of the European legal heritage of these systems; the present study hopes to contribute to the solution of this problem.

The problem of overstating the Islamic-ness of Arab legal systems is an interesting counterpoint to an earlier notion in academia, that the process of creating uniform legal systems in developing countries is hindered by "pockets of intense resistance from groups whose law has been preserved in some fashion."[7] In this view, Islamic law is a traditional remnant that exists in the lacunae and on the borderlands of the modern legal system. This is in some ways a useful and probably inevitable shorthand for the post-colonial state of affairs, particularly as Islamic law has a longer history in the region and did suffer some displacement by the rise of new legal forms. It also reflects something of the political reality, in that legal choices are often "sold" in this way – as a chance to preserve an element of traditional culture – by various kinds of conservatives. But political image is not necessarily synonymous with political reality, and what is really going on is the adaptation, and even creation, of Islamic, traditional and other forms of legal rules and practices, in order to serve contemporary needs – especially those of the state.

Among the constitutions of the Arab states, all except Lebanon[8] proclaim Islam the official state religion. The legal implications of this official enshrinement of Islam, however, have varied greatly from country to country. A few countries (such as Saudi Arabia) base their entire political order upon Islamic law, while others (Egypt, Kuwait, Syria, Qatar, Yemen) proclaim it a source of legislation to varying degrees, and still others (Jordan, Morocco) remain constitutionally silent on the issue of how Islamic law is to operate. Even where *shari'a* is formally recognized as the primary source of legislation, the actual character of the legal system departs significantly from a "purely Islamic" order, incorporating laws and procedures of various origins, both indigenous and foreign. The legal systems of most Arab states are thus most properly characterized as "dual systems," in that they are neither entirely Islamic nor entirely civil or secular. (These terms and their merits are discussed in greater detail below).

I argue that these dual legal systems are neither accidental nor anomalous but rather represent purposive choices by the state for dealing with a host of political

6 Lama Abu-Odeh, "The Politics of (Mis)recognition: Islamic Law Pedagogy in American Academia," *American Journal of Comparative Law* 52:4 (2004): 789–824.

7 Sally Engle Merry, "Legal Pluralism," *Law & Society Review* 22:5 (1988): 869–896. She cites Geertz (1983) as a proponent of this view of the development of law.

8 Lebanon's post-Taif constitution makes no reference to Islam except to provide that Christians and Muslims have equal representation. Syria's constitution lacks an explicit statement that Islam is the official religion but achieves similar effect by providing that the religion of the president must be Islam and that *shari'a* is a "main source" of legislation.

issues, particularly the need for legitimacy. Dual legal systems provide a flexible framework for social regulation, the exercise of state power and the maintenance of popular legitimacy in various sectors of society. In this chapter, I first examine the types of duality found in states, offering a rough typology for classification, and then examine the consequences of dual legal systems for political contestation, with particular attention to feminist and Islamist demands for legal reforms. I argue that the two elements of dual systems do not exist in isolation from one another; rather, each strand has affected the other in terms of content and procedures. This cross-pollination, even though limited, helps to shape the character and content of political contestation. If dual systems are maintained in their current forms in the states where they now exist, this will serve a limiting function to preclude certain kinds of political demands and forestall others. If, however, as I think is more likely in the long term, Islamic law becomes subsumed in the state-created legal systems of the region, formerly ostensibly static social practices will become subject to political reform in a new and potentially democratic way.[9]

As the purpose of this chapter is to examine the politics of legal dualism in relation to the state and its development, I have focused on the formal aspects of law rather than treating the law in a broader anthropological sense as the entire constellation of controlling norms and consequent penalties within a society. While this second approach to law has much to recommend it as a basis for understanding social organization more broadly, the present concern with the formal political order and state legitimacy precludes this treatment of law. Also, in analyzing the potential political consequences of dual systems and their future development, I have largely excluded states, such as Saudi Arabia, in which the system relies on non-Islamic law to an extremely limited extent. Although non-Islamic law exists in these systems, it has not yet become a significant characteristic of the political order nor, consequently, an important factor in political development, and thus the conclusions I draw about the truly dual legal systems are probably of little relevance to such cases.

Legal Pluralism

This study of dual legal systems is informed by work in the field of legal pluralism. The concept of legal pluralism is one that has been widely examined in social science literature of recent years.[10] Originally, the study of law and society

9 A third alternative, for state legal and political systems to be replaced with Islamic ones, is an extremely remote possibility in all systems except the Sudan and so will receive little attention here.

10 Legal pluralism, sometimes called legal polycentricity, has been of particular interest to scholars of post-colonial studies and anthropology. For a notable example in the field of Middle Eastern studies, see Baudouin Dupret, Maurits Berger and Laila al-Zwaini (eds), *Legal Pluralism in the Arab World* (Boston: Kluwer Law International, 1999).

recognized the occasional coexistence of different systems of law within a single state, usually as the result of European colonialism and the consequent imposition of a foreign legal system onto an indigenous one.

However, this simple formulation of the concept of legal pluralism was soon found to be epistemologically and methodologically problematic. It was criticized for inappropriately reifying the concept of "law," and for treating it as a social phenomenon isolated, and isolable, from the rest of the social order.[11] An important corrective was provided by scholars who took a more anthropological approach, pointing out the diverse forms of rules of social order in societies. This is what Merry called the "new legal pluralism," entailing a recognition that "plural normative orders are found in virtually all societies" and that "not all law takes place in the courts."[12] The editors of a recent book on the subject characterized this distinction as between a lawyerly view of legal pluralism as merely "recognition by the state...of the existence of a multiplicity of legal sources which constitute its legislation" and a social-scientific understanding of a "plurality of social fields, producers of norms which are in partial interaction with each other. It entails depriving the state of its capacity as a social actor (as opposed to its multiple constituents) and, consequently not considering it merely as the monopolist of legal production, be it directly or indirectly."[13]

This trend away from legal positivism calls to mind the earlier trend in political science which moved the discipline from an exclusive focus on formal institutions to a broader and more useful understanding of politics. However, political science as a discipline later found it necessary to reinvigorate the study of formal institutions, such as the state, as respectable objects of scientific inquiry and theory. In somewhat the same vein, while recognizing the intellectual validity of the work in the field of legal pluralism, this essay will treat the concept of law in a fairly formalistic sense – not out of an affection for positivism, which I do not embrace, but in order to examine the political realities of state power and state claims to authority. This study does not seek to define the entirety of law-like norms in the Jordanian system or to assess the normative power of every social and political actor; rather, I want to investigate the ways in which the state has deliberately managed legal systems to meet particular political ends and the effect that this process has had on the formal political system.

Thus this study is about legal dualism more than legal pluralism; it is a straightforward treatment of the existence of two conceptually separate formal legal traditions within single political orders dominated by states. This is not to suggest that such legal traditions are the only social norms that serve to order society or that the state alone exercises the power of creating and wielding norms. Rather,

11 See John Griffiths' prefatory essay in *Legal Pluralism in the Arab World* for a concise discussion of this problem.

12 Sally Engle Merry, "Legal Pluralism," *Law & Society Review* 22:5 (1988): 869–896.

13 Dupret, Berger and al-Zwaini (eds), *Legal Pluralism in the Arab World*, xi.

the focus on dualism is meant to provide a treatment of a specific manifestation of legal pluralism, within a political context sharply defined by the state and its powers. A treatment of non-state legal forms in the region would be valuable, but it is not the project of the present study.[14]

Legal Dualism: Islamic and "Modern" Law

The term "legal dualism" is not new; it has been used to describe a variety of cases in which a single state system recognizes two legal systems, whether applying to different sectors of the population or to different issues. Thus legal dualism has characterized the situation of Aborigines in Australia, blacks in Lesotho, Palestinians in the Occupied Territories, British and Chinese residents of colonial-era Hong Kong and the relative powers of church and state in thirteenth-century Spain. (The term has also been applied in international relations, in the context of international versus national law).

The legal dualism of the Arab states is fairly well-known; in nearly every state in the region, "modern"[15] law coexists to greater or lesser degree with Islamic law, or *shari'a*. In some countries, both separate bodies of law and separate court systems are maintained by the state; this is the case in Jordan and Qatar. In others, specific areas of social life have been reserved to *shari'a*, but judicial power has been unified in a single state-created court system, as is the case in Egypt. The arrangement of code and court in a particular country is, of course, a product of historical circumstance; for example, in Jordan as in several other cases, indigenous practices of *shari'a* were combined with the reformed civil and criminal codes of the Ottoman Empire. The Ottoman codes were modeled, in form and in content, upon nineteenth century European codes, particularly the French Code Napoléon. Other countries, such as Qatar, received their "modernized" codes from the British,

14 See, for example, Omar Razzaz, "Contestation and Mutual Adjustment: The Process of Controlling Land in Yajouz, Jordan," *Law and Society Review* 28:1 (1994): 7-39, in which the author makes explicit use of the concept of "autonomous social fields" developed by scholars of legal pluralism.

15 The term "modern" is used here with some trepidation; the current manifestations of *shari'a* in these systems often have equal claim to "modernity" in content, procedure and antecedent. However, I retain the modern/traditional terminology not only because it predominates in the literature on law in the Arab world but because participants in these legal systems themselves see the two fields in that way, as will be discussed below. I hope to make clear in this chapter that both terms are subject to politicization. Also, modern need not be taken to mean exclusively Western, in contrast with indigenous tradition; it can indicate something about the development of particular forms of state organization. Thus one could identify a modern/traditional legal dichotomy at certain periods in European legal development, when the rise of the modern state legal system began to subsume jurisdiction formerly held by the church through canon law.

while Saudi Arabia, which was never directly colonized, maintains a legal system entirely based upon *shari'a*.[16]

In most cases, *shari'a* persisted (although usually in altered form) primarily in the area of family law. This is because, I argue below, of both the greater specificity of *shari'a* in this area compared with other areas, such as commercial law, and the desire of the state to preserve traditional social forms and hierarchies. Most states maintain "personal status codes" that govern marriage, child custody, divorce and inheritance, and such codes are drawn (ostensibly) directly from *shari'a*. (For non-Muslims, equal provision is made for the existence of religious law governing the issues of personal status; thus countries with Christian minorities allow every recognized sect to maintain its own (canon-based) family law and, in the case of Jordan, its own courts with jurisdiction over such law).[17]

Thus it seems clear to many observers that the duality that characterizes most Arab legal systems involves a clear distinction between religious and secular law, with secular law predominating in most areas of law and religious law being reserved for "private" issues such as family relations. However, I argue that the duality is in fact much more complex, and more sophisticated, than it initially appears. Both "Islamic law" and "modern law" have become symbols subject to facile treatment that does not recognize the internal complexities of the two types of law.

First, the *shari'a* embodied in family law is in no way a static artifact of "original" unaltered *shari'a*; the content and form of such laws have been subject to reform by states and, increasingly, to contestation by various political actors. Amira Sonbol characterizes this as "modern *shari'a*,"

> whereby the formal law may have been defined on the basis of Qur'an, hadith, consensus and analogy, but the actual selection and final interpretation of the law is very much the construct of modern nation-states and hence shows great affinity to laws constructed and practiced by non-Muslim societies.[18]

However, the image of *shari'a* as an unchanging artifact of tradition persists, not only because of Western scholars' tendency to treat Islam as exceptional[19] but

16 It is worth noting, however, that even in the case of Saudi Arabia, non-*shari'a* forms of law exist, such as international legal obligations and particular commercial provisions not covered by *shari'a*.

17 The Christian and Jewish family laws that exist in several states are not examined here because they are not a chief component of legal dualism. Dualism persists because of the perceived necessity of maintaining both Islamic and "modern" law; religious laws of other communities exist only as a necessary corollary to the maintenance of Islamic family law.

18 Amira Sonbol, "Questioning Islamic Exceptionalism: *Shari'a* Law," *Arab Studies Journal*, 6:1 (1998): 76–86, 77.

19 See Sonbol. Also, numerous works on the world's legal systems treat Islamic (and other) religious law as minor exceptions to the reach of modern law.

because of Islamists' political claims about the value of *shari'a* in a society and the nature of legal authority. In the context of *shari'a* versus "modern" law, such thinkers talk about "the *shari'a*" as though there is only one unified and uniform body of Islamic law, and as though this law is a direct product of divine will rather than of human interpretation and construction. In fact, *shari'a* itself contains diverse principles and rules. The practice of adapting the formulation of Islamic law to a particular social reality is not new; it has characterized the formulation of Islamic law since its origin.[20] Another important caveat is suggested by Ann Elizabeth Mayer, who points out that the discriminatory character of the *shari'a*-based family laws is not simply a function of Islam, but has to do with a dynamic that has affected the family laws of all the Mediterranean countries.[21] Therefore, not only can these laws not be taken to represent some essential and unchanging element of Islam, but their gender discrimination must be considered as a social product rather than a purely religious one.

Modern law is often considered synonymous with secular law, a treatment which of course has some basis in reality. However, the two are not conceptually the same, and the distinction is important. While modern law is predominantly secular, and its rationales of authority are entirely secular, it is distinguishable from other forms of law which might equally be called secular, such as customary law. A key feature of "modern" law is not only that it is secular, but that it is a symbol and an agent of Weberian rationality and its associated bureaucratic developments. This rationality might be more claimed than real, as modern law is certainly in part a product of cultural habit and tradition. Nonetheless, the idea of rationality is key to the content and operation of modern law; laws are made by human design and decision, as necessary to meet the needs of human society. They are not received from God (although moral principles which inform the law may be) but are achieved through the use of human reason.

In a comparison of Islamic and modern law, this distinction could be characterized as "legislated" versus "unlegislated" law. Modern law relies upon legislation to produce laws, and the power of legislation extends across all social issues; that is, any issue that seems to require public regulation is one that the legislature may properly take up. In contrast, Islamic law is often represented as "unlegislated," in that basic laws are a product of divine revelation, their practical interpretation is entirely in the hands of jurist-scholars, and the proper subjects and scope of legislation are determined by Islam, rather than by human reason. In other words, "God and not man is the source of law in a Muslim society...Neither any individual, although he be a king, nor any class or group of people, nor the

---

20 N.J. Coulson, "Islamic Law," in J.D.M. Derrett (ed.), *An Introduction to Legal Systems* (Sweet and Maxwell: London, 1968), and J. Schacht, "Law and Justice," in Holt, Lambton and Lewis (eds), *Cambridge History of Islam*, vol. 2, part 8 (Cambridge: Cambridge University Press, 1970).

21 Ann Elizabeth Mayer, "Reform of Personal Status Laws in North Africa: a Problem of Islamic or Mediterranean Laws?" *Middle East Journal* 49:3 (1998): 432–446.

state, nor even the people as a whole has a right to make law."[22] Legislatures, in this context, may not legislate as their members see fit upon issues for which there already exists Qur'anic teaching because human reason may never supersede divine law. Where rules can be formulated, this activity is undertaken only to give practical expression to divinely-ordained law, not to create law itself.

We find elements of this distinction in many political statements about the law, which is why it is relevant to the current discussion. Both Orientalists[23] and Islamists are often inclined to present Islamic law as entirely divine in nature and thus either (a) not suitable for use in a democracy (according to Orientalists) or (b) not subject to flaws arising from human weakness and poor judgment (according to Islamists).[24] Similarly, the element of deliberate choice in creating law has, in Western systems, been somewhat overstated and, indeed, pursued as a political goal.[25] Upon examination, we find that Islamic law is not a single cohesive body of clear prescriptions, but a collection of general principles whose interpretation and practice have varied considerably over time and space.[26] Furthermore, the existing provisions for *shari'a* are in large part a direct product of legislatures and in most cases form part of a country's collection of legal codes. Likewise, law in Western countries has been heavily influenced by tradition, rather than being simply a product of legislation and other reason-based rule-making. The influence of social tradition is most clear in the area of common law, but the weight of traditional practices and community values is commonly recognized by Western judges operating within "legislated" systems. Certainly the "legislated/unlegislated"

---

22 Charles J. Adams, "Mawdudi and the Islamic State," in John Esposito (ed.), *Voices of Resurgent Islam* (New York: Oxford University Press, 1983), 115.

23 "Orientalists" were originally simply those scholars who studied the Near and Middle East, but the term has now come to refer to a particular orientation toward Arab and Muslim societies as inherently different from, and even a polar opposite to, Western ones. The most well-known criticism of Orientalism is that of Edward Said (see *Orientalism* (New York: Pantheon Books, 1978)).

24 Some Islamists, although by no means all, would agree with the argument that Islamic societies are unsuited to democracy – because Islam ordains a more perfect social order, not because Muslims are unable to achieve democracy. It is ironic that the position that Islam is antithetical to democracy is taken up both by some who value Islam and by some who disparage it.

25 The French Revolution, for example, had among its programs the improvement of the political order by, among other things, reconstructing the legal system such that law would be purely a product of the people (via their chosen legislators) rather than the product of undemocratically-empowered judges. By making the legal code as explicit as possible, it was believed that the influence of judges as interpreters of the law could be entirely eradicated. This position was later relaxed in the face of practical difficulties. For a useful explanation of this development, see John Henry Merryman, *The Civil Law Tradition*, 2nd edition (Stanford: Stanford University Press, 1985).

26 See, for example, Judith Tucker, *In the House of the Law* (Berkeley: University of California Press, 1998).

law distinction can be a useful one, but it is important to recognize that elements of tradition (and religion) and elements of human reasoning have been integral components of both kinds of systems. Once this is clear, it becomes easier to recognize the political purposes of certain claims about the nature and content of law. These claims have formed an important part of the critique of the Arab state from both external and internal observers.

Thus the duality of these legal systems is more complex than it first appears. While the contrast between them is in many ways one of appeal to different types of authority (and thus political organization), the reality of political and legal development has precluded the drawing of clear lines between tradition and modernity. Certainly the partisans of the two systems see themselves as ranged on a battlefield of tradition(al religion) and modernity, and the states that have created and managed dual legal systems have used the conceptual differences to appeal to different sectors of society. However, the real flexibility of legal duality has been recognized and utilized by political actors in pursuit of goals on all points of the political spectrum.

Islamic Law and the State

The chief variation in dual legal systems in the Arab world lies in the state's treatment of Islamic law. By and large, as described above, Arab states have civil and criminal codes and procedural codes attached to them, which take a basically European form and derive, in fact, from European codes by way of the Ottoman Empire. They differ, however, in terms of the degree to which they incorporate Islamic law into the state's legal order, and in the manner of doing so.

It is generally true that Islamic law "survives" in modern Arab states in the area of family law and has in most cases been replaced in other areas of law, such as penal codes. Among the states whose legal systems can be characterized as dual, I identify three types of treatment of Islamic law. The first, in Jordan, Syria, Lebanon and Iraq, involves the maintenance of a separate *shari'a*-based personal status code along with a separate system of *shari'a* courts to deal with issues within the bounds of this code. The second approach, as in Egypt, Algeria, Morocco, Tunisia and Kuwait, is the maintenance of a separate personal status code but no separate *shari'a* court system. Personal status laws are enforced by the regular courts (those which also hear civil and criminal cases); in the case of Egypt, these are heard by judges trained in *shari'a*. The third type of system is that of Bahrain and Qatar, in which personal status law remains uncodified, but separate *shari'a* courts exist to deal with matters of marriage, divorce, child custody, inheritance – the range of issues normally treated by personal status codes where they have been codified. In this third type of system, judges are directed to apply the classical law of the relevant madhhab, or school of jurisprudence.[27] However, even in cases where the personal status law has been codified, the codes themselves often instruct judges to rely on the classical texts of a particular school (or the predominant principles of *shari'a*) to fill in areas not detailed by the legislation itself.[28]

What explains these forms of incorporating *shari'a* into state legal systems? Certainly one must acknowledge the role of historical circumstance; these states have colonial histories that shaped their political systems to a large degree, and the lack of a direct experience of colonization is one of the factors explaining why Saudi Arabia, for example, does not have a fully dual legal system. Another factor is simple practicality; countries such as Qatar found it administratively useful to develop non-*shari'a* based legal codes for issues of commerce, citizenship and other topics not given detailed treatment in Islamic law.[29] Family issues are quite explicitly organized in all the schools of jurisprudence, and so that area of law ostensibly continued to function as it always had – except, of course, that family law had not "always" operated in any single way, and significant reforms were introduced at or after independence by legislatures and executives intent on forming an administratively operable and a politically governable state. But the common perception is that family law has been "preserved" by the state, and it is that perception that shapes the law's political role. I argue that these considerations influence the state's choices about maintaining an official realm of *shari'a* within its authority and that these choices are important for the course of political contestation and development in the dual-system states.

The continued presence of Islamic law in an "official" capacity could be regarded as a mere anachronism, a holdover of tradition in societies that have not fully modernized. Orientalists in particular see the retention of Islamic law as evidence of the basic incompatibility of Western concepts of rights and freedoms with Islamic society.[30]

The maintenance of dual legal systems could be regarded, as one author argues, as a shortcoming of Arab political orders.[31] The problem, in this view, is not that dual legal systems represent an insufficient degree of modernization but

27 There are four schools of jurisprudence in Sunni Islam: Hanafi, Maliki, Shafi'i and Hanbali. Hanafi was the predominant school of the Ottoman Empire and consequently predominates in Jordan, Egypt, Sudan, Syria, Iraq and among Sunnis in Lebanon. The Hanbali school predominates in the Gulf (except in Kuwait, which uses the Maliki school), the Maliki in North Africa and the Shafi'i in Yemen. There are two Shi'a schools, the Ja'fari (predominant in Bahrain) and the Zaydi, which is used by Shi'a minorities in a few countries.

28 This is the case in the Jordanian Law of Personal Status, for example. See also Jamal J. Nasir, *The Islamic Law of Personal Status* (London: Graham and Trotman, 1986).

29 A. Nizar Hamzeh, "Qatar: the Duality of the Legal System," *Middle Eastern Studies* 30:1 (1994): 79–90.

30 See Sonbol, "Questioning Exceptionalism."

31 Nabil 'Abd al-Fattah, "The Anarchy of Egyptian Legal System: Wearing Away the Legal and Political Modernity," in *Legal Pluralism in the Arab World.*

that the actual practice regarding modern law tends to discredit both the law and the political order that "owns" it, due to inconsistencies in application and the (accurate) perception that legislators everywhere are the captives of executives, whose project the dual legal system primarily is. This promotes a disregard of modern law and a nostalgia for familiar and consistent laws, such as those arising from custom. Where possible, people may turn to customary and religious law to solve their problems; the existence of not only other laws but other legal rationales that are not only familiar but even endorsed by the state may create a basis upon which to formulate political demands based upon an authority distinct from that of the state.

It is clear that law is a tool for political legitimation, in all types of political systems. The extent to which states are able to use that tool effectively is debatable; Nathan Brown's important study of Arab law[32] suggests that states may achieve much less than they (and their observers) believe in this regard. However, while legitimation is certainly not perfectly managed by the ordering of legal systems, I believe that the deployment of particular types of law in particular areas, as is the case in the dual legal systems, serves an important legitimating function for Arab states. While this legitimation is sometimes undermined by the state's inconsistent treatment of law (and recognizing that the state itself is not an internally uniform, monolithic entity), I argue that this is because legitimation is not the state's only goal, nor the goal of every aspect of the state. States and their agents also seek to maintain executive power and (in non-democratic or weakly democratic cases such as those treated here) to control political contestation, keeping it within manageable parameters. Thus the Jordanian state proclaims free speech, (although somewhat declawing the constitutional guarantee with phrases like "within the limits of the law" and "provided that such [speech] does not violate the law"[33]) while reserving the right to jail those who criticize the king.

With regard to the use of dual legal systems to legitimate the state, I believe that states tend to treat the two systems differently. The "traditional" or Islamic sphere is offered as a proof of cultural authenticity, which serves to help legitimate the state with "traditional" sectors of society; this legitimation serves indirectly to control contestation from that sector, as those who are satisfied with the maintenance of traditional social forms will not need to agitate or petition the state on these grounds. On the other hand, the "modern" sphere serves partly as a source of legitimation among domestic democrats and external powers by proving

32 Nathan Brown, *The Rule of Law in the Arab World* (Cambridge: Cambridge University Press, 1997).

33 Jordanian constitution (1952), Chapter 2, Article 15. This formulation also appeared in the previous constitution (of Transjordan, 1947). The Egyptian, Syrian and Lebanese constitutions contain similar language (see Egyptian Constitution, 1971, Part 3, Articles 47 and 54; Syrian Constitution, 1973, Part 4, and Lebanese Constitution, 1996, Article 13).

the state's secular character, its ability to manage modern forms of government and (in terms of civil liberties protections and egalitarian provisions) its good faith in democratization. However, this legal arena also serves as a direct control on political order, by allowing the state to manage both participation (by organizing elections laws, etc.) and contestation (by restricting speech, etc.) to its own best advantage.

Two Cases

1. The State Constraining Islamic Law

An interesting issue regarding state power at the nexus of Islamic and "modern" law is raised by Kilian Bälz, in his study of the "battle over the veil" in Egyptian schools.[34] Readers may recall the controversy, which began with the Egyptian government's ban on face-covering veils (*niqab*) worn by girls in public schools. The government sought by this action to prevent public display of affiliation with the Islamist opposition; the law was challenged by parents who argued that it was unconstitutional to forbid their daughters to veil in public. The Egyptian constitution declares the "principles of Islamic *shari'a*" to be the main source of legislation and also provides for religious freedom.[35] The Supreme Constitutional Court found in favor of the government, holding that the ban on *niqab* in schools was constitutional. The legal issue at stake, Bälz explains, was the understanding of "legislation" and the extent to which the state was limited by the "principles of Islamic *shari'a*."[36] Islamic law is not a "legislated" body of law, and thus the question arises of how the state is to incorporate it into its legislative duties. The solution reached by the Egyptian Supreme Constitutional Court is instructive in understanding the state's powers and purposes in the context of dual legal systems; the court held that while it was indeed bound by the principles of *shari'a*, the court itself reserved the right to decide what the substance of Islamic rules is. Bälz argues that "[i]t is exactly this 'substantialization' of Islamic legal rules within the secular legal order that allows the latter to maintain its autonomy;"[37] rather than Islamic law constraining the state, the state deploys Islamic law (and limits it) for its own ends.

---

34 Kilian Bälz, "The Secular Reconstruction of Islamic Law: the Egyptian Supreme Constitutional Court and the 'Battle over the Veil' in State-Run Schools," in *Legal Pluralism in the Arab World.*

35 Articles 2 and 46, respectively.

36 Bälz, 231.

37 Ibid., 233.

2. The State Constrained by Islamic Law?

Is the provision of Islamic law, then, merely a rhetorical strategy by the state, intended hide the weaknesses of secular states beneath a cloak of religious and traditional legitimacy? I believe not; the state's relationship with Islamic law is intended to satisfy real social needs (by preserving familiar practices) and political demands. Furthermore, and tellingly, the state can find itself constrained by claims about Islamic law even when it does not wish to be.

The Jordanian municipal elections of 1999 provide an example of this sort of effect on state administrative practice. Although the issue in question was not one of *shari'a* itself, it involved the question of proper Islamic dress for women, which is, in the opinion of many Muslims, a practice mandated by Qur'anic injunction. As noted in Chapter One, the majority of Jordanian women wear a form of hijab involving a headscarf but do not cover their faces. Some women do wear the face-concealing form of hijab (called niqab), however, and in advance of the 1999 municipal elections, a government official announced that such women would be required to remove their face veils to prove their identity to polling place officials.[38] This sparked a public outcry, particularly from the Islamic Action Front, Jordan's largest and best-organized political party. The IAF, and indeed most people, considered it inappropriate for veiling women to be forced to show their faces to unrelated men in public.

The government's plan to have women show their faces was part of an attempt to reduce electoral fraud, considered to have been significant in municipal elections of 1995. Amman Governor Qaftan Majali asserted that some male voters in that election had disguised themselves as veiled women in order to vote, and that some veiled women had voted more than once.[39] In order to prevent such fraud, therefore, election officials would match the voter's face to his or her identity documents. This would have presented no problem if polling places were staffed with female officials, but Majali made it clear that women would have to reveal their faces to the head of the polling place "regardless if the president is a male or female."[40]

The government's goal of preventing voter fraud was unexceptionable, but they did not account adequately for the intersection of administrative policy and Islamic practice. Even after objections arose, the governor maintained that women would be required to unveil in front of men, rather than offering the obvious solution of providing a female official at each polling place to whom women could reveal their faces. The Islamic Action Front, an opponent of the government, might have been expected to use this issue as evidence of the government's disrespect

38 See "Government demands that veiled women show faces in upcoming municipal elections," *Jordan Times*, July 12, 1999, 3.

39 Rana Husseini, "Governor reiterates demand that women uncover faces in tomorrow's municipal elections," *Jordan Times*, July 13, 1999, 3.

40 Quoted in "Government demands that veiled women show faces in upcoming municipal elections," *Jordan Times*, July 12, 1999, 3.

for Islam; however, the party took the interesting position that this policy was a violation of individual women's civil rights to freedom of religion. Rather than making the issue one of public morality and Islamic authority, the IAF primarily used the language of democratic rights claims, and did so very effectively. The governor promptly amended his policy, and in the end, policewomen, female army officers and female government doctors were provided at polling places for the identification of veiled women.[41] The "*shari'a*" position won out over the state's policy, but interestingly, it did so by deploying democratic rather than religious arguments.

Certainly garden-variety political and administrative considerations were at work here in addition to the nexus of Islam and state policy. The government wanted to prevent voter fraud; the Islamists wanted to ensure the turnout of conservative women, who are some of their staunchest supporters. However, the issue is interesting here for its lesson about the constraints on the state. Even for such a widely-supported goal as ensuring fair elections, the state finds it necessary to construct its policies to allow for the operation of Islamic rules; even though most people do not choose to follow this interpretation of Islamic dress requirements, the state cannot ignore them.

"Cross-Pollination" and Political Development

The political implications of dual legal systems stem, somewhat paradoxically, in part from the fact of separation of the codes and their historical-philosophical bases and in part from the fact that the codes are *not* entirely separate. One political effect, the one most clearly intended by the state, is that the existence of two codes serves not only practical purposes but ideological/legitimation ones, as discussed above. Another effect, more potential in my view than actual, results from the cross-pollination between the two systems of law and influences the process of political development in ways that suggest parallels with Western experience.

Shari'a and modern law have interacted and exerted influence over one another both in their content and in their procedures. Not only is the modern law subject to contestation on Islamic (and traditional) grounds, the *shari'a* is increasingly structured to partake of the forms and principles of the non-Islamic system. *Shari'a* has also persisted as a "residual" category of law, as when the Jordanian civil code provides for matters not encompassed by the code to be decided according to the rules of "Muslim jurisprudence" and, in the absence of applicable rules, according to the principles of *shari'a*, custom and equity in that order.[42] Thus there are several points at which one element of the dual legal system "bleeds over" into the other.

41 Francesca Ciriaci and Mohammad Ben Hussein, "Rural residents show more enthusiasm than urban counterparts in elections," *Jordan Times*, July 15–16, 1999, 3.

42 The Jordanian Civil Code of Muslim Jurisprudence, 1976, Article 2, paragraphs 2, 3 and 4.

It must be conceded that this blurring of the practical distinction between the two seems to have had little effect on the conceptual and rhetorical distinctions, which operate as though the two systems were isolated from one another. That is, people still think and talk about the systems as though they were entirely distinct in form and rationale, despite the willingness of activists to borrow from one another's playbooks in terms of their political competition.

However, the early signs of cross-pollination may indicate an important trend for political development: perhaps Islamic law will come to play the same role in modern Arab states that (Christian) canon law played in the development of European states. This is not to assert that Islamic and Christian law are equivalent legal forms; Christianity is not a law-based religion in the same way that Islam and Judaism are. The development of European legal systems, however, involved an initial separation not only between temporal and sacred authority but in the areas of life assigned to the legal jurisdiction of one or the other of the two authorities. Early European temporal powers were concerned with the areas of (secular) law developed by the Romans, the law that forms the basis of modern civil-law systems such as most of those in Western Europe and Latin America (as distinct from the common-law system of England and its former possessions).[43] The authority of the state expanded over time to include issues once held to fall within the jurisdiction of spiritual authorities, and in the process, canon law became subsumed within the state's legal system, combining with Roman law to produce the basis of the civil law systems in existence today. Canon law's contributions were primarily in the areas of family law, criminal law and legal procedure.[44] Islamic law seems to play a similar role in Arab states, although in a different context; the separation of temporal and spiritual authority is more valued by the former than the latter, whereas in Europe both the church and the state regarded their spheres as separate. But the essentially secular basis of most Arab states' authority, while supplemented by claims to Islamic cultural authenticity, suggests a course of political development that should not be expected to eradicate Islamic law in order to achieve modernity. Rather, Islamic law could come to serve the law of the state by preserving cultural forms and principles that are indigenously valued, contributing to state law the most developed areas of *shari'a*. If this process is underway, Egypt is probably farther along than Jordan, having already incorporated *shari'a* courts into the civil ones, just as ecclesiastical courts were once subsumed by the civil courts of Europe.[45]

---

43 For an excellent explanation of the history of the development of the civil law tradition, see John Henry Merryman, *The Civil Law Tradition.*

44 Ibid., 10–11.

45 A further point of comparison between the development of law in European and Arab states could be made regarding commercial law. In Europe as in the Arab world, this body of law developed separately from civil, criminal and religious law, in order to serve the practical needs of merchants. This is perhaps an issue best left to specialists in that area, however, so it is not dealt with here.

Another possible comparison between Western and Arab legal development, which I advance somewhat tentatively, is the potential similarity between *shari'a* and common law as it now operates in countries such as the United States and the United Kingdom. The tentativity stems from a recognition that the two systems are different in some fundamental respects. Common law originated as judge-made law, whereby legal principles were "discovered" by judges ruling in particular cases; in theory, the principles already existed because of long-standing practice and common consent, and judges simply found them and applied them to cases. Islamic law, on the other hand, contains little scope for the judge (*qadi*) to create law, and requires him instead to apply pre-existing, divinely ordained principles and rules in manners specified (insofar as possible) by jurisconsults (*fuqaha*) who were scholars. However, my comparison is not of the types of law, which are quite different, but in their potential role in the legal system. In common law countries, the project of codification of the law, begun centuries ago, has long meant that the common law itself continues to operate only as a residual category of law, where statute is silent.[46] Several Arab systems make similar provisions for Islamic law; apart from its acknowledged (whether codified or uncodified) role in family law, Islamic law is treated as a residual category, with principles of *shari'a* to be applied in the lacunae of statutory law.[47] This practice would seem to contribute to the primacy of statutory law, which is generally (despite constitutional exhortations regarding *shari'a*) a product of legislatures. These legislatures do not, most would agree, yet represent the will of the people, but they do serve to entrench the notion of legislation as a social, rather than a divine, project.

I hasten to stress that it is not necessary for Arab legal systems to become identical to American or European systems in order for these countries to become politically "developed" or democratic. Rather than advocating a particular course or content of political development, this study is meant to examine existing forms and seek conclusions about potential future developments. Democracy will be best served, in any system, by the development of legal systems that value individual rights, free contestation and equal participation. However, the presence of Islamic law in the realm of the state should not be taken as prima facie evidence of underdevelopment or antidemocratic intentions; the discussion above has, I hope, demonstrated that the relationship between *shari'a*, political authority and the development of the political system is multilayered and complex, rather than a clear-cut divide between the forces of tradition and modernity.

---

46 Statutes always take precedence over common law; thus, if a statute differs from an established common law principle, it is the latter that gives way.

47 Bahrain (Judicature Law, 1971), Jordan (Civil Code, supra) and Yemen (Article 349 of Personal Status Law) are three countries that have made such provisions. According to George Sfeir, this practice originated with the Egyptian Civil Code produced in the 1940s by Abdel-Razzaq al-Sanhuri, which served as a model for the codes of several other states (see "Source of Law and the Issue of Legitimacy and Rights," *Middle East Journal*, 42:3 (1988): 436–446).

Dual legal systems exist in Arab states not because of the incontestable dictates of Islam, or even merely due to the accidents of colonial history. Dual legal systems continue to exist because they have been extremely useful for state legitimation. This has important implications for understanding the development of law as a part of the process of democratization. Increasing democratization calls into question the degree to which any area of law can rely, even rhetorically, on an authority other than the sovereignty of the people. However, the authority of the people as a source of law is insufficient for the protection of anything but the most limited notion of democracy. Any definition of democracy that includes a set of rights and liberties for the individual recognizes the need to protect those rights from the "tyranny of the majority" as well as the tyranny of the dictatorial government. Laws and legal systems are problematic for democracy, therefore, not only when they rely on authority other than popular consent but when their provisions and their operation deny the equal enjoyment of fundamental rights and liberties to all citizens.

As (or if) Jordan becomes more democratic, we should not expect to see Islamic law disappear from the Jordanian legal system. We can, however, expect to see *shari'a* provisions subjected to greater analytical and political scrutiny by the people, and thus to an accountability that is democratic in the broadest sense even where it may not be secular. If the contestation over the content and status of such laws works to extend legal equality and to protect liberty, then democracy will have been well-served by the people, and vice versa.

PART II
Laws and Legal Changes

Chapter 4
Criminal Law

> The ordinary administration of criminal and civil justice...contributes, more than any other circumstance, to impressing upon the minds of the people affection, esteem, and reverence toward the government.
>
> –Alexander Hamilton, Federalist Papers, #17

Criminal law in Arab countries catches public attention in the West only rarely, and then only on issues with a certain shock value, such as the amputation of thieves' hands in Saudi Arabia or honor killings in Jordan.[1] These phenomena are usually characterized as the ugly side of an undemocratic and less-developed foreign culture. However, I argue that such practices and the legal environments surrounding them should be understood as the product of a relationship among law, politics and culture that exists in all systems and is tied to political contestation and, ultimately, to state legitimacy. This relationship has especially important implications for democracy insofar as it defines the extent of equality and rights protection in a society.

Focusing on the crimes of rape and honor killing, this chapter considers criminal law in its role as both a locus of political debate and an influence on the fundamental makeup of the political system. Law has potentially greater social power than other elements of politics precisely because it does not appear to be primarily political; it is an arena for contestation not merely over policy choices but over the shared values on which the political system is based. It is simultaneously part of the debate about political choices and rights and a means of defining the terms and scope of that debate.

This political aspect of legal codes is not always recognized, since their most apparent function is a practical regulatory one; criminal law, in particular, seeks to regulate social conflict for the purpose of public order. Laws also affect and reflect shared notions of justice and morality; these concepts are important elements of the legitimacy that states need to undergird their political rule. Contestation over the requirements of justice and morality are thus a chief means by which law becomes overtly a matter of political choices. The political implications of conflict regulation are usually invisible, as such regulation appears more practical or natural than political, but questions of justice and morality have a prominent place in many political systems.

---

1 A version of this chapter was originally published in the Blackwell journal *Law and Society Review* 39:2 (2005): 315–348, and entitled "The Vanishing Victim: Gender and Criminal Law in Jordan."

Criminal Law as Politics

The statement above that law does not seem primarily political warrants further clarification. There is a large body of work on the anthropology and sociology of law, in which it has long been established that law and even crime itself are best understood as social constructs.[2] Law reflects dominant social values and at the same time helps to shape these values. Thus law indicates what interests in a society are most powerful, and "law in operation is an aspect of politics – it is one of the methods by which public policy is formulated and administered for governing the lives and activities of the state's inhabitants."[3] Furthermore, not only does law reflect power and interests within a society, it is also a means by which the state can serve its own interests, which is particularly important in the cases studied here.

Thus of course law is political, but it is less obviously political than election contests, party platforms, public demonstrations, or other political activities that clearly involve competition of different interests. Law is often regarded (not by scholars, perhaps, but by regular citizens) as an objective collection of rules – moral, certainly, but not really political (or even moral *rather than* political). Where the law is political, it is often constitutional, in the broadest sense;[4] that is, it appears less partisan-political and more about establishing and protecting the fundamental elements of society – the conditions that make civic life possible.

For example, murder is a crime everywhere, but this would not strike most people as a law that is political. It does not serve some identifiable political interest at the expense of others; rather, murder is "just wrong." But the outlawing of murder serves an important and fundamentally political purpose. It helps to define and protect what is necessary for society to exist. If we take the example a step further, laws about murder admit several exceptions and mitigations; these are perhaps more obviously an example of political choices in the law. We recognize, for instance, a difference between murder and justifiable homicide. This may appear to be merely a practical regulatory distinction, but it clearly incorporates society's (dominant) values about who is allowed to kill and what constitutes acceptable circumstances for killing. Obviously, if the law allowed white men to kill but not women or black men, it would tell us something important about norms of equality and power in that society. But when the law is less blatantly skewed to a particular interest or set of values, the political implications can be more difficult to tease out. Where legal provisions seem to deal with the fundamental necessities

---

2 See Richard Quinney, *The Social Reality of Crime* (New York: Little, Brown and Company, 1970).

3 Ibid., 37.

4 See Victoria F. Nourse, "Law's Constitution: a Relational Critique," *Wisconsin Women's Law Journal* 17:1 (2002): 23–56.

for social life, as in the original example above, the law seems less political, and thus less contestable.

This question – how political law is – is an important one in the criminal law issues described below. Debate over criminal laws that are particularly disadvantageous to women often involves assertions about the primacy of moral claims over merely political ones. Those who advocate changing the laws to redress inequality must counter the assertion that they are promoting individual (political) preferences over society's morality or cultural authenticity (discussed further below) – that is, that they are treating law as politics when really law is morality and cultural identity.

This chapter examines how and why criminal law plays a role in Jordanian political legitimacy. As contestation over legal inequalities and legally-reinforced social subordination becomes increasingly visible, the effect of the law on legitimacy becomes ever more apparent. The state's legitimation needs have been pursued through the toleration of a traditional practice, honor killing, that is increasingly at odds with the demands of the liberal strand of legitimation and increasingly controversial among the public. The outcome of contestation over this and other issues of criminal law will be an important indicator of prospects for legal equality and rights protections in the future, and thus of the prospects for democratization.

Gendered Criminal Law

The political purposes served by legal codes are perhaps most apparent in issues such as civil liberties regulation, but the same purposes can be served equally well, if not equally overtly, in ordinary criminal law. In the Arab world, as in many areas, criminal codes are markedly gendered, by which I mean that the definition of and penalties for certain crimes reflect societally-sanctioned notions of appropriate sex roles. This is most obvious in legal treatments of rape and domestic violence; statutes as well as police and judicial practice in these areas are widely recognized to reflect social mores about female and male sexuality, appropriate roles of marriage partners and so forth. This is true in every criminal justice system of which I am aware; the days are not long past when American court officials accused rape victims of inviting the attack by their manner of dress or behavior. In a similar vein, a man who punches his neighbor is guilty of simple assault, a crime to be dealt with by the public laws, while one who punches his wife is in many countries still considered to be acting within a semi-protected "private sphere" not subject to equal public regulation.

This gendering of law disadvantages women as victims of crime in order to serve a broader sociocultural purpose. The tension between individual rights and community interests exists in all legal systems; the rights of accused criminals, issues of community standards as a restriction on individual behavior and the state's interest in maintaining public order versus the individual's interest in limiting the power of the state are issues that all systems deal with in some form. It must also be acknowledged that most, if not all, legal systems seek to be appropriate to the societies they regulate by reflecting social norms and shared beliefs. What is notable about the issues examined here is that concessions to social practice or cultural tradition are reconciled with the legal system largely by altering the way the law applies in cases where crime victims are almost by definition female.[5] This is in keeping with the widespread practice, in state structures and in societies, of regarding women as the vehicles by which authentic culture is maintained; thus gender issues are fertile ground for efforts at cultural legitimation.[6]

When gender issues are related to the nature of a crime itself (as in rape, honor killings and domestic violence), the penal code departs from the general orientation toward the pursuit of justice for the wronged individual and privileges the social-order aspects of law. That is to say, in the case of most types of crime, the state seeks justice for the victim (and thus indirectly for society) by pursuing criminal punishment of the offender. However, in the gendered elements of criminal law that I discuss below,[7] the state seeks social justice – or more accurately social order – by means of redefining the victim as complicit in the crime, as perpetrator herself or simply as the available means for resolving a social conflict. Thus the victim disappears in that she is no longer visible as a victim to whom justice is owed and reappears as a means by which a problematic situation can be resolved to best serve the interests of the community.

Rape

Rape law in the Arab world has long been a target of criticism by women's rights activists and others. Rape is a crime that, when prosecuted, carries serious penalties

5 I do not mean to imply in the treatment below that rape is a crime exclusively against women. However, the laws at issue here treat it that way, and the social meaning of the crime is very much about women and honor. Rape of males raises similar gender issues about power and sexuality, but these do not inform the law or politics on the issue, as such crimes are not brought into public discourse.

6 Traditional practices not related to gender are also given occasional recognition in legal codes. For example, some codes provide for the payment of *diya*, or blood money, as partial redress for the killing of another. This practice recognizes the economic consequence to a family of a person's death, and *diya* amounts are adjusted accordingly. However, such traditions supplement, rather than circumvent, the practice of "regular" criminal law; laws of homicide still apply, and the state simply recognizes an additional interest to be served by the system, rather than redefining the system's interests as is the case in the gendered legal statutes.

7 This article addresses rape and honor killings, but not (other) domestic violence. Although domestic violence has received greater attention in Jordan in recent years, it is still very much a hidden phenomenon. Victims of domestic violence are generally unwilling to make their troubles public, and cases are rarely brought to prosecution.

for those convicted. The punishment in Jordan for rape of an adult woman is ten years' imprisonment;[8] in Egypt the penalty usually ranges from three years to life imprisonment.[9] In several countries, rapists can receive the death penalty although this usually requires that the crime be accompanied by special circumstances, such as abduction or a juvenile victim.[10] However, legal codes (and public attitudes) have also treated rape as a social conflict requiring resolution among all the affected parties. Reliable statistics on the prevalence of rape in societies are difficult to find,[11] as most observers believe that the vast majority of such crimes are unreported.[12] Furthermore, marital rape, which takes place exclusively within the sphere deemed private and does not raise issues of threats to social order, remains legal in Jordan, as in most countries of the region.[13] It is in cases where the

---

8 Lawyer Asma Khader, interview, Amman, April 1998. In February of 2008, the Jordanian courts sentenced a rapist to a 10-year prison term for the rape of a married woman in her own home; another rapist received a 15-year sentence for the rape of a married woman whom he had also abducted. See Rana Husseini, "25-year-old man handed 10-year term for rape, indecent exposure" and "Man gets 15 years for abduction, rape," *Jordan Times*, February 4–5, 2008.

9 U.S. Department of State, *Country Reports on Human Rights Practices*, 2002 (Egypt). www.state.gov/g/drl/rls/hrrpt/2002/18274.htm.

10 In Jordan, rape of a child under 15 is punishable by death although lawyer Asma Khader, interview, 1998, points out that the death penalty has usually been imposed in cases where the rapist also killed his victim. However, the death penalty is sometimes imposed in cases of child rape without additional aggravating circumstances; for example, in 2008, a man was sentenced to death for the repeated rape of a 14-year-old girl (Rana Husseini, "40-year-old man sentenced to death for raping minor," *Jordan Times*, October 30, 2008). Tunisia provides for the death penalty in cases of "rape of a female with violence," Morocco in cases of "rape of a minor leading to death" and Saudi Arabia in all cases of rape. (United Nations Economic and Social Council, report on Crime Prevention and Criminal Justice, June 8, 1995, at www.un.org/documents/ecosoc/docs/1995/e1995-78.htm).

11 Jordan publishes official crime statistics; reported cases of rape numbered between 29 and 63 annually between 1992 and 1996, while cases of indecent assault ranged from about 400 to just over 500 per year in the same period (in a population of about 5 million). The rate of indecent assault stayed relatively constant in the 1999–2007 period (between 411 and 558 cases annually), while the number of rape cases increased from the earlier period to between 88 and 152 cases annually. Curiously, there is no consistent trend in the number of such cases over time; for example, the government reported 142 rape cases in 1999 but only 86 and 88 in 2006 and 2007, respectively. Data are compiled from the *Statistical Yearbook*, Department of Statistics, and the Annual Report published by the Judicial Council.

12 For example, a Jordanian woman, raped by an intruder in her own home in 2007, so feared the shame attached to the crime that rather than report it, she kept silent and moved away to a different neighborhood. She eventually reported the rape months later when her attacker harassed her after encountering her in the street. See footnote 5 above.

13 United Nations Committee on Economic, Social and Cultural Rights, Press Release, May 12, 2000. See also U.S. Department of State Country Reports on Human Rights Practices for 1999 (Egypt, Jordan, Syria, Algeria). It is sometimes asserted (see the

crime becomes public that the law steps in, and even there, the law can provide a means for resolving the situation without prosecuting the crime.[14]

Under Jordanian law, it is possible for rapists to escape criminal prosecution if they marry their victims;[15] this was also the case in Egypt until 1999.[16] Because of family and societal pressures, rape victims often do agree to such marriages.[17] The law has permitted such a resolution out of recognition of the cultural value placed upon female virginity at marriage; "despoiled" girls and women are a source of shame for their families, innocent of wrongdoing though they may be. It is not unknown for rape victims to be murdered by family members in order to rectify the shame brought upon the family by the crime. In the Egyptian parliamentary debate surrounding the decree to remove the "marriage loophole," some lawmakers objected to altering the existing law on the grounds that it provided raped women with their only chance to marry, since after having been raped, no other man would

Rishmawi and Jewett articles, cited below) that Egypt's rape law applies to husbands, but this is not the case.

14 Judith Tucker points out that the history of Islamic legal practice also provides examples of the treatment of rape as a matter for compensation rather than strict criminal penalty. She cites the seventeenth-century mufti Khayr al-Din al-Ramli as instructing that a rapist who had abducted his victim should under some circumstances be allowed to compensate her by payment of *mahr* (dower payment to a bride) rather than face the penalty for unlawful intercourse (stoning or flogging). See Tucker, *In the House of the Law* (Berkeley: University of California Press, 1998), 16.

15 Penal Code (Jordan), Law No. 16 of 1961, Article 308. See also Mona Rishmawi, "The Legal Status of Palestinian Women in the Occupied Territories," in Nahid Toubia (ed.), *Women of the Arab World: the Coming Challenge* (London: Zed Books, 1986) and IRWAW report on Jordan, October 27, 1997, submitted to the United Nations as CEDAW/C/JOR/1 and /2. A medical examiner who assists in police investigations of such crimes suggested that this provision is no longer active (Dr. Hani Jahshan, interview, June 1999), but it remains part of the legal code, and underreporting of rapes in general makes it impossible to determine how many such crimes are "privately" resolved this way. Once a rape is reported to the police, regulations require that the case be referred to prosecutors. (Family Protection Unit, Public Security Directorate, interview, November 1998).

16 Penal Code (Egypt), 1937, Article 291. This article was cancelled by Presidential Act #14 of 1999 (confirmed by Parliament), published in the Official Gazette, No. 16, 2 (April 22, 1999).

17 It is important to note that neither the legal nor the cultural aspects of this situation are unique to the Arab or Muslim world. For example, Brazilian law provides that a convicted rapist can escape punishment by offering to marry his victim (U.S. Department of State Country Report on Human Rights Practices, Brazil, 2003). Likewise, in Guatemala, "criminal responsibility for rape or certain other sexual crimes is extinguished upon the perpetrator's marriage to the victim," according to the Inter-American Commission on Human Rights (Fifth Report on the Situation of Human Rights in Guatemala, OEA/Ser. L/V/II.111, 2001). The same was true in Peru until 1999, Colombia until 1997 and Mexico until 1991.

want them.[18] Rape law has, in statute and in practice, privileged the protection of social order over the provision of individual criminal justice.[19]

The marriage loophole, where it exists, is clearly a means by which to rectify a social problem (the social standing of a raped woman and her family) rather than to punish a crime. In general, it is clear that the practice privileges broader social interests, especially those of the victim's relatives, over the interests of the victim herself. Arguments about the presumed benefit to the otherwise unmarriageable victim of a rape are tenuous, as marriage to a violent attacker could hardly be more suitable than remaining unmarried, even recognizing the economic and social disadvantages facing unmarried women. It is worth noting, furthermore, that even this practical solution has its shortcomings, as rapists often divorce their wives/victims soon after marrying to avoid criminal charges. Jordanian law attempts to close this avenue of escape from marriage by providing for resumption of prosecution if the rapist arbitrarily divorces his wife/victim within three years of marrying her.[20] He could, however, divorce his wife for cause, such as not bearing children.[21] The claimed traditional aspect of the practice is tenuous as well, since the Egyptian law itself dates from 1904 at the earliest.[22] Nor is it an element of Islamic law, and the mufti of Egypt, Sheikh Nasr Farid Wasel, has condemned the practice of pressuring girls and women to marry their attackers as contrary to the principles of Islamic marriage.[23] However, the marriage loophole was created and used for the purpose of providing social problem-solving rather than criminal justice, and it addressed the social practices surrounding raped women and family

18 "Egypt's president voids law setting free rapists who marry victim," Associated Press, April 5, 1999.

19 As one author put it, Egyptian rape law punishes offenders, but "while this may be an attempt to protect the psychological and physical health of women, it is more likely an attempt to maintain both the purity of women and the honor of the family." Jennifer Jewett, "The Recommendation of the International Conference on Population and Development: The Possibility of the Empowerment of Women in Egypt," *Cornell International Law Journal* 29:1 (1996): 191–223, 200.

20 Article 308 of the Penal Code; cited in International Women's Rights Action Watch report on Jordan submitted to the United Nations as CEDAW/C/JOR/1 and /2, October 27, 1997.

21 There is little information about the fate of such women, or even how often such divorces occur, which is not surprising given that the purpose of such a marriage in the first place was largely to avoid the social shame for the woman's family consequent upon rape. In general, however, the stigma attached to divorce varies from case to case, and many divorced women eventually remarry.

22 Tarek el-Tablawy, "Egypt Debates Rape Law," Associated Press, April 6, 1999. Other AP reports refer to the same 1904 date for the start of the practice, although the *Middle East Times* identified the source of the actual statute as dating from the 1930s, probably because the current criminal code was enacted in 1937 (*Middle East Times*, issue 99, 7).

23 "Legal loophole for rapists closed," *Cairo Times*, 28 April 1999.

honor, rather than the crimes against individual women. The problem of the social existence of a raped woman is settled by having the rape victim disappear, to be replaced by a wife.[24]

Honor Crimes

In recent years a great deal of international attention has focused on the phenomenon of "honor killings," particularly in Jordan and Pakistan. Honor killings are murders carried out by family members against girls and women who are believed to have committed a sexual indiscretion, or to have caused gossip related to sexual behavior, that besmirches the honor of the family. The concept of honor (*sharaf*) has to do with social standing on the basis of moral behavior; men's honor is intimately connected to the sexual chastity of their female relatives. Thus a woman's or girl's bad conduct would not only embarrass her family, but would impugn the honor of the entire family, particularly the men, who have the right and duty of defending this honor. This conception of honor distinguishes such killings from otherwise-similar "crimes of passion" that are well-known in most legal systems. While claims of reduced responsibility on the grounds of rage are often claimed as mitigating circumstances by the perpetrators of honor killings, the justification for the killing is socially understood not as the temporary loss of control produced by passionate anger, but the social harm and loss of honor caused by the woman's behavior.

This phenomenon is often regarded, in the Western media and among its local advocates, as specific to either Arab constructions of honor or Islamic values, but in fact, similar practices relating to honor and female sexual behavior are found in other regions, as well. In particular, the lenient treatment of men who kill their wives is well-known in many systems. From dowry deaths in India to the "legitimate defense of honor" in Brazil, many legal systems have found formal or informal ways to excuse or mitigate the penalties for wife-killing.[25] Many readers will be familiar with similar practices in the American system, in which husbands who murdered their adulterous wives received little or no penalty for the crime. In the American case, this phenomenon arises from a variety of sources – common law, statute, judicial interpretation and jury practice. Blackstone wrote,

---

24 Feminist scholars have noted a similar phenomenon in American law and society, as well. See Matoesian, (1993) regarding the "social facticity of rape." The argument is that the juridical treatment of rape tends to define and recast it in such a way that rape often becomes, in the view of the law, consensual sexual intercourse. The rape disappears to be replaced with sex, and if there is no crime, there is no victim. This is quite similar to the process described above wherein the victim disappears to be replaced with a wife.

25 See Melissa Spatz, "A 'Lesser' Crime: A Comparative Case Study of Legal Defenses for Men who Kill their Wives," *Columbia Journal of Law and Social Problems*, vol. 24 (1991): 597–638.

for example, that a man who killed his wife's lover upon discovering them in adultery was guilty of manslaughter, rather than murder, being assumed to have acted in a passionate rage.[26] Until the 1970s, statutes in Texas, New Mexico and Utah recognized a husband's discovery of his wife's adultery as grounds for justifiable homicide.[27] Judicial interpretation in Georgia created a rule allowing a man to kill his wife's (or, in this case, daughter's or fianceé's) lover in order to stop an adulterous relationship; interestingly, the Georgia rule also applied to wives, unlike the provisions in other states.[28]

Although it is widely believed that these statutory and judicial rules allowed men to kill their adulterous wives with little or no penalty, it appears that in fact we must look elsewhere for the source of the toleration of wife-killing in the American case – these rules allowed only the killing of the spouse's lover, *not* the adulterous spouse.[29] The widely-known practice of letting wife-killers off with light penalties seems to be primarily a product of the application of crime-of-passion provisions and the sympathy of jurors (for most of history, exclusively male) for cuckolded husbands. The American case is thus not exactly similar to the phenomenon discussed in this chapter because the concept of honor is less important in the American context than the common-law concept of a husband's property in his wife,[30] but in other respects the judicial treatments bear a strong resemblance. The legal path has different scenery, but the destination, where murder charges are reduced to manslaughter or the act is excused altogether, is very much like that in the Jordanian case, as discussed below.

The legal treatment of wife-murders has also received a great deal of attention in Brazil, where explicitly honor-based defenses were common until recent years. A man who murdered his wife or girlfriend was often exempted from any penalty

---

26 Blackstone's *Commentaries on the Laws of England*, Book 4, Ch. 14. Blackstone explains that such killing, while manslaughter, "is however the lowest degree of it: and therefore in such a case the court directed the burning in the hand to be gently inflicted, because *there could not be a greater provocation*. Manslaughter therefore on a sudden provocation differs from excusable homicide *se defendendo* in this: that in one case there is an apparent necessity, for self-preservation, to kill the aggressor; in the other no necessity at all, being only a sudden act of revenge." Emphasis added; see note 30 below.

27 See Jeremy D. Weinstein, "Adultery, Law and the State: a History," *Hastings International Law Journal* 38:1 (1986): 195–238 and G. Kristian Miccio, "Notes from the Underground: Battered Women, the State, and Conceptions of Accountability," *Harvard Women's Law Journal* 23 (2000): 133–172.

28 Weinstein, 234–235.

29 Weinstein, 1986. He notes, however, that until the 1920s the Texas statute was interpreted to allow the killing of the wife as well.

30 Miccio (2000) cites an English case from 1708 in which the court commented, "adultery is the highest invasion of property….[A] man cannot receive a higher provocation" (161). The language here is very similar to that of Blackstone, cited above.

if he was found to have acted in "legitimate defense of his honor."[31] The so-called defense of honor often involved the (actual or alleged) adultery of the wife but was also a successful defense for a playboy who had been kicked out by his wealthy girlfriend and responded by gunning her down in the street.[32] It was not until 1991 that the Brazilian Supreme Court rejected such defenses,[33] and reports suggest that in the interior regions of the country, trials often still incorporate them. Similarly, in Haiti, the current penal code provides that men who murder wives or their lovers upon discovering them committing adultery in the conjugal home are excused from penalty; wives who kill husbands under identical circumstances do not benefit from this excuse.[34] In both the Haitian and Brazilian cases, the origin of these provisions can be traced to the legal systems of the colonial European powers, France and Portugal respectively.[35]

In addition to these examples of similar practices in non-Arab, non-Islamic countries, honor killings are also known among Christians in Jordan and other Arab countries, leading some observers to attribute it to a "tribal mentality" rather than religion or Arab culture as a whole.[36] However, despite its questionable position as an inherently Islamic or Arab practice, the question of whether the practice is appropriate on traditional or religious grounds is at the center of the social understanding and political relevance of honor crimes in the Jordanian case.

In Jordan, girls and women have been killed for adultery, pre-marital sex, flirtations, speaking to or corresponding with males outside their families, being seen in the presence of an unrelated male and marrying against the wishes of their families. Honor killings are most often carried out by the brother or father of the victim, rather than the husband, but the decision to kill is often a family one. For example, in the case of a woman murdered by her father and a brother, with the assistance of another brother and a nephew, "the four held a meeting that night and decided to kill her to cleanse their family's honour."[37] It is not uncommon for a family to have a minor, usually a brother of the victim, commit the killing because juveniles receive lighter penalties. There is little reliable demographic information on the victims and perpetrators, but the crime is often associated with

31 Inter-American Commission on Human Rights, Fifth Report on the Situation of Human Rights in Guatemala, document OEA/Ser.L/V/II.III, 2001.

32 James Brooke. "Machismo on Trial: the feminist backlash to Brazil's 'crimes of passion,'" *Washington Post*, December 6, 1981. The verdict was later overturned after loud public protests from women's rights groups.

33 Jim Brooke, "'Honor' Killing of Wives is Outlawed in Brazil," *New York Times*, March 29, 1991.

34 U.S. Department of State Country Reports on Human Rights Practices (Haiti), 2003. www.state.gov/g/drl/rls/hrrpt/2003/27902.htm.

35 The effect of French law in the origin of honor-crime statutes is also discussed below.

36 Senator Leila Sharaf, interview, Amman, July 1999.

37 Rana Husseini, "Four charged with complicity in premeditated murder," *Jordan Times*, August 20, 2007.

conservative sectors of society, rural areas and poor families. It is not limited to these groups, however, and anecdotal evidence suggests that the question comes up even in mainstream, urban, professional families. In conversation, those from Jordanian families sometimes told me that honor killings mostly take place among the Palestinian population, while Palestinians were more likely to depict it as a "tribal Jordanian" phenomenon. People from educated backgrounds tended to attribute the phenomenon to the lower classes.

As with rape, reliable statistics are difficult to find because such crimes often go unreported or masquerade as accidents or suicides.[38] In recent years there have been around twenty recognized honor killings each year in Jordan, which may represent a decline from the late 1990s, when the number of known cases was between 25 and 30 per year out of a total murder rate of approximately 100 per year.[39] Many observers, including the police, doubt the accuracy of these numbers and believe that the actual rate of honor killings is much higher.[40] The practice of honor killings occurs throughout the region, but no government produces reliable or official statistics. NGOs such as Human Rights Watch occasionally compile reports on honor killings, but it is generally accepted that the data on the frequency of the practice are unreliable. Statistics, whatever their quality, are in any case available only for recent years; the very issues of honor and shame that provoke honor killings have precluded the public discussion and tracking of such crimes until very recently.

A review of the most complete available record of honor killings, the *Jordan Times* newspaper, revealed 21 reported honor crimes, involving 22 victims, in the one-year period between November 1, 2007 and October 31, 2008.[41] Of these cases,

38 Jordanian medical examiner Dr. Hani Jahshan, of the National Institute of Forensic Medicine, reports that many young female suicides are the result of direct pressure or threats by families who believe the girls have dishonored them (interview, Amman, 1999). Also, some alleged suicides are in reality homicides; in April 2008, a father was charged with murdering his daughter, whose death had originally been considered a suicide, after the victim's sister told police that the suicide report had been false. See Rana Husseini, "Man charged with killing daughter," *Jordan Times*, April 11, 2008.

39 Honor killings are not reported as a separate category in crime statistics, but a reliable source has for several years been provided by journalist Rana Husseini in the daily *Jordan Times*. Ms. Husseini tracks honor crimes by following police cases and court proceedings; in 1998 she reported that officials believe that approximately 25 of the known murders in 1997 constituted honor killings and cited an average of 25–30 such killings per year, and in 2008 she cited "medical sources" who put the annual rate of honor killings at approximately 20 (Rana Husseini, "New penal code to be tougher on crimes against women, children – justice minister," *Jordan Times*, February 18, 1998 and "Man charged with manslaughter of his niece," *Jordan Times,* October 5, 2008).

40 Interview with officers of the Family Protection Unit (1999) and numerous statements by activists.

41 This is a tally of crimes first reported during this period; they may have occurred earlier than November 1, 2007. The cases were identified by the suspect's outright claim to

20 were homicides and one an attempted murder in which the victim survived the attack. Women and girls were 20 of the 22 victims, and 70 percent of the attacks were perpetrated by the victim's brother. The most common methods of killing were shooting (38 percent of cases), stabbing (33 percent) and strangulation (24 percent); in one case the victim was drowned, and often the victim was beaten before the murder. Killers in such cases are so confident of social and official approbation that they commonly surrender themselves to the police; in at least 70 percent of the cases during the review period, the killer went to the police himself, often with the murder weapon, and described what he had done, sometimes even re-enacting it.[42] In one case, a man even took his sister's corpse to the police station in the trunk of his car in order to show the officers her body.[43]

Honor Crimes and the Penal Code

The Jordanian, Egyptian, Syrian and Lebanese penal codes[44] provide reductions or elimination of penalty for murders committed for reasons of honor. The statutes have traditionally specified that the victim is female, that the perpetrator is a male relative of a certain degree (usually brother, father or husband)[45] and that the circumstances of the victim's behavior justify the crime (catching a wife in the act of adultery, for example).[46] Until recently,[47] the Jordanian statute, Article 340 of the Penal Code, provided that:

> 1. He benefits from an exculpatory excuse who surprises his wife or one of his female unlawfuls [*muharim*, a woman related to him by a close enough degree to preclude marriage between them] in the act of adultery with another man and kills, wounds, or injures one or both of them.

---

have killed for reasons of honor or citing of such honor-related justifications as the victim's alleged sexual misbehavior.

42 In two cases, it was not reported whether the victim had turned himself in, and in only one case was the accused reported to have maintained that he was innocent even after being charged.

43 Rana Husseini, "Man charged with premeditated murder of his younger sister," *Jordan Times*, May 11, 2008.

44 Article 340 of the Jordanian Penal Code, Article 237 of the Egyptian Penal Code, Article 548 of the Syrian code and Article 562 of the Lebanese code (amended 1999).

45 In the Jordanian case, perpetrators are usually brothers or fathers and more rarely husbands. This differs from the examples cited of the United States, Brazil and Haiti, where women killed for honor or sex-related reasons are nearly always killed by husbands or boyfriends.

46 A more detailed analysis of the statutes themselves can be found in two very useful articles by Lama Abu-Odeh, 1996 and 1997.

47 In December of 2001, the text of Article 340 was amended. These changes are discussed in more detail below.

> 2. The perpetrator of a killing, wounding or injury benefits from a mitigating excuse if he surprises his wife or one of his female ascendants or siblings with another in an unlawful bed.[48]

The terms of the law provide for reductions of penalty to male perpetrators only; women who discover husbands or relatives committing adultery were not accorded similar treatment here or elsewhere in the law. Furthermore, the term "honor" is nowhere mentioned in the article, yet it is the basis of the social understanding of the law's role. It is widely understood that the behavior encompassed by the statute's description would discredit the honor of a woman's (male) relatives, and that the law is meant to account for the natural response to such a provocation.[49]

This is the article of law around which the honor crimes debate in Jordan has been centered. However, it is interesting to note that this statute does not reflect the predominant social practice, nor is it legally relevant in terms of judicial practice. Lama Abu-Odeh has investigated the issue of court practice and found that for much of the country's history, Article 340 was rarely, if ever, used in the courts.[50] This is no doubt in part because of the difficulty of meeting the circumstances required by the article, which refers to catching the couple in the act. In practice, women and girls are usually killed well after whatever act they are believed to have committed and often merely upon the suspicion of bad behavior or for causing gossip that embarrasses the family. One man who suspected his sister, a married mother of five, of "immoral behavior" waited for her outside her home and shot her repeatedly;[51] a 13-year-old boy strangled his 14-year-old sister to death with a phone cord for "talking with men over the phone."[52]

Also, by the terms of the statute, killing the male partner to the adulterous or indecent act would also qualify a man for a lighter or waived punishment, but in practice, it is almost invariably women who are killed. The law thus does not reflect the entirety of social understanding of the circumstances in which killing is a justifiable response to honor affronts, nor does it predominate in actual judicial

48 Article 340, Jordanian Penal Code of 1960 (my translation). The items above are often translated "benefits from an exemption from penalty" (paragraph 1) or "benefits from a reduction of penalty" (paragraph 2); while this is certainly the substantive outcome of the provision, the precise language of the law refers to the nature of the *excuse* as exculpatory (full) or mitigating (partial), and does not actually mention "penalty" or "punishment".

49 In the words of parliamentary deputy Mahmoud Kharabsheh, "What do you expect from a man who walks into his house and finds his wife in bed with another man? Give her a rose?" Quoted in Husseini, 2000f.

50 Lama Abu Odeh, "Crimes of Honour and the Construction of Gender in Arab Societies," in Mai Yamani (ed.), *Feminism and Islam: Legal and Literary Perspectives* (New York: NYU Press, 1996), 157–159.

51 Rana Husseini, "Deputy accuses West, Zionists of instigating campaign against 'honour crimes'," *Jordan Times*, May 20, 2000.

52 Rana Husseini, "Boy, 13, claims honour crime in strangulation of sister, 14," *Jordan Times*, February 24, 2000.

treatments of honor killers. Nonetheless, its presence in the penal code has become a matter for political contestation and has provoked one of the most vibrant and widespread debates in Jordan in recent years.

These killings are crimes that would under other circumstances constitute murder. In many cases the acts are premeditated, and they are typically extremely violent; victims are not merely quietly done away with to restore family honor, they are killed with multiple stab wounds or gunshots, bludgeonings or strangling, occasionally in public. One woman killed by her brothers and husband was reportedly stabbed 50 times.[53] A case in the Jordan Valley involved a man who killed his pregnant sister by repeatedly running over her with a pickup truck;[54] another pregnant woman was stomped to death by her brother and (in an unusual twist) her sister-in-law.[55] One father electrocuted his teenage daughter by binding her hands with wire and connecting it to an electrical outlet and then waiting 15 minutes for her to die.[56] A Jordanian medical examiner has described honor killings as "more violent" than other murders,[57] and yet the killers routinely receive extraordinarily light sentences, sometimes as little as three months. As with the marriage loophole for rapists, the law allows the crime victim to disappear; her death is redefined as something like a justifiable homicide, her own actions (or alleged actions) become an element in the crime and the murder victim vanishes, leaving in her place a wicked woman who had to be killed for the honor of her family and the morality of society.

The Political Debate over Article 340

In 2001, Article 340 was amended by the government as part of a package of amendments to the Penal Code.[58] The complete exculpatory excuse, formerly found in the first clause, was removed; paragraph one now reads very much like the old paragraph two regarding mitigating excuses:

---

53 Rana Husseini, "Two women killed in reported 'honour crimes'," *Jordan Times*, April 14, 1999.

54 Rana Husseini, "Courts sentence man to one year after killing sister with car, three men to five months after shooting," *Jordan Times*, July 31, 1999.

55 Rana Husseini, "Deir Alla woman slain in suspected honor crime," *Jordan Times*, November 4, 2001.

56 Rana Husseini, "Man convicted of murdering daughter walks free," *Jordan Times*, May 1, 2008. The killer received a six-month prison sentence but was released upon conviction because he had served the time while awaiting trial.

57 Dr. Hani Jahshan, interview, June 1999.

58 Article 9 of Temporary Law No. 86 for the year 2001, published in the Official Gazette December 31, 2001 (translations below are mine). I thank Ra'eda Freahat of the Jordanian National Committee for Women for providing me the text of the amendments set against the original text. These amendments are also available (in Arabic) at www.lob.gov.jo.

> 1. He benefits from a mitigating excuse who surprises his wife or one of his female ascendants or descendants or sisters in the commission of the crime of adultery or in an unlawful bed and he kills her immediately or kills the one committing adultery with her, or kills them both together, or attacks her or both of them causing death, wounds, injuries, or permanent disability.

Paragraph two is the more significant innovation, allowing wives to benefit from an honor-related excuse in some circumstances:

> 2. The wife who surprises her husband in the commission of the crime of adultery or in an unlawful bed *in the marital home* benefits from the same excuse if she kills him immediately, or kills the one with whom he is committing adultery, or kills them both together, or attacks him or both of them leading to death or wounding or injuries or permanent disability. (emphasis added)

The third paragraph specifies that no one claiming an Article 340 excuse can simultaneously benefit from a self-defense claim allowed in other articles of the Penal Code.

There are several notable features in the amended text. First, the reference to adultery is now a reference to "the crime of adultery," a change in language that seems to stress the wrongdoing of the victim. This treatment is consistent with the understanding of honor-related murders as caused by the victim's honor-damaging actions, and it does not alter the meaning of the text, but it suggests an effort to make a symbolic concession to the defenders of the practice of honor killings. This is particularly meaningful in light of another penal code amendment offered alongside the changes to Article 340; although little noted, the government quietly increased the criminal penalties for adultery at the same time it "reformed" the honor killings law.[59]

Second, the paragraph allowing women to benefit from honor-related excuses would seem to equalize, to some degree, the law's treatment of male and female killers and male and female wrongdoers, as it recognizes a husband's adultery as a provocation to the wife. However, only wives, not sisters, mothers, or other female relatives are covered by this provision, and the adultery must take place in the marital home. This is meant to answer the objections of conservatives that a wife who catches her husband with another woman cannot be sure that the other

---

59 Adultery is addressed in Articles 282–284 in the Penal Code, amended by Temporary Law No. 86 for the year 2001, Articles 6–8. The penalty for adultery was raised from a range of six months to two years to a range of one to three years. However, this change is also primarily symbolic, as adultery is usually kept secret even when discovered by a spouse, in order to avoid shame to the family. As a result, criminal prosecutions for adultery are extremely rare. I thank Dr. Omar al-Jazy of the law firm Aljazy and Company for explaining the legal text and prosecutorial outcomes relating to adultery (personal communication, November 2008).

woman is not a legally-permitted additional wife.[60] Murders of husbands by wives are extraordinarily rare in Jordan,[61] so this amendment appears to be an effort to introduce greater gender equality into legal texts in a way that is unlikely to prove relevant to social or legal practice. Indeed, many critics of the law objected to the notion that allowing murder on a more equal basis, rather than reducing excuses for murder, was a desirable form of equality at all.

In any case, as the discussion above suggests, these changes may have little effect in the actual exercise of law, as the article is virtually never used in criminal proceedings, and there is little expectation that the amendment will produce changes. One activist remarked that the change "is merely symbolic and will not… decrease the number of women killed in the kingdom for reasons of honour."[62] This prediction was unfortunately borne out by the number of honor killings in 2002, which at 22 was the highest in four years.[63]

Perhaps most importantly, the changes to Article 340 were made in the form of a "temporary law" issued by the government while Parliament was out of session; such laws must be reviewed and ratified by Parliament when it returns to session. The law has since been debated several times in the Lower House, and each time it has been rejected. The Senate, which is appointed by the government rather than popularly elected, has approved the amendment and sent it back to the Lower House for reconsideration at least twice since 2003.

The tactic of "temporary laws" is generally used by the government to overcome parliamentary opposition to its plans and is seen as an authoritarian element of the Jordanian political system. Its use on this issue reflects both the opposition of Parliament (discussed below) to changing the law, and the possibly growing determination of the regime to settle what has become a thorny issue of political debate. The course of that debate, from its inception to the recent changes in law, provides a valuable perspective on political contestation, culture and law in a developing system.

60 Jordanian marriage law permits Muslim men to have up to four wives at one time; they need not notify their current wife before contracting a new marriage although there have been efforts to amend the law to require notification. In practice, polygamy is not very common, and third and fourth wives are particularly rare.

61 Homicides of any kind by women are rare; according to court reports, women committed only six percent of homicides on average between 1999 and 2006. See Judicial Council, *al-Taqrir al-sanawi 'an 'umaal al-mahakim li-'aam 2006*, at http://jc.jo/files/docs/jc-report-2006.pdf.

62 Emily Nafaa, quoted in Rana Husseini, "Women activists set their eyes on 2002 polls after positive legislative changes," *Jordan Times*, January 3, 2002.

63 This is not, however, a clear indication that honor killings are on the rise. In 2003, the number of reported honor killings was 17, according to Amnesty International (*Report 2004 – Jordan*, at web.amnesty.org/report2004/jor-summary-eng. (2004). The annual official numbers are believed to represent only a fraction of the honor killings carried out each year.

Honor crimes became an issue of public debate in Jordan in large part due to the attention the issue has received in the *Jordan Times*, an English-language daily newspaper in Amman.[64] Reporter Rana Husseini has made a practice of reporting honor killings and trials of such killers, relying on statements by police and court proceedings. Her reporting has become one of the most reliable sources of information on honor killings in Jordan and has helped to spark public debate on the practice and the law. Other activists have also campaigned for changes in the law and in police and judicial practice, and once the issue began to receive significant attention, members of the royal family became involved as well.

An indication of the extent to which honor crimes have become a leading issue of public debate was the appearance in August 1999 of a political cartoon on the topic. This cartoon, drawn by leading editorial cartoonist Imad Hajjaj, was published both in the Arabic-language daily *Al-Rai* and, in English translation, in the *Jordan Times*. At the time, the Pan-Arab Games were underway in Amman, accompanied by fervent expressions of national pride; Hajjaj's cartoon effectively mocked the irony that people could be proud of a nation that condones the murder of its own women. The cartoon, one of Hajjaj's beloved Abu Mahjoob series, depicted a young woman reading a newspaper story about the Arab Games, then underway in Amman. The young woman says to her father, "Oh dad, I wish you would let me play sports. I promise I won't wear shorts. Maybe I will become a famous athlete, and win medals and make my country proud…" Her father, watching television on the couch, says without looking up, "My dear, you remind me of your cousin Najwa. She was a fast runner. I remember we ran 20 miles before we managed to shoot her." The cartoon's appearance made quite an impact and was regarded as an indicator of the new public importance of the issue. Hajjaj's cartoon was also considered daring in its black-comedy take on honor killings, an approach very much in line with his other, extremely popular, work.

Once the public debate over honor killings was launched, it centered around the proposed elimination of Article 340 from the penal code. In 1998, the Jordanian National Committee for Women, which is headed by the sister of the late King Hussein, Princess Basma, appealed to the government to change the law. Later that year, a group called the Campaign for the Elimination of So-Called "Crimes of Honour" was formed by Rana Husseini and other young activists in Amman; this group led a petition drive to support the cancellation of Article 340.[65] While they

64 The Arabic-language press in Jordan has given much less attention to honor killings; when reported at all, they are usually limited to a small paragraph giving only the fact of the murder, the initials of the victim and perpetrators and occasionally the relationship between them. The *Jordan Times'* audience is primarily well-educated Jordanians and foreigners, who are less likely to view it as a "private" matter that should remain hidden.

65 For an excellent description of the campaign and its political effect, see Stephanie Nanes, "Fighting Honor Crimes: Evidence of Civil Society in Jordan," *Middle East Journal* 57:1 (2003): 112–129.

collected over 15,000 signatures,[66] they also received condemnation from some quarters for embarrassing Jordan by inviting international criticism.

Support for the cancellation of Article 340 has come largely from liberal elites and the royal family, while opposition to it is centered in conservative sectors of society and the Islamic Action Front party. The two camps on this issue reflect the two types of legitimation pursued by the Jordanian state; one appeals to the egalitarian-rights language of democracy, while the other appeals to the cultural authenticity of indigenous tradition and to the principle of national self-determination. This is not to say, of course, that the liberal camp does not value tradition, or that the conservative camp does not value democracy; rather, the two positions represent a disagreement over how these should be incorporated into the political system. The debate over honor crimes has thus become a reflection of fundamental issues of Jordanian political development.

The arguments for canceling Article 340 included that it was inappropriate for a modern society, that it violated women's rights to equal treatment under the law, that it granted male relatives the power of extrajudicial execution and that it violated Jordan's obligations under international law.[67] Some have pointed to the occasions on which "innocent" women have been killed as a reason to change the law,[68] but the predominant view among those who advocate change is that *no* such killings are justified, whatever the woman has done.

Not all those who advocated changing the law are secularists; the king's advisor on Islamic Affairs, Sheikh Izzeddin al-Khatib al-Tamimi, has condemned Article 340 as contradicting *shari'a*[69] and Nawal Faouri, a prominent (and female) Islamist, has suggested that the law has encouraged misguided individuals to kill, an act forbidden by God.[70] In February of 2000, the al-Azhar Ifta Council, a prominent Sunni religious law body, issued a *fatwa* (legal opinion) holding that individuals do not have the right to kill adulterous female relatives.[71] According

66 Rana Husseini and Dina Hamdan, "Senate upholds decision on Article 340, reject gun draft law," *Jordan Times*, February 22, 2000.

67 Jordan has signed and ratified the Convention on the Elimination of All Forms of Discrimination Against Women; upon ratification, this treaty became formally part of Jordanian law, although no one has yet sought legal redress under the terms of the treaty (Professor Salah Bashir, interview, Amman, 1998).

68 For example, former deputy Dr. Hammam Sa'eed cited the killing of innocent women in order "to silence the gossip" as a reason, along with its un-Islamic character, to eliminate Article 340 (quoted in Noura Wazani, "Article 340 of the Criminal Law is not fair to women," *ArabDaily* (Amman) May 23, 1999).

69 Rana Husseini, "Sabeel to publish survey on 'crimes of honour,'" *Jordan Times*, February 22, 2000.

70 Rana Husseini, "Lawyers, judges, intellectuals condemn national campaign against Article 340," *Jordan Times*, March 10, 2000.

71 Rana Husseini, "Al Sabeel survey weighs in against amending Article 340," *Jordan Times*, February 23, 2000. This condemnation of honor killings has precedent in Islamic legal history, as well. Judith Tucker (1998: 166) cites the eighteenth-century mufti

to one religious scholar, honor killings are "the result of a deeply rooted tradition falsely attached to Islam."[72] Religious arguments are deployed on both sides of the debate, and thus the issue does not necessarily represent a clash between Islam one hand and democracy or human rights on the other. Rather, both sides recognize the practice as a traditional one, and they differ in their views of the proper role of this tradition in society. Islam has become an important element in the debate because of views on both sides about the relationship of the traditional practice of honor killings to Islamic law and principles.

Although religious and other figures, including the late King Hussein, have condemned honor killings as contrary to Islamic law and principles, many of those who endorse the practice and advocate retaining Article 340 hold that the law is consonant with *shari'a* and suitable for an Islamic society. In February of 2000, the newspaper al-Sabeel, a pro-Islamist daily, conducted a survey and found that 78 percent of female respondents and 77 percent of males were in favor of keeping Article 340 in its current form.[73] A majority of respondents agreed that the campaign against honor crimes was a result of international pressure, and 81 percent agreed that honor killings occur because *shari'a* is not implemented in Jordan. The survey is not a reliable indicator of general public opinion in Jordan,[74] but it may well represent the opinions of al-Sabeel's primary audience. It also conforms to the editorial position of al-Sabeel, which generally agrees with the Islamic Action Front.

The IAF's position on the honor crimes issue has strongly favored retaining the article on the grounds that it promotes a virtuous society in accordance with the principles of *shari'a*. Specifically, the practice of honor killings is regarded as a roughly equivalent substitute for the *shari'a's* death penalty for adultery. It is important to note, however, that the *shari'a* penalty (even if it were part of the criminal code in Jordan, which it is not) applies only at the direction of a judge, after a trial in court in which four reliable witnesses to the actual act of adultery are produced. The circumstances of honor killings do not meet these requirements,

---

'Abd al-Fattah al-Tamimi as holding that brothers have no special role in the "chastisement of a sister suspected of *zin'a*" (extramarital sex).

72 Sheikh Hamdi Murad, in Rana Husseini, "'Crimes of Honour': One year in, amendments to Article 340 appear to have made little difference," *Jordan Times*, December 22, 2002.

73 Rana Husseini, "Al Sabeel survey weighs in against amending Article 340."

74 This survey appears to have a number of methodological shortcomings. Participants were said to be taken from a "random sample," but the questionnaire was circulated partly via the Internet and partly in person, so the quality of the sample is questionable. (It is difficult to get a random sample for a survey in Jordan because of significant variation in people's access to communications media). Also, of the five questions asked, four were worded to prompt responses consonant with al-Sabeel's editorial position on the issue. For example, participants were not asked what they believed causes honor killings but whether they agreed that honor killings happen because the Islamic laws on adultery are not implemented in the Jordanian code.

not only because of the invariable absence of four witnesses to an act of adultery but because they are extra-judicial and often concern "damage to family honor" from some act other than adultery, as described above. Some of those who regard honor killings as justifiable on a *shari'a* basis are simply not clear on the stringent requirements of the law and so see the death of the "adulterous" woman as the meaningful element. Others, however, are perfectly aware of the difference between honor killings and the *shari'a* treatment of adultery; their endorsement of the practice of honor killings considers them "pro-*shari'a*" rather than part of the *shari'a*, on the grounds that they serve the same end of public morality. This may not be the self-serving disingenuity it first appears, as there is certainly a basis in Islamic thought for regarding the *shari'a* as a moral as well as a legal code. Noel J. Coulson described it as follows:

> The Islamic *Shari'a* is, in our terminology, both a code of law and a code of morals. It is a comprehensive scheme of human behavior which derives from the one ultimate authority of the will of Allah; so that the dividing line between law and morality is by no means so clearly drawn as it is in Western societies generally.[75]

Thus honor killings are, like the penalties for adultery, a means by which to secure the morality of Islamic society. The *shari'a*'s silence on what to do about immoral (female) behavior short of adultery is filled in with a traditional practice that seems, to its advocates, to reflect Islamic principles. Opponents of the practice may consider this a flawed argument, but it carries social weight nonetheless.

These claims about the compatibility of honor killings with *shari'a* raise the broader issue of the relationship between Islamic law and custom. Islamic law, like other legal orders, does not exist in a cultural vacuum. Since its inception, Islamic law has existed alongside, and sometimes consciously taken into account, cultural practices that did not originate within the Islamic system itself. The payment of *diya*, or blood money, for example, was a pre-Islamic practice modified by Qur'anic teaching, and the practice continues today, recognized as having both Islamic and customary authority. Coulson explains that in the first century and a half of the Islamic era, existing customary law "remained the accepted standard of conduct unless it was expressly superseded in some particular by the dictates of divine revelation."[76] This changed as Islamic theology and philosophy grew more sophisticated, and eventually classical legal theory (from the tenth century onward) "express[ed] to perfection the notion of law as the comprehensive and preordained system of God's commands," independent (in theory) of both social practice and human reason."[77] However, Islamic law in practice depended on the

75 Noel J. Coulson, *Conflicts and Tensions in Islamic Jurisprudence* (Chicago: University of Chicago Press, 1969), 79.

76 Ibid., 4.

77 Ibid., 7.

reasoning of jurists, which "served to perpetuate standards of the customary law if it did not expressly reject it."[78]

This inevitable role for human reason, situated in and reflecting real human contexts, helps to explain the diversity in Islamic legal teaching and practice over time and from place to place. Coulson attributes, for example, the differences regarding women's legal capacity in the Hanafi and Malaki schools to the different social environments in which they were developed.[79] Judith Tucker describes the seventeenth century *mufti* Khayr al-Din al-Ramli as "draw[ing] on his knowledge of local custom and human nature in order to fashion legal decisions that were well suited to the specific contexts of the cases at hand."[80] Not only does Islamic law as practiced come to reflect and accommodate some customary practices, the process was apparently, at least at some stages, a deliberate one, with custom being accommodated by legal scholars and judges particularly where it seemed to serve the good of Islamic society.

Current claims about the compatibility of certain customs, such as honor killings, with Islamic law, therefore, cannot be dismissed as mere attempts to bestow an additional source of authority upon a challenged practice. Rather, we should examine these claims in the light of the history of the interaction between Islamic law and customary law. Efforts to "Islamize" a customary practice or rule are relevant here for their importance in politics rather than in the development of Islamic legal theory, and so I cannot fully address the question of the quality of historical precedents for specific claims, as these do not generally arise in the political context. Rather, the claims are interesting for what they reflect about understandings of Islam, authority and social practice; the fact that the same custom can be both hailed as Islamic and condemned as un-Islamic reveals the contingent nature of the incorporation of both Islam and custom into politics and law.

Other arguments for the retention of Article 340 in whole or in part suggest that to remove it would usher in widespread general sexual immorality, that the proposed changes are a conspiracy by foreign interests who seek to destroy Jordanian society by dismantling its traditions and that, in the frank words of one member of Parliament, "if [Article 340] is canceled men will not have control over women."[81] These elements seem to be linked around the issue of what constitutes authentic Jordanian culture; in this view, it is Islamic, has certain traditions of social control of women and is non-Western, and thus those who would preserve Jordan must do what promotes Islam, what safeguards traditions and what resists foreign influence. Several Islamists have denounced attempts to change the law on

78 Ibid., 19.

79 Ibid., 27–28.

80 Tucker (1998), 16.

81 Deputy Usama Malkawi, an attorney from Irbid, quoted in Rana Husseini, "Opposition to Article 340 driven by 'Zionists, Western interests,' says Oweideh," *Jordan Times*, February 25, 2000.

honor crimes as a "Zionist plot." Another argued that canceling the article was a "call to spread corrupt morals and obscenity and will bring total destruction to our society."[82] Clearly, the stakes could hardly be higher.

The argument about a foreign conspiracy to destroy Jordanian tradition is one of the most popular components of the Islamist-led opposition to changing the honor crimes law; this is somewhat ironic, since the law itself is originally a product of the French criminal code. The Napoleonic Code contained a provision commuting the sentence of a man who killed his wife after catching her in the act of adultery in their home. This provision was eliminated from French law in 1975, long after it had been incorporated into many legal systems in Europe and European colonies during the nineteenth and twentieth centuries. French law arrived in the Arab world in part through the Ottomans, who had reformed their legal system on the French model, and through French colonial involvement in Egypt.[83] The source of the early honor crimes provision in Egyptian criminal law can thus be traced to Article 324 of the 1816 French Penal Code;[84] Jordan and other countries of the region have laws heavily influenced by the Egyptian system and the Ottoman/French legal heritage.

When asked about the issue of the "Islamicness" of Article 340, Dr. Abdul Latif Arabiyyat, then Secretary-General of the Islamic Action Front, made the following argument in favor of keeping the article: he insisted that it is an important marker of valuable traditions and religious prescriptions for behavior, while also arguing that the law is originally French and thus should not be characterized in the foreign press as an element of Islamic law.[85] Asked to reconcile the apparently contradictory positions that the law is essential to local culture and that it is foreign in origin, he argued that in the absence of the state's adoption of full Islamic law, society must do what it can to control immoral behavior, and this law serves that purpose and so serves Jordanian culture. This view that the absence of *shari'a* is to blame in honor killings is endorsed by other Islamists and even by the head of

82 Mohammad Oweideh, quoted ibid.

83 For the relationship between French and Ottoman law and the development of law in Arab states, see Nathan Brown, *The Rule of Law in the Arab World* (Cambridge: Cambridge University Press, 1997).

84 I am grateful to Dr. George Sfeir, formerly of the Library of Congress, for tracing this specific legal lineage for me (personal communication, October, 2000).

85 Interview with Dr. Abdul Latif Arabiyyat, April 2000. It is not surprising, given this political characterization of the honor crimes law as Islamic, that Western observers often confuse the issue. See, for example, Spatz 1991. She writes, referring to honor crimes laws, that "as currently interpreted in many Islamic countries, Islamic law provides defenses for men who murder their wives for committing adultery." This is not accurate, either as an assessment of the provisions of honor crimes laws or as an attribution of their Islamic origin. In all of the cases in which separate statutes exist, they are not part of the country's *shari'a*-based family law codes but of the state-created criminal code. Simply put, not all laws in Muslim countries are "Islamic law."

the Jordanian Bar Association, who goes further to state that "the absence of full implementation of *shari'a* is responsible for all corruption in our society."[86]

The Jordanian state, as embodied in the royal family and the king's chosen prime minister, has advocated the elimination of this law. One reason for this is that members of the royal family have probably sincere principles regarding women's rights. However, personal royal opinion would, in other political circumstances, be subjugated to interests of state, and so we can be confident that additional factors are at work in producing the state's new position. Opposition to the honor crimes law has reached a point where legitimation needs are no longer well-served, and the issue has become a divisive one placing contradictory and very public demands on the state. If the law could be eliminated, the reform itself might serve to legitimate the regime and political system to another segment of society, those who have generally liberal outlooks.

The royal element of the state has consistently favored eliminating the law, and one of King Abdullah's early acts upon his inauguration in 1999 was to instruct the Prime Ministry to redraft the relevant section of the law and submit the changes to Parliament for approval.[87] The appointed upper house of Parliament endorsed the government's proposal. However, the popularly-elected lower house refused to make the proposed changes, going so far as to condemn the originally-proposed change because it "legalises obscenity and is detrimental to the morals of women."[88] Thus the regime resorted to the "temporary law" procedure in 2001, between parliamentary sessions, which has produced the current state of limbo, as the temporary law is repeatedly rejected by the lower house and endorsed by the upper.

It is somewhat unusual for the typically docile parliament to thwart the expressed will of the monarch and his government so openly, but members of Parliament are apparently confident that popular opinion favors keeping the law in place. The parliamentary debate has centered neither around the rights of women not to be killed for violating social norms nor around the number of women and girls killed who later prove to have been innocent of the acts attributed to them but around the maintenance of legal protection for an established social custom.[89] Not the rights of women but the nature of society was the question considered relevant in evaluating the law and its purposes. As a result, proponents of eliminating

86 Quoted in Rana Husseini, "Lawyers, judges, intellectuals condemn national campaign against Article 340," *Jordan Times*, March 10, 2000.

87 Rana Husseini, "Justice ministry committee cancels article allowing for reduced penalty for honour crimes," *Jordan Times*, July 22–23, 1999.

88 Quoted in Dina Hamdan, "King expected to call extraordinary session," *Jordan Times*, February 23, 2000.

89 That the legal issue arises at all is an indication of the contestability of the social practice; presumably a universally-accepted practice would spark no such challenge. The dual nature of Jordan's legal system also raises the stakes in the legal debate, since challenges to the practice have a legal tradition of their own on which to base their authority.

Article 340 have constructed arguments along the same lines, leading to the prevalence of statements about the injustice of such killings from the point of view of *shari'a* (discussed above). However, despite these attempts, the ability to define cultural authenticity and claim to be its protector has been most successfully demonstrated by the Islamists and their allies on this issue. A government minister recently conceded that government efforts to change the law were being thwarted by "strong conservative powers in the Jordanian community that are fighting any efforts geared toward this problem."[90]

Thus, despite its marginal utility in criminal law, Article 340 has become the locus of political debate over the proper role of tradition and the protection of culture in the criminal law system. At its creation, this statute served the legitimation interests of the state by permitting the continuation of a traditional practice without burdensome state interference; its amendment serves the state's legitimation interests with a different sector of society. Both the state and its opponents (internal and external) recognize that the debate over this article is a debate about cultural legitimacy, and the contestants each seek to claim it for themselves.

The Law in Practice: Gender-Neutral Texts, Discriminatory Outcomes

Legal systems are more than mere collections of statutes; the practice of judges and police in investigating, prosecuting, ruling and sentencing are a significant element of the legal order. For example, while criminal codes define crimes, police and prosecutors decide with which crime an alleged criminal is charged, and judges and attorneys make decisions about the laws that may apply in terms of mitigating or aggravating circumstances. Thus, in the area of judicial practice we find further elements of the gendered nature of the legal system.

Article 98: "Bad Acts" and "Fits of Fury"

As mentioned above, the now-famous Article 340 of the Jordanian Criminal Code has not actually been used in court in many years.[91] Crimes of honor continue to occur, and perpetrators continue to receive light sentences (often a few months, or even less if the killer is a juvenile). However, few crimes meet the standard of Article 340, which refers to catching the woman *in flagrante delicto* of the act of adultery (*hal at-talabbus bil-zina,* or in the amended language, *bi-jarimat al-zina*).

---

90 Minister of Political Development and Minister of Parliamentary Affairs Mohammad Daoudiyeh, quoted in Rana Husseini, "Gov't working to eliminate legislative discrimination against women – Daoudiyeh," *Jordan Times*, June 27, 2004.

91 Abu Odeh (1996) finds no evidence of the use of Article 340 after the late 1960s. Also, a Jordanian attorney interviewed said that he can recall perhaps two cases in the last 15 or so years in which Article 340 might have been used and agrees that it is no longer an active part of the criminal code (Professor Salah Bashir, October 1998).

Many, if not most, honor killings are carried out on the basis of suspicion, much of which proves later to have been unfounded.[92] Article 340 does not, therefore, apply, and killers and the courts have found another law much more useful in providing for reduced penalties – Article 98, which provides for a reduction of penalty for one who commits murder in a "furious passion." The full text of the article reads: "The committer of a crime who undertakes it in a furious passion produced by a bad [*ghair muhiq,* lit. unrightful] or dangerous act performed by his victim, benefits from a mitigating excuse."

This law is generally equivalent to the "crime of passion" laws found in many legal systems. Article 98 makes no mention of the sex of the victim or perpetrator, and can apply to any case of murder carried out in the heat of furious passion. It has been widely applied in honor cases on the grounds that men (and boys) who suspect a female relative of shameful behavior would obviously be overcome with rage and unable to control their actions. Judges often cite in their rulings the "bad or dangerous action on the part of the victim" that, according to the statute, must have occurred to justify the fit of fury. There is little evidence, however, that they give much critical consideration to whether the act was literally bad or dangerous (rather than just offensive to the perpetrator) or whether the alleged act even occurred at all. Apparently, the suspicion of a bad act is not only sufficient to cause a murderous rage, but the rage can be presumed when a bad act (or the suspicion thereof) has been alleged. Then, in all but the most obvious cases of premeditation, the perpetrator's actions will be held to have occurred while in the grip of this fury.

A number of observers have noted that Article 98 is more important than Article 340 in the actual prosecution of honor killers, but an interesting point has generally been overlooked. The murder victim is essentially redefined by this law as a guilty party herself – the committer of a "bad or dangerous act." In a 1999 case, the court granted an Article 98-based reduction of penalty because the murdered woman engaged in "wrongdoing" by "going out with strangers and engaging in sexual activity, considered a risk in our conservative society."[93] In another case, a man with a long history of domestic conflict had an argument with his wife in which she threatened him with a knife if he did not leave the house. In response, he took the knife from her and stabbed her repeatedly, killing her. The court eventually decided that he should benefit from a reduced penalty, and held that "the victim's actions violate the traditional and religious beliefs and marriage duties which stipulate that the wife should respect, obey and serve her husband,

---

92 Interview with a Jordanian medical examiner, Dr. Hani Jahshan, Amman, 1999. He reports that young girls who have been accused of illicit sex nearly always prove upon post mortem examination to have been virgins.

93 Quoted in Rana Husseini, "Courts sentence man to one year after killing sister with car, three men to five months after shooting," *Jordan Times*, 31 July 1999. The woman in this case was killed by her uncle and father after being released from protective custody, an issue discussed below.

and thus constituted dangerous actions against her husband."[94] The husband's act was not considered by the court to be one of self-defense in response to an assault with a knife but one of justifiable rage at his wife's violation of her proper role, and the "danger" posed by the wife lay in her failure to conform to traditional norms about wifeliness, not in the physical harm posed by the weapon.

A victim need not even have been literally guilty of a "bad act," as in many cases the woman or girl suspected of an affair later proves to have been a virgin. It is the man's rage that is the active component of this law, and his suspicion of the woman's guilt justifies that rage and its consequences. The victim becomes not only responsible for her own murder but a perpetrator of a "bad act" herself, and so no longer a real victim. This point is made explicitly by then-chief judge of the High Criminal Court in Jordan, Mohammed Ajjarmeh, who said:

> Nobody can really want to kill his wife or daughter or sister. But sometimes circumstances force him to do this. Sometimes, it's society that forces him to do this, because people won't forget. *Sometimes, there are two victims – the murdered and the murderer.*[95]

The effect of Article 98 in reducing penalties for honor-related murders is substantial. The penal code's rules regarding mitigating circumstances suggest that they should reduce a death sentence to imprisonment with hard labor or life imprisonment, a life imprisonment sentence to a limited-term imprisonment, etc.[96] However, in the cases involving "fit of fury" arguments that apply to honor killings of women, sentences are especially light, sometimes only a few months' imprisonment. In a 2002 case, the court handed down a seven-month prison sentence to a man who had murdered his pregnant sister by stabbing and shooting her, citing the application of Article 98 to the case. Notably, only two months of the sentence were for the killing of his sister. Two months were for causing the death of her fetus, two for illegal possession of a weapon, and one for theft of the

---

94 Court ruling quoted in Rana Husseini, "Man released after serving one year for murder of wife," *Jordan Times*, March 21, 1999. The Criminal Court originally found that the man did not benefit from an Article 98 excuse because he was known to have frequent violent quarrels with his wife. The Court of Cassation (appellate court) ruled that he should benefit from a reduced penalty and returned the case to the lower court, which issued the finding cited here.

95 Quoted in Douglas Jehl, "For Shame: a special report: Arab honor's price: a woman's blood," *New York Times*, June 20, 1999. Emphasis added.

96 Jordanian Penal Code, Article 99, regarding reasons for lightened sentences. This article was part of the 2001 amendments to the Penal Code, which would have increased minimum sentences, but its status is still in limbo. As of 2008, sentences as light as a few months' imprisonment are still handed down in honor-killing cases in which Article 98 is applied.

shotgun used in the crime.[97] Despite increasing public attention to sentencing and growing criticism, light penalties are still common; of 11 sentences imposed in honor-related cases in the past year (November 1, 2007 to October 31, 2008), six were for imprisonment of less than a year and a half.[98] In each of the six cases, the court applied Article 98 to reduce the punishment. By contrast, in the six cases in which the court did not find that Article 98 applied, sentences ranged from seven and a half years imprisonment to the death penalty. (The death penalty, however, was imposed in a case in which the court rejected the defendant's claim that his wife had dishonored him and thus found that he had no basis for a claimed fit of fury).

Although the basis for an Article 98 claim concerns passion rather than honor, the distinction between the two is often blurred by the courts. In one case, the court reduced a charge of premeditated murder to manslaughter because "the defendant committed his crime in a fit of fury to cleanse his honour,"[99] suggesting that the fury and the honor problem are functionally, if not legally, linked. Judges' decisions generally evaluate victims' sexual misbehavior (or alleged misbehavior) as "dangerous" and thus responsible for the killer's murderous rage. In a case involving a victim killed by her brother after she was accused of having affairs and leaving home without her husband's permission, the judges ruled that "the victim…did not care about the culture or her family's reputation…she tarnished their image by violating her own honour, which the court considers a dangerous act."[100] Dangerous, indeed, as it served as an excuse for her murder; her killer received a three-month sentence. But it is not the danger to the victim that the court has in mind but the danger to the family's reputation; in a similar case, the court ruled that a murdered woman's alleged immoral behavior was "dangerous… especially to the defendant [her brother], since in our customs and traditions a man is valued by his sister's behavior and honour among his community."[101]

---

97 Rana Husseini, "Murder charge reduced to misdemeanor in Azraq crime of honour case," *Jordan Times*, June 12, 2002.

98 There were 13 reported judgments in honor-related cases in this period (compiled from *Jordan Times*). One was an acquittal. Of the twelve cases in which sentences were handed down, nine were original convictions and three were the result of appeals of earlier sentences (this tally counts only primary offenders, not accomplices). Sentences ranged from three months imprisonment to the death penalty.

99 Quoted in Rana Husseini, "Courts sentence man to one year after killing sister with car, three men to five months after shooting."

100 Quoted in Rana Husseini, "Egyptian gets two months for murdering his Jordanian wife," *Jordan Times*, April 4, 2008. (This is not the case mentioned in the headline). Another notable aspect of this case was that the victim was gunned down in the offices of the regional governor after her father and another brother signed a pledge that they would not harm her. She had been in police custody for an unstated reason after leaving home.

101 Quoted in Rana Husseini, "19-year-old handed reduced sentence for murdering his sister," *Jordan Times*, September 23, 2008.

Thus, despite the revisions to Article 340 described above, Article 98 continues to be a virtual guarantee of light sentences for perpetrators of honor killings. In response to the increasing recognition of the problematic applications of Article 98, in 2004 the government proposed a change in the penal code.[102] This change, the status of which remains somewhat murky, would raise the minimum punishments allowed by Article 98. (The punishments themselves are specified in Article 97, which would also be amended). At present, the articles allow death or life-imprisonment sentences to be reduced to one year's imprisonment and lower sentences to be reduced to as little as six months' imprisonment. The proposed changes would make the minimum penalty five years' imprisonment.

A number of activists and observers have argued that, as Article 98 is the problem, it is Article 98 that must be amended.[103] However, amending the language of the article will have little effect on its application; the text of this law is gender-neutral, and thus the problem lies more in its use than in its language. Unless the amendments specify what may be considered a "wrong and dangerous act" or in some other way limit judicial discretion, the use of the "crime of passion" defense would remain unaltered, and the legal treatment of murdered women as culpable in their own homicides can be expected to continue as described above.

In the Jordanian legal system, as in others, judicial practice is shaped by both text and context; the interpretation of statutes is inevitably affected by dominant social mores and the shared values of a culture. This is perhaps even more evident in countries such as Jordan, which operate largely within the civil law tradition and thus do not rely on precedent as a controlling factor in judicial decisions. Earlier court decisions can have an advisory effect on a case but not a binding one.[104] This is meant, in civil law countries, to give the (legislatively-created) text of the law a paramount role, in order to limit the undemocratic power of judges to make law.[105] However, judges' decisions are not made in a vacuum containing only the facts of the event and the text of the law, and so it is to be expected that judges' own attitudes and principles, shaped not only by their profession but by their social surroundings, will affect the treatment of crimes in the courtroom. This has long been a complaint of those concerned with honor killings, who attribute the light sentences for such murders to judicial

102 Rana Husseini, "Amendments to Penal Code proposed," *Jordan Times*, July 7, 2004.

103 See, for example, Janine Clark, "The Conditions of Islamist Moderation: Unpacking Cross-Ideological Cooperation in Jordan," *International Journal of Middle East Studies* 38:4, 539–560.

104 Information on the role of precedent in the Jordanian system was provided by attorney Salah Bashir and retired judge Farouk Kilani.

105 See John Henry Merryman, *The Civil Law Tradition,* 2nd edition (Stanford: Stanford University Press, 1985).

discretion as much as to legal text.[106] There is also a widespread perception that judges must make decisions consonant with the wishes of the regime; one rare attempt at judicial review, in which a judge criticized the regime's handling of a "temporary law," resulted in the judge's subsequent removal from the bench.[107] In short, judges do not enjoy a great deal of independence; consequently, judicial decisions are believed to represent the interests of the politically powerful as well as the social force of traditional values. Given the lack of judicial independence and the royal family's clear position on honor killings, it is somewhat interesting that judges have not tended to assign harsher penalties in such cases. This is not really an example of judicial independence, however, but of the degree to which powerful conservative interests are reflected in the judiciary.

Dropping the Charges: The Recognition of Private Interests in Public Prosecutions

An additional source of light sentences in honor-killing cases is the practice known as "dropping the charges." Criminal prosecutions in Jordan are public; that is, they are undertaken by the state rather than by private individuals. However, Jordanian law adds a private component to criminal prosecutions. The victim, or in homicide cases the victim's family, may drop charges against the accused, effectively offering a personal pardon or renouncing the personal right inherent in the matter. Dropping the charges does not end the case; the prosecution of the crime proceeds, and the accused may still be convicted, but any criminal penalty will be reduced. The dropping of charges is taken into account as a mitigating factor in punishment and reduces a sentence, generally by the degree specified in Article 99 of the Penal Code, which deals with mitigating factors in general.[108] The effect is often to reduce the punishment by half although the reduction is at the judges' discretion; thus, the death penalty often becomes a 20-year prison

106 Lawyer Asma Khader and medical examiner Dr. Hani Jahshan, among others, attributed the lenient treatment of honor killers to attitudes of judges (interviews, cited above).

107 This was the well-publicized 1998 case involving the Press and Publications Law. Judge Farouk Kilani of the Court of Cassation was transferred and then "involuntarily retired" after he ruled that the law was invalid because the government had exceeded its authority in enacting it while Parliament was out of session. Government statements denied that Kilani's retirement was a punishment for the ruling, but it was generally regarded as such and as an example of the lack of judicial independence from the executive power (interview with Farouk Kilani, Amman, March 1999).

108 The mitigating effect of "dropping the charges" was established by appellate court jurisprudence rather than statute, and judges have discretion as to its application in any case, but the practice is routine and its effects on sentencing highly predictable. I am grateful to Dr. Omar Aljazy for his explanation of the legal basis of this aspect of sentencing (personal communication, December 18, 2008).

term, a 15-year term becomes a seven-and-a-half-year term, and so forth across the board.

Like Article 98, this aspect of the law is not specific to honor crimes, crimes within families or crimes against women. However, it does take a particularly interesting twist in honor killings. It is the victim's nearest relatives (usually the father) who have the right to drop charges. In honor killings, the victim's nearest relatives are almost always the perpetrator's nearest relatives as well; a brother who murders his sister will have the charges "dropped" by the victim's father, who is also his father.

This practice, while gender-neutral on its face, is deeply problematic for two reasons: it grants power over public prosecutions to people who have a personal interest in the outcome for the accused, and it leads, particularly in combination with the application of Article 98, to shockingly light punishments for individuals who have committed murder.[109]

There is nothing necessarily wrong in principle with recognizing the private interests inherent in criminal prosecution. These private interests could be pursued separately through the civil courts (as in the case of "wrongful death" suits in the United States), but incorporating them as an aspect of public prosecutions is not unique to Jordan; the statements of victims' relatives are often allowed at the sentencing phase of American trials. In an earlier era, the ability to "drop the charges" might have served the purpose of preserving social order by defusing family or clan conflict; in homicide cases in which the victim and the perpetrator are from different families, the "wronged" family could show mercy to the family of the perpetrator and perhaps preclude further rounds of retaliation. However, the practice of "dropping the charges" in the context of family violence allows those likely to have been *complicit* in the crime a say in the punishment. Even if family members were not complicit, allowing them to secure lighter punishments for honor killers lowers the disincentives to commit such killings, and it suggests that these kinds of murders are more tolerable, or even justifiable, than others because the family values the freedom of the killer more than the life of the victim.

Protective Custody

A final example of judicial or prosecutorial redefinition of the victim concerns the issue of protective custody. As a matter of police and government practice, a woman or girl who is believed to be a likely victim of an honor crime (for

109 Of the eleven honor-related sentences handed down from November 2007 to October 2008, charges were dropped in at least seven cases (in one case the family did not drop charges against a husband who killed his wife for what were believed to be financial motives, and in the others the issue was not reported). In every case where charges were dropped, the victim was a close blood relative of the perpetrator, and so her family was also his family, with an interest in protecting him from punishment.

example, one who has run away from home or who has engaged in pre-marital sex) can be placed in protective custody to prevent her relatives from harming her. (This decision is made by the district governor and not by the courts). After a period of time, her father or other male guardian may be allowed to sign a statement for the governor promising not to harm his daughter, and she will be released into his custody. In practice, women and girls are sometimes killed after being returned to their families. In a 1998 case, a 17-year-old girl ran away from home in connection with an affair with her boyfriend (who was later charged with statutory rape).[110] When her father came to claim her from police custody, they were reluctant to release her because it was believed that he would kill her. Despite police objections, the governor ordered the girl released to her father, who took her to a park and slit her throat and then turned himself in to the police, announcing that he had killed his daughter in the name of family honor. The following year, a girl who had been in protective custody at the Juweideh prison for three years was released to the custody of her father, who signed a pledge not to harm her. One month later she was murdered in her sleep by her brother, who claimed to have been acting on his father's instructions and to protect the family's honor.[111]

Stories like this are well-known, and in an attempt to forestall such killings, the governor of a district may require the father or brother to sign a guarantee pledging that he will not harm the woman or forfeit a monetary penalty (usually JD 5,000)[112] if he does. Of the 21 reported honor crimes from November 2007 through October 2008, five victims had been in police or protective custody prior to the crime and were released to their families, and in four of these cases, the father or brother had signed a pledge not to harm the victim. These written guarantees are clearly an ineffectual means of protecting potential victims.

Women and girls who are not released into a relative's custody must remain in detention. The police responsible for many cases of protective custody report that most girls and women in this situation are detained willingly, as they have no other option.[113] However, some are held for a period of several years and have little hope of release: honor killings have been known to occur many years after the original offending incident, which makes releasing these women from custody at any point a risky option in many cases.

---

110 Lt. Taghreed Abu-Sarhan, Public Security Department's Family Protection Unit, interview, November 1998. She expected the man to receive a penalty of approximately three months' imprisonment for the murder. This story was also reported in the *Jordan Times* (Rana Husseini, "Criminal Court upholds 'fit of fury' arguments," *Jordan Times*, March 25–26, 1999); the father was found guilty of manslaughter and sentenced to nine months in prison.

111 "Brother waits three years to cleanse family honor," *Arab Daily* (Amman), May 23, 1999.

112 Around US$7,050, a significant sum in a country with an annual per capita income of US$7,995 in 2007.

113 Ibid.

The legal basis for protective custody is not entirely clear. A legal statute gives district governors the power of preventive detention to temporarily incarcerate persons believed to be on the point of committing a crime.[114] However, the text of this statute clearly refers to the prevention of crime by detaining the potential perpetrator, not the potential victim. That this statute is the legal basis for the practice has been confirmed by several observers, who attribute the broadening of the law's application to both the power of governors to order administrative detentions and to the lack of practical options that police and other authorities have in such cases. Until 2007 Jordan had no women's shelters to which women at risk could be sent, and it is generally believed that if the police detain one male relative to prevent an honor crime, the killing will simply be carried out by someone else. It is therefore far easier to detain the woman herself. As the Interior Minister remarked in response to a question about the practice, "We cannot lock up an entire tribe or family. We really do not like or want to imprison women, but what can we do? The concept of [family] honour is socially imbedded in our society."[115] Placing the woman in custody requires, in order to conform to the letter of the law, that she be redefined as the potential criminal, rather than the potential victim. While it is clear that some officials do see these women as victims, it is also acknowledged that in most cases the woman has done something to have caused her family to want her dead. This negotiated understanding of the victim as criminal goes well beyond the rhetorical – until very recently, women and girls in protective custody were held at the women's prison in Juweideh, for many years simply mixed in to the regular female criminal population. Again, the victim vanished, in this case literally, as she disappeared behind the walls of a prison, administratively if not legally reconstructed as a perpetrator rather than a victim.

Conclusion

This analysis of criminal law and judicial practice demonstrates the persistence of legal texts and practices that disadvantage women by privileging social interests, including the interest in maintaining traditions, over the interests of the individual crime victim when that victim is female. While traditional elements of culture necessarily, and perhaps properly, affect the legal system governing a society, it is notable that in regard to gender issues, cultural practices generally trump legal rights that would otherwise operate. In order to preserve specific cultural practices regarding the social control of women, female crime victims are essentially redefined as perpetrators or as means of social problem resolution, such that the

114 This is among several executive powers held by governors that enable them to enforce social order and prevent conflicts from spreading, as when one family retaliates against another and personal incidents become grounds for communal strife.

115 Quoted in Rana Husseini, "Interior Ministry seeks cooperation to put an end to honour crimes," *Jordan Times*, June 29, 2004.

victim disappears and her interests can be sublimated to those of other actors. The state not only permits these practices to continue, it creates and manages the legal system in such a way as to seek legitimacy from the combination of different kinds of legal authority. Other actors, such as the state's opponents, make use of these legal elements in similar ways. Thus we find that the law on murder does not merely serve the interest of public safety; it also feeds a debate about the permissibility of the extrajudicial killing of women in order to benefit society by preserving certain norms of sexual behavior and social control.

The purpose of this chapter was not merely to describe the deplorable condition of women in the area of criminal law. The legal treatments of rape and honor killing also tell us something about law's constitutive role in the political system. Law is not the sole constitutive foundation of politics, of course, as much of politics is not law in either the positive or the anthropological sense. However, law plays a particularly important role in the political aspects of hegemony and legitimation, and those are exemplified by the issues discussed above. The criminal law discussed here is a subject of contestation among political actors with different interests, and it is a tool of the state in the promotion of the state's own interests. It is common for law to play these roles in any system, but in this case the politics of law extends even further, combining the two roles in a way that has great potential for defining the political landscape. The state's regulation of law partakes of the contestation among other political actors in order to address the risk (or benefit) to the state arising from these conflicting social forces. In other words, responding to the competition over the definition of hegemonic norms in society is important for the state's pursuit of legitimacy.

The relationship between law and hegemony is well-recognized in recent literature.[116] The cases above demonstrate, however, that this hegemony should not be understood as a reflection of a single dominant interest. If it were, then honor killings might simply be defined in law as justifiable homicides, or the "shameful" conduct of women later killed for honor would itself be criminalized. The law as it stands represents hegemonic values but also indicates that those values are at times ambiguous or even conflicting. This allows, or even necessitates, contestation over the content and use of the laws to work out their social meaning, which presents the possibility of changing not only the laws but the broader social understanding of acceptable behavior and rights. This is what we see when different political actors debate changes to, or preservation of, the law.

If the example of law's hegemonic role focuses on society, then the issue of legitimation brings the role of the state to the forefront. It has perhaps always been recognized that law can be used to serve the interests of the state, whether through the antique notion that the law *is* the interest of the state ("*l'état, c'est moi*") or the

---

116 See, for example, Joseph Massad, *Colonial Effects: the Making of National Identity in Jordan* (New York: Columbia University Press, 2001) and Mindie Lazarus-Black and Susan F. Hirsch, *Contested States: Law, Hegemony and Resistance* (London: Routledge, 1994).

more modern notion of political crimes that is so useful to authoritarian regimes. Law also "tends to legitimate the existing social order," but as one scholar puts it, "we don't know…the mechanics of law's constitution (the 'how' it happens as opposed to 'that' it happens)."[117] This study cannot answer the question of 'how,' but perhaps it can suggest a place to look for the answer. I argue that the Jordanian state has, with regard to gender and law, staked out a tenuous position based on its need to balance two not-always-compatible sources of legitimacy: claims about cultural authenticity and claims about democracy and human rights. If the state wants to take advantage of the legitimating effects of law, it must align itself with the "existing social order" being legitimated. The problem, again, is that social orders are not static and not univocal (and neither are states, for that matter). The social order is fluid, and its features and prescriptions are contested, as in the honor killings debate. Therefore, the state balances different sources of legitimation, and both are evident in the legal issues described above. The Jordanian state wants to claim the mantle of cultural authenticity by allying itself with traditional practices, and it wants to claim the mantle of democracy by redressing legal inequalities and rights violations. One arm of the state seeks to preserve the law for the former purpose, while another seeks to change it for the latter.[118]

Thus the topic of gender and criminal law has implications well beyond "women's issues" and goes to the heart of the development of the Jordanian political system. The principles and practices enshrined in law are important for the political system, and not merely because the preservation of traditional social hierarchies in special areas of law contradicts the logic of democracy. The contestation over which conception of rights and freedoms should serve as the foundation of the political order is more than merely a negotiation of the "rules of the game." Rather, it is a determinative element in the character of the system itself; the nature of the system will be a product of the legitimacy upon which it rests.

Many readers will have noticed the parallel between victim-blaming in Western societies, particularly in the case of rape, and the treatment of victims of rape and honor crimes in the cases discussed here. This demonstrates that while the practices described above may seem completely foreign to a Western observer, the legal and political phenomena are in fact quite comparable across systems. Thus the lessons of this case tell us something not only about law in Jordan or the Arab world, but about the nature of law in political systems more generally. In particular, the extent to which gendered legal systems serve legitimation claims has important implications for the process and outcome of the development of political systems. Personal rights and freedoms, equality

117 Nourse, 36.

118 For an extensive treatment of the relationship between law and state interests in the Jordanian case, see Massad, 2001, in particular his discussion of the state's use of juridical discourse in fundamental constitutive issues like national identity.

before the law and the proper sources of authority in the legal and political order are contested issues whose resolution will be strongly determinative of chances for the future of political liberalization and democratization in Jordan.[119]

119 Of course, the existence of legal discrimination against women does not preclude the eventual development of democracy in a political system. The extension of rights to women long after they have been secured by men is a pattern long established in other countries; throughout Europe, the Americas and elsewhere, legal systems shed their discriminatory elements only gradually. However, this is a circumstance of history and not integral to the development of democracy itself; there is no logical necessity for women's rights to appear only after those of men. The current process of development in the Jordanian system is based upon political demands for individual rights, participation and the transfer of political power to the people. To perpetuate legal disadvantages of the female half of the population can only undermine the very logic of the development process itself.

Chapter 5
Nationality Law

Nationality law exists to define the state's citizenry; it establishes a formal relationship that is the legal basis of claims of rights and duties between state and individual. Thus, this is an area of law that would seem to be entirely within the purview of the state in terms of its creation, content and objectives. Deliberate choices by the state can be expected to operate here to a great degree, and this area of law is tied quite directly to the state's own goals rather than serving additional primary purposes, as is the case with criminal law and social order. An investigation of nationality law provides important information about the state's own understanding of its relationship to individual citizens and their rights. Nationality law, like criminal law, is notably gendered, and this provides a further basis on which to evaluate the state's choices in pursuit of cultural legitimacy.

This chapter investigates Jordanian nationality law and related laws of other Arab states in order to demonstrate that the unequal treatment of women in these laws is a deliberate element of policy in pursuit of state interests, rather than only a result of latent traditionalism or legal inertia. Female citizenship is, in Jordan as in much of the world, a significantly different quality than male citizenship, and this difference reflects not only the attitudes of the state's agents and supporters but the state's perception of its interests in the areas of demographics and legitimation.

The gendered aspects of many Arab nationality laws are fairly well-known; for example, in Jordan (as well as Egypt, Lebanon and elsewhere), women – but not men – who marry non-citizens cannot pass their own citizenship on to their children or their spouses. The practical problems arising from such laws, in particular regarding residency, state services and civil rights, have been well-documented. However, the various political purposes that such laws serve, and the reasons for their continued existence, require further investigation.

These laws, and their seemingly firm entrenchment in state legal systems, may appear at first glance to be explicable either as remnants of earlier social practices or as tokens of traditionalism, but neither of these explanations is sufficient to explain the existence and purpose of such laws. I argue that gendered nationality laws, which have several sources, serve a dual purpose: they facilitate state claims to legitimacy through the maintenance of traditional practices, and they serve a demographic purpose in managing the perceived nature of the citizenry. In the Jordanian case, for example, officials claim that the law is meant to prevent an influx of young Palestinian men from the Occupied Territories to Jordan. Upon analysis, the demographic arguments reveal that the state's (and its agents') view of female citizenship precludes the equal treatment of women, as they are not the same kinds of citizens as men.

This chapter presents (1) the historical development and current content of nationality laws, (2) implications of current applications of the laws and (3) state choices about nationality law. I then analyze the laws in terms of their political effects and purposes and the state interests that are addressed by maintenance or reform.

Citizenship and Nationality

There is an extensive literature on women's political rights in the Arab world[1] and elsewhere and abundant evidence that women's citizenship rights are, across the globe, generally inferior to those enjoyed by men. The issue of citizenship itself is an expansive one, ranging from electoral participation to civil liberties to access to state services to military service. Thus, studies of women's citizenship often cite the levels of female participation in voting, the proportion of female members of legislatures, the protection of women's rights, the state's provision of social services such as health and child care, and so forth.

The aspect of citizenship upon which I will focus here is nationality, as it is the most basic element of an individual's relationship to a state and is a consideration prior to the fuller expressions of citizenship in public and political life. The question of whether a person is a citizen of a given state is the initial question in determining that person's civil and political rights, and an assessment of the quality of a person's nationality is the basis for understanding the nature of citizenship and its variation within a state's population. It is important to clarify the terms used here, as diverse understandings are possible. By "nationality," I mean the formal relationship between a person and a state, what is termed in Arabic legal codes *jinsiyya*. In English, the word "citizen" (Arabic *muwatan*) describes this relationship, and in international law the term "national" is commonly used; the distinction between the two is often rather imprecise.[2] I use the term "citizen" in order to avoid the inadvertent implication that nationals may be members of nations as distinct from states, as the focus of study here is the latter. The term "citizenship" can mean, in a limited sense, this formal connection between person and state, but in political science and other scholarship it generally denotes the whole range of a person's political standing and consequent rights and duties. Thus I have attempted to be

1 See Laurie Brand's *Women, the State and Political Liberalization: Middle Eastern and North African Experiences* (New York: Columbia University Press, 1998), Selma Botman's *Engendering Citizenship in Egypt* (New York: Columbia University Press, 1999) and Suad Joseph (ed.), *Gender and Citizenship in the Middle East* (Syracuse: Syracuse University Press, 2000).

2 For an interesting treatment of the difference between *jinsiyya* and *muwatana*, see Uri Davis, "*Jinsiyya* versus *Muwatana*: The Question of Citizenship and the State in the Middle East: the Cases of Israel, Jordan, and Palestine," *Arab Studies Quarterly*, 17:1 and 17:2, 19–50.

consistent in distinguishing the narrow concept of nationality from the broader concept of citizenship, while pointing out the necessary connection from the former to the latter.

The history of nationality is characterized by two approaches whose predominance has varied over time and location. *Jus sanguinis* is the concept that ties nationality to blood, as when Germany recognizes as Germans all those who are born to a German parent, even if they are born in another country. *Jus soli*, by contrast, is the concept of territorially-based nationality, wherein one derives citizenship by virtue of having been born within a state's territory, as is the case in the United States. Examples of both approaches can be found throughout the world, with many countries now recognizing both types of claim. The United States, for example, grants nationality to all those born on its soil and also to those born to American parents abroad.[3] The reliance on one concept or the other can serve political purposes, such as the preservation of a particular ethno-national group or the management of a multiethnic state. *Jus sanguinis* is the approach that receives preferential treatment in Jordan, but as will be discussed below, some provisions have been made for *jus soli* claims to a limited degree. It should be noted that these concepts of nationality both refer to claims by right of birth; the acquisition of new nationalities by adults is a separate issue, and most states provide for some means of naturalization after the fulfillment of certain requirements.

Nationality Laws

Ottoman Law

The earliest law establishing rules for nationality in the modern Arab world was the Ottoman Nationality Law of 1869.[4] This law provided that "every person born of Ottoman parents or whose father was an Ottoman is an Ottoman."[5] This article is similar to provisions found in current Arab nationality laws, establishing a right of nationality based on paternity. The Ottoman law differs from later laws by mentioning both parents, but the article makes it clear that the father's Ottoman

3 However, one element of sex discrimination persists in American nationality law. A child born abroad to unmarried parents has an automatic claim to American nationality if the mother is American, but proof of paternity before the age of eighteen is required if it is the father who is American. This law (8 USC §1409) has been upheld by the Supreme Court twice in recent years (*Miller v. Albright* 523 U.S. 420 (1998), *Nguyen v. INS* 533 U.S. 53 (2001)). This law is based on assumptions about the nature of maternal versus paternal ties to children; it is probably also meant to limit potential citizenship claims from the offspring of American servicemen abroad.

4 January 19, 1869 Law Concerning Ottoman Nationality (Arabic). In all citations of French- and Arabic-language sources herein, translation is by the author.

5 Ibid., Article 1.

nationality is both necessary and sufficient for a right-of-blood nationality claim by the child. A more significant difference between the 1869 law and current Arab laws is found in the provision that every individual born in Ottoman territory to foreign parents could obtain Ottoman nationality by request within three years of reaching the age of majority. This territorial basis for nationality is not reproduced in the nationality statutes of the Arab states in the post-Ottoman period. The Ottoman law also provided general rules for the acquisition of Ottoman nationality by adults (by special act or by virtue of request after a period of residence within Ottoman territory) and the obtaining of foreign nationalities by Ottoman subjects.

The Ottoman law also made provisions for the nationality of married women. Article 7 provides that:

> The Ottoman woman who marries a foreigner may recover her Ottoman nationality if she is widowed, by a decision to that effect on her part within a three-year period of the death of her husband. This rule applies only to her person; as for her property, it remains subject to the laws and regulations that governed it before.[6]

The law assumed that a married woman would automatically acquire the nationality of her husband and lose her original nationality; this was the practice throughout the world, including the United States, at that time. There were no provisions for a married woman to retain her own nationality, making her citizenship derivative of her husband's rather than held by the woman in her own right.

Ottoman nationality law was replaced by the laws of various states after the Treaty of Lausanne (1923), which provided that residents of the former Ottoman Empire should have their nationalities transferred to the states governing each country. The treaty stipulated that married women would follow the condition of their husbands and that minor children would follow the condition of their fathers in all nationality matters.[7]

Egyptian Law

As is often the case, Egyptian law is important in this area because of its influential effect on Jordanian and other Arab statutes. The earliest Egyptian law of nationality dates from 1926 and designates former Ottoman citizens as Egyptians.[8] It further provides that children born, in Egypt or abroad, to an Egyptian father shall be considered Egyptians; this formulation has remained constant throughout amendments to the Egyptian nationality law and is used in other Arab laws in nearly identical language. The law also grants Egyptian nationality to children born to Egyptian mothers and unknown fathers, to unknown parents and to a

6 Ibid., Article 7.

7 Treaty of Lausanne, 1923, Part 1, Chapter 2, Article 36.

8 *Decret-Loi sur la Nationalité Egyptienne du 26 mai 1926.*

foreign father who was also born in Egypt, when the father has ties to an Arabic-speaking or Muslim country.[9]

Article 18 granted Egyptian nationality to foreign women who married Egyptian men and allowed this nationality to be retained even after dissolution of the marriage, unless the woman lived abroad and regained her original nationality. Egyptian women who married foreign men were held to lose their Egyptian nationality for the duration of the marriage if by marrying they acquired a foreign nationality; Egyptian nationality could be recovered on request after the marriage ended.[10] (The law did not make provisions for Egyptian men who acquired a second nationality by virtue of marriage to a foreign woman; that would have been an extremely rare case at the time). Furthermore, a foreign man's acquisition of Egyptian nationality conferred it upon his wife unless she declared within one year that she wished to retain her original nationality, and the acquisition of foreign nationality by an Egyptian man likewise caused his wife to lose her Egyptian nationality (which was replaced by the new nationality) unless she declared that she wished to retain it.[11]

The provisions relating to nationality by birth remained fairly constant over time even as the nationality law was amended, while those governing the nationality of married women have undergone some modifications. Law No. 160 of 1950 provided that Egyptian women who married foreigners could retain their Egyptian nationality unless they declared an intention to acquire their husbands' nationality,[12] and an amendment provided for foreign women married to Egyptians to maintain their original nationality unless they petitioned to have it changed (instead of having to petition to keep it).[13]

The most recent Egyptian nationality law, Law No. 26 of 1975, maintains most of the earlier provisions regarding nationality by birth, with the exception that nationality granted through an Egyptian mother (as in cases of unknown fathers or fathers of unknown nationality) is available only to children born in Egypt and not to children born to Egyptian mothers abroad.[14] As in the 1950 law, a woman's nationality is changed at marriage only if she requests it, rather than automatically following the nationality of the husband.

The regulations regarding the nationality of married women could appear as practical safeguards against the complication of dual nationality, except that the same laws provide rules by which Egyptians who are male can maintain both Egyptian and foreign nationalities. Furthermore, even the recent law does not treat as problematic the acquisition of a second nationality by a husband who marries a foreign wife. It is not the loyalty to two states which appears to be problematic

9 Ibid., Article 10.

10 Article 18.

11 Article 19.

12 *Loi n. 160 de 1950, relative a la nationalité égyptienne*, Article 13.

13 Ibid., Article 9, as modified by Law No. 194 of 1951.

14 Law No. 26 of 1975 Concerning Egyptian Nationality, Article 2, paragraphs 2 and 3.

for the framers of the law but the possibility that a wife could owe loyalty to a different state than her husband. Thus, nationality laws both reflect and reinforce social values about family structure, and they translate family hierarchies into the realm of the state.

Jordanian Law

As indicated above, nationality laws of the Arab states are markedly similar due to the borrowing that takes place among the legal systems of the region.In addition, in the 1950s, Jordan, Iraq, Saudi Arabia, Yemen, Egypt, Libya, Lebanon and Syria signed an agreement on nationality law in order to regularize practices in the region.[15] One of the topics of the agreement was the nationality of married women; the agreement provided that Arab women who married Arab men from other countries would automatically acquire the husband's nationality unless they requested otherwise but could reclaim their original nationality and residence in their country of origin upon the termination of the marriage. No provision was made at the time for Arab men to acquire the nationality of their (Arab) wives, nor does any such provision currently exist.[16]

Jordan's nationality law of 1928, like Egyptian law, based nationality upon the father's possession of Jordanian nationality at the time of the child's birth. It also contained an entire chapter on the nationality of married women and minor children, a telling category. While every individual (except in the rare cases of statelessness) acquires a nationality by right of birth, only those who are legally subordinate to another individual require special rules regarding how their nationality can be altered by subsequent circumstance. That is, women and children may have their nationality altered by the acquisition or loss of the "head of family's" nationality; an adult male could have his nationality altered only by voluntary naturalization into a new nationality and renunciation of a former one. Arab nationality laws gradually came to permit married women the right to retain their own nationality during marriage, if they so wished, a process similar to that in other areas, but the presumption of nationality rules remains that the wife's nationality will generally follow that of the husband (and that the converse is not considered).

The nationality of children remains almost absolutely determined by that of their fathers. According to the Jordanian Nationality Law of 1954 (currently in force),

> He shall be considered Jordanian:[17][...]

---

15 Agreement of April 5, 1954, Concerning some of the Rules of Nationality among the States of the Arab League.

16 Arab men can acquire the nationality of their wives only through the ordinary process of naturalization, as any Arab foreigner might do; marriage to a female citizen is irrelevant in this process.

17 Law No. 6 of 1954, Law of Jordanian Nationality; Article 3.

3. Everyone born of a father who enjoys Jordanian nationality.
4. Everyone born in the Hashemite Kingdom of Jordan from a mother who bears Jordanian nationality and a father whose nationality is unknown or who has no nationality or whose paternity cannot be legally proven.
5. One born in the Hashemite Kingdom of Jordan from unknown parents and who is considered a foundling in the Kingdom as a newborn and nothing can be proven to the contrary.

The importance of the father in determining an individual's claim to Jordanian nationality is reinforced elsewhere in the law. Article 9 provides that "the children of a Jordanian are Jordanian, wherever they are born."[18] Although Article 2 of the law defines the word Jordanian (*'urduni*) as "every person possessing Jordanian nationality in accordance with the rules of this law," the meaning here is specifically masculine and is not understood to be gender-neutral as it is elsewhere in the law.

As in the Egyptian law, Jordanian nationality can be claimed through the mother only in the effective absence of a father, but the child must be born on Jordanian soil. Effectively, foundlings and children of Jordanian mothers are in the same position with regard to their claim to nationality. Thus, on examination, we find that a woman's nationality is not transmissible to her child even as a secondary option; rather, the nationality of such children is based on their birth in Jordan without a known automatic (father's) nationality. While some have characterized this as a case where maternal nationality is allowed to be transmissible, I consider it a case where the state allows *jus soli* claims to nationality where no *jus sanguinis* claim, to any nationality, would be possible and the individual would consequently be stateless. That is, it is the fact of birth within Jordanian territory without a father's nationality that gives the child a claim to Jordanian nationality, not the child's relationship to a Jordanian mother. Uri Davis has written that "[m]odern citizenship in the Middle East is predicated, as it ought to be, on *jus soli*;"[19] I must disagree, as a *jus sanguinis* claim to nationality not only appears in all the Arab codes but is, in fact, the chief and standard means by which nationality is currently granted.[20]

---

18 "*Awlad al-'urduni, 'urduniyeen 'aynama wulidu.*"

19 Uri Davis, "State, Nation, and People," in Butenschon, Davis and Hassassian (eds), *Citizenship and the State in the Middle East* (Syracuse: Syracuse University Press, 2000), 62.

20 Some laws, such as those of Jordan and Egypt, also contain articles declaring the nationality of those who received nationality under previous laws, etc., but this does not infringe upon the basic *jus sanguinis* foundation of the nationality law.

International Law: CEDAW

Jordan and several other Arab states are parties to the United Nations Convention on Elimination of All Forms of Discrimination Against Women.[21] This treaty obligates parties to grant women and men full political and social equality, and it contains in Article 9 a specific requirement regarding equal nationality rights for men and women. The article states that:

1. Parties shall grant women equal rights with men to acquire, change or retain their nationality. They shall insure in particular that neither marriage to an alien nor change of nationality by the husband during marriage shall automatically change the nationality of the wife, render her stateless, or force upon her the nationality of the husband.
2. Parties shall grant women equal rights with men with respect to the nationality of their children.[22]

This article was not popular among the Arab signatories. Like other Arab signatories, Jordan specified several reservations to particular articles of the treaty, including Article 9, paragraph 2. No explanation was provided with the reservation, but subsequent comments make clear that the state does not wish to be required to alter its nationality law to conform to this treaty provision. Numerous statements by Jordanian representatives to the United Nations make clear that in cases of conflict between Jordan's domestic laws and its treaty obligations, the latter take precedence.[23] Consequently, treaty obligations could, in theory, provide grounds for a successful court challenge demanding the alteration of the nationality law, and so it was important to exclude equal nationality rights from Jordan's CEDAW obligations in order to preserve the existing disparity in domestic law.

Other countries have expressed similar reservations to Article 9, paragraph 2. Iraq and Lebanon exempted themselves without explanation.[24] Algeria, Kuwait and Tunisia stated that the article would conflict with their domestic nationality laws but offered no substantive explanation. Morocco likewise cited its Nationality Law, further claiming that the provisions for nationality to be transmitted from the

21 Jordan signed the treaty on December 3, 1980 and ratified it on July 1, 1992. While the ratification bound Jordan to uphold the treaty's provisions, and the government made periodic reports to the CEDAW commission as required, the treaty's text was not published in the Official Gazette until July 25, 2007, incorporating the provisions into national law.

22 United Nations Convention on the Elimination of All Forms of Discrimination Against Women (1979), Article 9.

23 See, for example, documents filed by Jordan in connection with its obligations under the International Covenant on Civil and Political Rights (CCPR/C/SR.332 and CCPR/C/1/Add.55, both 1981). The precedence of treaty obligation over domestic law was also confirmed by a Jordanian law professor (Salah Bashir, interview, October 1998).

24 Iraq, alone among the Arab countries, also objected to paragraph 1 of Article 9. Libya and Yemen registered no reservations to Article 9.

mother in the case of a stateless or unknown father served to guarantee each child the right to a nationality, but did not specify the reasons for preferring paternal to maternal nationality.

Egypt provided the most explicit statement of reasons for its reservation to Article 9, claiming that it did not wish to prejudice the

> acquisition by a child born of a marriage of the nationality of his father. This is in order to prevent a child's acquisition of two nationalities, since this may be prejudicial to his future. *It is clear that the child's acquisition of his father's nationality is the procedure most suitable for the child* and that this does not infringe upon the principle of equality between men and women, since it is customary for a woman to agree, upon marrying an alien, that her children shall be of the father's nationality.[25]

This statement reflects attitudes about paternal importance widely endorsed by governments (and people) in the region, and it raises several interesting questions. First, it is unclear in what way dual nationality would be prejudicial to a child's future; it might more readily be regarded as an advantage. Egypt recognizes dual nationality, particularly for the children of Egyptian fathers and non-Egyptian mothers, and makes special provisions for such dual nationals in its consular practice and immigration regulations.[26] Clearly the state is not, in general, interested in preventing "a child's acquisition of two nationalities," since its own law and supporting procedures provide for exactly this circumstance. Second, despite the state's assertion, it is in fact *not* clear that the acquisition of the father's nationality is most suitable for the child. The cases in which the issue of maternally-transmitted nationality has become most salient involve children born and continually resident in Egypt, for whom Egyptian nationality and the consequent access to public facilities and civil rights would be preferable to the foreign nationality of their fathers. Finally, it is unclear upon what basis the final assertion of custom rests; the question of a woman's agreement or disagreement on the nationality of her children does not arise in Egypt, since the law does not provide a choice, and in any case the existence of a custom is not evidence of the neutrality or desirability of that custom.

What seems clear is the devotion of the state to the principle that fathers, and fathers alone, are heads of household. The state is willing to allow women to determine the nationality (and consequent residency and civil rights and status) of their children only in the effective absence of a father, and, as I pointed out

---

25 Reservation filed by Egypt upon signing the treaty, July 16, 1980. Emphasis added.

26 Facilities Offered by the Ministry of Interior to Egyptian Nationals Living Abroad (2008) specifies the procedures for Egyptians to register the acquisition of a second nationality (while retaining their Egyptian nationality) and for dual nationals to enter and exit the country via expedited procedures.

above, even these limited rights of maternal nationality transmission are territorial at heart, as they generally now require that the woman give birth within the state's territory.

"Waiting for the Government's Mercy": Consequences of the Nationality Law for Women and Their Families

The practice of denying women the right to transmit nationality to their children and husbands has led to a host of social problems for families and individuals affected by these laws. These non-citizen family members are denied many of the services of the state, such as education and employment. A Jordanian woman's foreign husband is eligible to reside in the country only with a residency permit from his employer, not by virtue of his marriage to a citizen; children likewise require residency permits, even those born in Jordan.[27] These consequences of the nationality law pose a particular burden for poor families who cannot afford private education and health care.[28] Children from these families often end up working illegally or begging in the streets, and their precarious position puts them at great risk of exploitation. Until the law is changed, making these children (and spouses) eligible for citizenship, families can do little but "wai[t] for the government's mercy," as a news report recently put it.[29]

The government has estimated that as many as half a million children in Jordan are ineligible for citizenship because of the legal distinction between citizen mothers and citizen fathers.[30] This number refers only to children with Palestinian fathers; thus the total number of individuals whose citizenship is affected by this law is even greater. Estimates of the number of children affected in Egypt suggest that nearly one percent of the population could be in this situation.[31] In the Jordanian case, the large numbers of potential claims to citizenship are cited by the government not as a reason to change the law, but precisely the reverse;

27 An interesting effect of the law is that children of Jordanian mothers and foreign fathers may more easily get residency permits via their non-citizen fathers, whose work-related residency permits include minor children, than through their citizen mothers, who would be required to prove that the fathers cannot financially support the children and that they, the mothers, can.

28 The government's policy on public education changes periodically; non-citizen children in Jordan have sometimes been allowed to attend public schools if they have residency permits and security and health clearances. In 2006, the Ministry of Education announced that these children would no longer be eligible for public education, a policy apparently reversed in 2008.

29 Rana Husseini, "Women seek equal rights under Citizenship Law," *Jordan Times*, December 28, 2007.

30 Ibid.

31 Cynthia Johnston, "Egyptian law penalises children of foreign men," Reuters, in *Jordan Times*, May 22, 1999, 7.

extending citizenship to so many would be a serious threat to the public purse – and, the subtext suggests, to public security. The government has announced and then backed away from proposals to change the law in the past, on the basis that amending the law is "not possible because it means granting citizenship to around half a million Palestinians in Jordan."[32]

That the situation is considered an important one is clear from the attention it receives from women's and human rights organizations. When the General Federation of Jordanian Women voted on a "Women's Agenda" for the 1997–2001 period, of 26 identified priorities, changing the nationality law to allow Jordanian women to give nationality to their non-Jordanian spouses and children ranked fourth.[33] More recently, the organization SIGI/Jordan (see Chapter 9), among others, has held seminars on the issue of citizenship rights, and the National Center for Human Rights and the Jordanian National Committee for Women have issued repeated calls for the government to amend the nationality law and eliminate sex discrimination in citizenship.[34]

The burdens resulting from discrimination in the nationality law have been amply documented; while many have mentioned the issue of women's rights in this context, the focus is generally on the problems facing the children and families as a consequence of the law. My purpose here is to examine the phenomenon not as a social problem but as an issue of legal equality. Certainly it is important that the children and husbands cannot receive citizenship, but the concern here is the implications of women's inability to transmit it. I argue that this indicates that the nationality of women is different not only in degree but in quality from that of men, and that the state regards the two sexes as very different kinds of citizens.

It is difficult to assert a single clear objective by states in maintaining different provisions for the nationality of men and women; one can find in different sources arguments ranging from national security to economic pragmatism to burdens on state resources to custom and tradition. Jordanian Interior Ministry officials have said that the nationality law is designed to prevent an influx of Palestinian men seeking jobs, as the country cannot bear the pressures of an increased population.[35]

---

32 Former Interior Minister Samir Habashneh, quoted in Rana Husseini, "Women seek equal rights under Citizenship Law," *Jordan Times*, December 28, 2007.

33 General Federation of Jordanian Women, "Women's Agenda for the Next Parliamentary Period 1997–2001" (September 15, 1997). The agenda specified that this desired change was "in order to keep families intact." The top-ranked concerns were the rights of divorced women, access to health care and child protection; the nationality law outranked other issues such as a quota for women in Parliament (#6), canceling the honor crimes law (#26) and entitling women to their own passports without male approval (#9).

34 The NCHR reports of 2005 and 2007 called for granting men and women equal rights to transmit citizenship to their children. The NCHR and the JNCW have both linked the nationality law to Jordan's reservation to Article 9 of CEDAW and called for the reservation to be withdrawn in conjunction with amending the law.

35 Interview with Dr Barakat Nimr and Mr Adil al-Hadeed of the Interior Ministry, Amman, August 24, 1999.

When I asked what the difference was between population growth from female citizens and male citizens, they replied that women might marry foreign men who are too poor to support them and thus place a burden on welfare resources; they were also concerned that foreign workers (mostly poor laborers who are not well-regarded in Jordan) would want to marry Jordanian women just to get citizenship. The officials went on to argue strongly that the Jordanian state does not discriminate between male and female citizens, that the nationality law would probably soon be changed and that the chief obstacle was culture and traditions.

However, when I asked if the law was meant to reflect an Islamic understanding of the family, they stated that there is no connection between religion and nationality and also that customs and tradition have nothing to do with law. Nonetheless, it seems to me that the rules on paternal transmission of nationality are almost certainly related to Islamic practices such as the requirement (also incorporated in Jordanian law) that children be named after their fathers.[36] Judith Tucker likewise suggests that nationality rules can be seen as analogous to the transmission, in Islamic law, of an individual's status as free or slave through his father rather than his mother.[37]

The inconsistency in claims about the purposes of the law seems to arise from attempts to articulate the several interests served by the current law; the law's discrimination against women is not merely a patriarchal artifact but serves numerous state interests (which themselves may be formulated on the basis of patriarchal assumptions about women's roles). A representative of the Ministry of Justice suggested in March of 1999 that the ministry planned to change the law and would draft a new proposal,[38] and this notion was put forward publicly again in 2002 by the Ministry of the Interior, but as of 2008, no such changes have yet been introduced for parliamentary debate.

To be fair, one must acknowledge that the state is not a monolithic entity and that different agencies may well pursue separate and even conflicting interests. This internal diversity, combined with varying pronouncements to different audiences, complicates the identification of a state's interests. However, in the Jordanian case, the issue of the proportion of the population who are of Palestinian origin is clearly salient although still somewhat puzzling in terms of its effects on nationality law. The high proportion of Palestinians among the Jordanian citizenry (most estimates place it at about 60 percent) has long been a concern for the state, and this concern

36 Further support for this position is provided by a citation in Abla Amawi, "Gender and Citizenship in Jordan," in Suad Joseph (ed.), *Gender and Citizenship in the Middle East* (Syracuse: Syracuse University Press, 2000), 162. Amawi describes a commentator in favor of Jordan's CEDAW reservations as saying that transmission of nationality by mothers is "rejected by Islam. Almighty God says: 'Call them by the names of their fathers: that is [more just] in the sight of God,'" (Sura 33, verse 5).

37 Personal communication, June 2002.

38 Interview with judicial inspector Adel Khasawneh, Ministry of Justice, Amman, March 15, 1999.

has occasionally been publicly advanced as a reason for preventing women from transmitting nationality to their spouses and children.[39] The logic, apparently, is that Palestinian women would bring in Palestinian men from outside Jordan, and produce children who would increase both the population size and the proportion of Palestinians among the citizenry. If, however, the only concern were the expansion of the Palestinian segment of the population, the problem of Palestinian men with Jordanian citizenship marrying Palestinian women from abroad would be considered equally problematic, which it is not.[40]

The Patriarchal State: An Insufficient Explanation

Clearly, even acknowledging the Jordanian government's concern over the Palestinian/Jordanian split in society, the fundamental idea is that children have a greater connection to the identity of their fathers than of their mothers. This is reflected in many aspects of social life, of course, including the naming of children after their fathers[41] and the greater authority given to fathers in law. On its face, this would seem to indicate that the state is reproducing and endorsing traditional social forms that exist separately from the state itself, rather than deliberately creating a system that privileges men over women.

39 An NGO conference on nationality, held in Amman in the summer of 1997, was attended by representatives from the ministries of Justice and Foreign Affairs, who spoke up to persuade the attendees that the nationality issue was one of national security and that they should not place it on their agendas for political action. This was reported to me by a conference participant.

40 Economic and national security concerns are also cited in the Egyptian case as reasons for limiting the transmission of nationality. I could find no evidence that the Egyptian government is concerned about children of fathers of a particular nationality, as Jordan is concerned with Palestinians, and reports suggest that the foreigners married to Egyptian women come from any number of European, African and Arab countries. However, government officials have argued that children of foreign fathers in general would be more loyal to the father's country and thus potential spies or fifth-columnists if they joined the military. See Neil MacFarquhar, "Egyptian Mothers Fight for Foreign Offspring's Rights," *New York Times* (online), May 14, 2001. One activist characterizes the Egyptian government's position as "exactly a clan punishing their daughter for marrying a man from outside the clan. This is a completely backward, tribal patriarchal mentality." Quoted in Hossam Baghat "Living on the Margins: a parliamentary proposal brings the long-ignored issue of citizenship to the fore," *Cairo Times*, May 10–16, 2001.

41 Jordanian naming practices give the child a personal first name, followed by the child's father's name as a middle name, paternal grandfather's name next and finally the father's surname as family name. Birth registration procedures do not allow deviation from this naming practice. Every person's identity is necessarily defined by patrilineal connections. Assumptions about the importance of fathers' names sometimes create odd or amusing situations for foreigners, as when a female friend of mine was asked by an official to explain how her father's name could be "Claire" (her middle name).

However, while the effects of the nationality law support aspects of patriarchal social forms, it is worth noting that even the desire to perpetuate such forms does not require the approach taken in the nationality laws. One could find an equally sound traditionalist, patriarchal basis for favoring the transmission of nationality by women to their children. The view that women are inherently the chief vehicles and transmitters of culture is well-established; both nationalist and Islamist groups have stressed the importance of women in producing the next generation and raising sons for the movement, inculcating in them the values of the nation.[42] This view of the social role of women would seem to suggest that perhaps they, above all, should be able to transmit nationality to their children.

Thus the nationality handicap of women is not a necessary product of a desire to promote traditionalism or patriarchy, and we must look further for the political significance of such laws. The treatment of women's nationality is not merely a result of concern for the nationality of children they may produce; it is, I argue, indicative of the state's understanding of women as citizens themselves. As one exasperated Jordanian newspaper columnist put it, if the state cannot treat men and women citizens equally, government offices could simply put up "pink and blue leaflet display stands, with the pink ones declaring that they carry the regulations for those who don't qualify for full citizen benefits because they are women."[43]

In arguing that Jordan's gendered nationality law is not a mere automatic reflection of tradition and patriarchy, I do not suggest that it has no connection to these forces. Indeed, nationality law is reflective of the state's understanding of the dominant cultural position on women's roles and rights.[44] The Jordanian state is not divorced from its cultural environment; on the contrary, it takes explicit steps to partake of the legitimacy that comes from cultural authenticity, as I argue throughout this work.

However, the pursuit of legitimacy is a political project and so involves political choices; this is why gendered nationality law cannot be dismissed as an inevitable outgrowth of a traditional society. In this of all areas of law, the state is making deliberate choices, and it does so with an eye to its legitimacy. As I have already argued, the Jordanian state's legitimacy is based in part upon its claim to represent authentic local culture, a stance which requires the endorsement of some

---

42 One of the clearest Islamist statements of this position is found in the Charter of the Islamic Resistance Movement (Hamas), which identifies women as the key to the preservation of national identity and the transmission of culture. Similar sentiments are reflected in the statements of some Jordanians who view potential cancellation of the honor crimes law as a threat to society; a frequently heard argument is that "if women become morally corrupt, then the whole society will become corrupt." (Quoted in Rana Husseini, "Lawyers, judges, intellectuals condemn national campaign against Article 340," *Jordan Times*, March 10, 2000).

43 Nermeen Murad, "Not a full Jordanian citizen," *Jordan Times*, April 21, 2008.

44 This also explains why nationality laws in most other countries, including the United States, treated the nationality of women as different from (and inferior to) that of men, in many cases until quite recently.

(but not all) aspects of traditional society. The subordinate position of women would certainly fall into this category, and by endorsing the existing patterns of social power, the state partakes of the authority that those patterns have. Gendered nationality laws are thus a component of the state's legitimacy project and are, in fact, as much related to the liberal aspect of the state as to its traditional one.

The Liberal State and Its Failures

Gender-differentiated nationality rights are not a phenomenon limited to the Arab world, or to the developing world. The development of the modern liberal state and the concept of citizenship owe much to the liberal tradition, which, while it established a basis for political rights claims, did so incompletely. As Mary Ann Tétreault points out,

> [T]he brotherhood envisioned by liberal theorists from John Locke to John Rawls is exactly that, brotherhood. It rejects half of the dynastic concept of patriarchal rule, the rule of the fathers, but does not question the other half, the subjection of women to men and particularly of wives to husbands...Well into the twentieth century and virtually everywhere in the world, wives were the subjects of their husbands and thus could not be autonomous citizens.[45]

Thus we find limitations on women's citizenship in developed democracies as well as in authoritarian and developing systems. The idea that women's citizenship was different from men's has been most notably reflected in the denial of suffrage to women but has also affected women's nationality rights in various ways. The United States maintained for most of its history a practice of automatically assigning married women the nationality of their husbands and of conditioning the naturalization of immigrant women upon the gain or loss of nationality by their husbands. This, like denial of suffrage, is a means of mediating women's citizenship through a male guardian; married women did not need to vote because their political will was expressed by their husbands, and they did not need separate nationality because they would naturally follow that of their husbands. In the West, these practices were part and parcel of the doctrine of coverture, which treated married women as legal minors requiring guardianship, but in both the West and elsewhere it also reflected (and in some cases continues to reflect) the belief that women are ill-suited by their natures for the performance of public duties. Women are understood to be naturally emotional rather than rational and concerned with the home and private welfare rather than with the public realm and the commonweal, and thus they are unsuited for political roles. The liberal state

45 Mary Ann Tetréault, "Gender, Citizenship, and State in the Middle East," in *Citizenship and the State in the Middle East*, 77.

perpetuates such understandings of women, and thus legal orders derived from it will do likewise.[46]

State Legitimation

The liberal state is not, of course, the sole cause of what Laurie Brand has called women's "second-class citizenship."[47] Local customs, religious mores and the exigencies of the state are also important factors in determining the quality and degree of women's citizenship in general and nationality rights specifically. I have argued throughout this work that the Jordanian state faces significant legitimation needs that it satisfies in part through appeals to cultural authenticity. In such cases, the maintenance of laws that contribute to the preservation of traditional social forms can serve the state's interest by helping to legitimate it to particular audiences.

Simultaneously, the state may pursue different policies meant to appeal to other audiences. In the Jordanian case (some elements of) the state undertake legal reforms on gender issues when necessary or useful to please liberal elements and avoid them when such reforms would come at too high a cost in terms of displeasing traditionalist sectors.

With regard to nationality laws, reform is complicated by the broader legal environment granting fathers the primary agency in family matters. States have shown themselves unwilling to undo the current legal structure, and it is likely that reform will occur gradually from the margins, with an accretion of new policies to mitigate the objectionable effects of law.

In the meantime, however, it is important that nationality-law disparities based on gender not be dismissed as historical or cultural curiosities or as mere policy alternatives for demographic management. They should be recognized, analytically and politically, for their real importance in defining the standing of women in the eyes of the state. Citizenship is one of the key elements in political development, and the choices made by the state in this arena are indicative of both the relationship of the state to its citizenry and some of the principles upon which legitimacy is based.

46 Ibid., 75.

47 Laurie Brand, "Women and the State in Jordan: Inclusion or Exclusion?" in Haddad and Esposito (eds), *Islam, Gender and Social Change* (New York: Oxford University Press, 1998). Brand was writing specifically of the position of Jordanian women, but the term is applicable more broadly.

Chapter 6

Women's Access to Divorce: Religious Law as a Basis for Improved Rights

The two preceding chapters have addressed legal issues in the areas of criminal and administrative law; this chapter focuses on the arena of family law, and in particular on the issue of Muslim women's access to divorce.

Personal Status Law

Issues such as marriage and divorce in Jordan come under the jurisdiction of personal status law, which differs based on the confessional identity of the citizen; Muslims have one body of law based on *shari'a*,[1] and members of other sects have their own laws created by something like a church council; the personal status laws have their own corresponding courts (see Chapter 3). All personal status laws in Jordan are brought into existence through the action of the legislature, but in their nature and their operation these codes are unlike other laws in several important respects. Personal status laws are specific to each recognized religious sect because they serve a perceived need to respect divine law, and they are seen as protecting both the Islamic character of society in general and the religious rights of minorities. Non-Muslims from recognized sects (several sects or denominations of Catholics, Orthodox and Protestant religions as well as Jews)[2] have the right to have matters of marriage, divorce and child custody adjudicated by the laws of their religion rather than *shari'a*, and the maintenance of a *shari'a*-based Muslim personal status code for the vast majority of citizens serves the state's claim of local cultural authenticity.

One effect of the recognition of religious rights through multiple personal status codes is that every citizen must have a religious identity known to the state; identity cards and other documents note this identity because it is important for family-law purposes. For the most part, the state does not concern itself with individual citizens' personal beliefs; if you were born into a Christian family, you are a Christian for the purposes of the state. Whether you believe, or practice, your religion is irrelevant; your affiliation will not change unless you officially convert

---

1 Law No. 61 for 1976, Law of Personal Status for Muslims.

2 Although the Jordanian government recognizes Judaism as a religion, there are no reported Jewish citizens in Jordan and thus no operative Jewish personal status law currently.

to another recognized religion. The official recognition of religion, therefore, is not seen as conflicting with the constitutional promise of freedom of belief and opinion – believe what you like; the state just needs to know which law to apply to your marriage. The corollary is that everyone must have a religion; there is no civil marriage or divorce in Jordan and no "atheist" category for nonbelievers.

Another effect of this reliance on religious law is that members of different religions have different rights. Christians, for example, may convert to other religions because their religious law does not forbid it, but Muslims may not convert away from Islam; this would be apostasy, which is forbidden by *shari'a*. Several Christian sects do not allow divorce at all while *shari'a* makes divorce very accessible to men and significantly less accessible to women. The differences among the personal status laws are well-known and can to some extent be manipulated by individuals. One of my favorite examples is that of the Christian man who wished to divorce his wife. As divorce was forbidden in the law of his sect, he simply converted to Islam, at which point he had a legal right to divorce. After divorcing his wife, he went to his priest and confessed that he was very sorry for having left his religion and wished to return to the church. But while the church may have been ready to welcome the return of the prodigal, the courts took another view. The man's conversion to Islam had placed him under the jurisdiction of the personal status code for Muslims, not only with regard to divorce but for apostasy as well – he could not convert away from Islam and have that conversion recognized by the state. The court that ruled on this matter also took a dim view of the man's divorce, pointing out that he had divorced a Christian woman who had had no expectation that this could happen to her (as her husband was also Christian at the time of their marriage) and that she was, by the personal status law applying to her, ineligible to remarry, as divorces are unrecognized by her sect. Therefore, the court ruled, the ex-husband must pay her maintenance for the rest of her life.

Making several bodies of law simultaneously operative for different groups of citizens may seem a complicated approach to family law, but it is universal throughout the region, including in Israel, and is quite practical, both socially and politically. Consigning personal, daily life issues to the care of personal status law allows the state to adopt the pre-existing (or, as we shall see, allegedly pre-existing) practices sanctioned by religion as its own, without the necessity of contestation. The state benefits in terms of legitimacy by preserving sociocultural elements that serve to order life in a familiar way for most people. The state's abstention from apparent and direct legislative creation of these laws does not, however, reduce its complicity in and responsibility for the practices maintained under personal status law. In adopting religious law for the purposes of the state, the state effectively lends its authority in support of this body of social regulation. Thus the state may be held accountable in this realm as well, since it seeks to benefit by using traditional formulations of religious law to enhance its political need for cultural authority.

Personal status law is the locus of many of the gendered legal prescriptions that serve to perpetuate inequality between men and women, but political contestation on these issues is more difficult as a challenge to these laws can be characterized as a challenge to God's authority, not just the state's, as the state has designated these issues as governed by divine rather than political authority. This does not mean, however, that such issues are depoliticized; the content of the personal status law for Muslims, in particular, is a focus of interest for several NGOs concerned with women's rights and is also a tool which serves the interest of traditionalist forces by distributing power in a way that tends to preserve social forms that effectively constrain women. Although there is very little, if any, outright challenge to the personal status law framework itself, or to its religious basis, the content of the personal status law has become a top priority in many women's concerns regarding social change.[3] In recent years, both activists and the government have sought to improve women's rights to divorce, to limit men's rights to take additional wives, to raise the minimum age for marriage and to improve child custody arrangements. While a plan was under discussion in 1999 to undertake a complete overhaul of the Muslim Personal Status Law, these changes have been pursued only piecemeal over the past decade, and divorce has emerged as the most controversial of the personal status issues.

Khul' Divorce

It has long been recognized that Muslim women are at a significant disadvantage vis-à-vis men in their access to divorce. The modern personal status laws have not contained provisions for "no-fault" divorce; the only means of divorce have been those found in *shari'a*. There are certain circumstances under which a wife can request a divorce in court, by demonstrating that her husband has done her serious harm, but this process is cumbersome and highly dependent upon the attitude of the judge and the rules of the relevant personal status law; even women who are victims of domestic violence do not find it easy to obtain divorces on grounds of harm. In contrast, Muslim men have the power of unilateral divorce by repudiation, or *talaq*.[4] *Talaq* divorce can be pronounced by the husband at will, without the ruling of a court and without any statement of grounds or cause. The

3 A September 1997 project sponsored by al-Kutba Institute for Human Development, the General Federation of Jordanian Women and the Konrad Adenauer Foundation brought together representatives of local-level women's groups in order to form an agenda of women's concerns for the next four years. The top priority expressed by these women was to change the personal status laws in order to give women more protections with regard to divorce, polygamy and child custody. The success of this agenda is visible in the 2001 amendments to the personal status law addressing precisely these issues, but as the changes are not yet legally secure, women's groups continue to advocate legal reforms.

4 *Talaq* actually encompasses more than one form of divorce, and the verb is often used to describe the act of any form of divorce, but the noun tends to be used to distinguish unilateral divorce by the husband from other forms of divorce, particularly *khul'*. For a concise description of the several forms of divorce in classical Islamic law, see Esposito and

declaration of *talaq* three times by the husband effects an irrevocable divorce, after which the couple cannot remarry unless the wife has been married and divorced or widowed in the interim.[5] *Talaq* divorce has not been the target of substantial reforms or challenges; the only aspects that have been subject to state regulation are the question of whether the wife must be told of the divorce, whether it must be registered with or approved by the courts and other functional questions. The right of *talaq* itself has never been erased or seriously limited.

Efforts to improve the position of women with regard to divorce, therefore, have focused not primarily on restricting talaq or ameliorating its effects, but on giving women greater abilities to divorce by their own will. This has been pursued, in Jordan and other Arab states, by seeking legal recognition of a form of divorce known as *khul'*. A *khul'* divorce is initiated by the wife, who need not demonstrate that she has been harmed but only that she loathes life with her husband and wishes to be divorced in order to keep from falling into sin (generally taken to mean an unwillingness to allow her husband his "marital rights," that is, sexual intercourse). An essential condition of *khul'* is that the wife must give up her financial claims related to the marriage. This means that she cannot have alimony or maintenance payments and that she must return her *mahr* to her husband. (The *mahr*, usually translated as "dowry," is the payment to the bride by the groom upon marriage and is often gold or cash that is a source of financial security for the wife). In effect, *khul'* divorces allow women to buy themselves out of marriages that have become undesirable to them; both the Egyptian and the Jordanian codes use the word "ransom" (iftadat) to describe the wife's renunciation of her financial rights. *Khul'* divorces are irrevocable.

Khul' divorce was added to the Jordanian personal status law for Muslims in 2001 although its status has not been permanently settled. As in the case of the penal code amendments discussed in Chapter 4, the changes to personal status law were made as "temporary legislation" while Parliament was out of session. In addition to adding a provision for *khul'*, the government amended marriage and child custody provisions; the age of marriage was raised to 18 for both men and women (it had been 16 for boys and 15 for girls), polygamy was limited by requiring a man wishing to take a second wife to notify the first wife and demonstrate that he was financially capable of supporting two wives and custody rules were changed to give women greater visitation rights.

The amended personal status law sets out two paths to *khul'* divorce. The married couple may agree to the divorce, in which case the wife returns her

DeLong-Bas, *Women in Muslim Family Law*, 2nd edition (Syracuse: Syracuse University Press, 2001).

5 This is the practice of *tahlil* marriage. For an excellent explanation of the practice and its legal bases, see Barbara Stowasser and Zeinab Abul-Magd, "*Tahlil* Marriage in *Shari'a*, Legal Codes, and the Contemporary *Fatwa* Literature," in Barbara Freyer Stowasser and Yvonne Yazbeck Haddad (eds), *Islamic Law and the Challenges of Modernity* (Walnut Creek, CA: Alta Mira Press, 2004).

mahr and renounces her financial rights, and the court pronounces the divorce. Alternatively, and more significantly, the wife may also obtain a *khul'* divorce without the husband's consent. In this case, she must petition the court, making an

> explicit declaration that she hates life with her husband and that there is no way to continue marital life between them and she fears that she will not keep to the limits of God because of this hatred, and she ransoms (*iftadat*) herself by giving up all her marital rights and divorces her husband and returns to him the dowry that she received from him.[6]

The court must then attempt a reconciliation (*sulh*) and, if unsuccessful, assign arbitrators to continue reconciliation attempts for up to 30 days. If reconciliation is not completed, the court must then pronounce the divorce final.

When Parliament convened after the 2003 elections, the changes to the personal status law were the subject of heated opposition, mainly from members of the Islamic Action Front. The lower house voted to reject the amendments, and the measure has since been sent back and forth repeatedly, as the Senate approves the changes and the lower house refuses them. The situation is very similar to the debate over the changes to the honor-killing provisions in the penal code, and this similarity is not coincidental; these amendments are regarded by conservatives as ushering in an era of sexual license and immorality that would threaten the foundations of society. A parliamentary deputy, and member of the Islamic Action Front, described women who would seek such divorces as "women of comfort and leisure who don't care about their families,"[7] and another described them as wanting to "divorce their husbands to pursue affairs with other men."[8] These are not objections to divorce in general, only to divorce initiated by women.

Some Islamists, however, have indicated their willingness to accept the *khul'* law. Former IAF secretary-general Dr. Abdul-Latif Arabiyyat characterized it as a choice between "bad and worse;" divorce is a bad thing, but intolerable marriages are worse. "It is a human right to remove injustice from oneself, the woman through *khul'* and the man through *talaq*."[9] This, in his view, is one of the ways that Islam provides justice and equality. He added, however, that many women use *khul'* for the wrong reasons.

The question of "how Islamic" the practice of *khul'* is has become central to the debate on whether it is a permissible addition to the law; at the time of this

---

6 Law No. 82 for the year 2001, Amending the Personal Status Law (Provisional). Available (in Arabic) at www.lob.gov.jo; translation by author.

7 Deputy Ali Utum, quoted in Sahar Aloul, "House rejects khuloe law by a narrow margin," *Jordan Times*, June 28, 2004.

8 Deputy Muhammad Abu-Faris, quoted ibid.

9 "*Min haq al-insan an yarfa' al-thulm 'an nafsih, al-mar'a bil-khul' wal-rajul bil-talaq*," quoted in "*Khul'* represents 80% of cases pending before the Jordanian courts," *Ad-Dustour* (in Arabic), December 23, 2006.

writing, some members of the Jordanian parliament were planning to seek a *fatwa* (religious legal opinion) on the provisions of the 2001 amendments to the Personal Status Law.

Khul' in Principle – Innovation or Restoration?

Jordan was not the first Arab state to consider *khul'* as a means of expanding Muslim women's access to divorce. In fact, the Jordanian provision is remarkably similar in its language and content to the Eygptian *khul'* provision that came into force in 2000, the year before the Jordanian temporary law was enacted. Between 2000 and 2007, six Arab League member states added explicit *khul'* provisions to their family codes, and another three had similar provisions for wife-initiated divorce not labeled as *khul'*.[10] There has clearly been a recent resurgence of interest in *khul'* as an element of personal status laws.[11]

What accounts for the current popularity of such provisions? The efforts to improve women's access to divorce might be understood in the context of the demands of the women's movement and of rights advocates to improve the status of women by eradicating sex discrimination in the law. Both advocates of *khul'* and its opponents have presented the matter as a significant change in the marital power structure – advocates of gender equality hail *khul'* as redressing an unjust disparity, and unreconstructed patriarchs deplore it as an assault on husbands' religiously-sanctioned power and, by extension, on religion itself. They may both be right – and wrong. *Khul'* provisions do serve to empower women in an important respect (*hooray!* shout the feminists), and they represent a willingness to alter the traditional structure of *shari'a*-based marriage regulation (*haram!* cry the conservatives). However, the *khul'* amendments, in Jordan and elsewhere, are far from equalizing men's and women's roles and power in marriage. And while these amendments have emerged from increasing demands for legal reform by women's groups and rights groups, they have taken a form that is actually far more conservative than it may first appear.

While Islamists and others have decried *khul'* as an impermissible innovation that is contrary to Islamic law, the practice in fact has a well-known history in pre-modern *shari'a*. Stowasser and Abul-Magd point out that "various divorce practices, including *khul*...were liberally used" in Syria and Palestine in the

10 See Lynn Welchman, *Women and Muslim Family Laws in Arab States* (Amsterdam: Amsterdam University Press, 2007) for a collection of these divorce provisions, as well as other family law texts.

11 *Khul'* provisions have long existed in the personal status codes of Morocco, Algeria and Libya, all of which follow the Maliki school of *shari'a*, which has the most well-established *khul'* jurisprudence. However, it has been a general rule that the husband's consent is required, unlike in the newer *khul'* provisions. Tunisia, also a Maliki country, has equalized men's and women's access to divorce by prohibiting extra-judicial divorce and allowing either spouse to sue for divorce in court.

seventeenth and eighteenth centuries,[12] and classical legal sources use the term *khul'*, describe its practice and set out its rules from very early in the Islamic era.[13] There is a generally-recognized Quranic basis for *khul'* in Surah II (The Cow), verse 229:

> And it is not lawful for you that ye take from women aught of that which ye have given them; except [in the case] when both fear that they may not be able to keep within the limits [imposed by] Allah. And if ye fear that they may not be able to keep the limits of Allah, in that case it is no sin for either of them if the woman ransom herself.[14]

The language of the Quranic verse is mirrored in the Jordanian (and Egyptian) laws, particularly the phrases about the "limits imposed by Allah" (*hudood Allah*) and the wife "ransom[ing] herself" (*iftadat bihi*).

In addition to the provision in the Qur'an, there are several hadith sources that have informed the rules of *khul'* in Islamic law. Arabi cites the Maliki jurisprudence on *khul'* as relying on two reported examples, the Prophet Muhammad's own divorce initiated by his wife Sawda, who feared he would neglect her out of preference for his younger wife 'Aisha, and the divorce of his Companion Thabit bin Qays, initiated by his wife not out of a claim of harm or potential harm but simply because she strongly disliked him.[15] These examples have been sufficient in Maliki jurisprudence to establish the right of a wife to plead for dissolution of the marriage in exchange for compensation paid by her to the husband. While these are drawn from Maliki jurisprudence, they have been put to similar use in Shafi'i, Hanbali, and Hanafi jurisprudence.[16] Although the jurisconsults of the four schools have differed as to the technical requirements of *khul'*, such as whether the wife's payment may exceed the amount of her *mahr*, the existence of a *shari'a*-sanctioned avenue of *khul'* divorce would seem incontrovertible.

It might therefore seem that *khul'* is more a restoration of earlier *shari'a* than an innovation, which ought to assuage the outrage of religious conservatives. However, Arabi points out an important distinction between the Egyptian (and Jordanian) *khul'* provisions and the pre-modern practice: whatever their differences as to the details of *khul'*, predominant opinion in all four legal traditions agreed that this type of divorce required the consent of the husband. The modern *khul'* laws allow for the divorce to proceed even without the husband's consent, and it is in this respect that they go farthest toward establishing women's independent right to divorce, and likewise farthest away from the earlier *shari'a* rules of *khul'*.

12 Stowasser and Abul-Magd (2004), 168.

13 Oussama Arabi, "The Dawning of the Third Millennium on *Shari'a*: Egypt's Law No. 1 of 2000, or Women May Divorce at Will," *Arab Law Quarterly* 16:1 (2001), 2–21.

14 From the widely-used Pickthall translation, available with many other translations at the Online Quran Project, at www.quran-online.net.

15 Arabi, 8–13.

16 Ibid., 13–16.

Interestingly, however, this departure from the historical jurisprudence on *khul'* is not necessarily an example of progressive thinking about *shari'a*, but of conservatism. The Egyptian *khul'* provision was subjected to a court challenge on constitutional grounds; a divorced husband claimed in a 2002 case that the *khul'* law violated Article 2 of the Egyptian constitution, which requires that the "principles of *shari'a* are the principal source of legislation."[17] The divorced husband argued that the new law was invalid on the grounds that it allowed *khul'* to proceed without the husband's consent, in contradiction to the *shari'a* requirements. The court's opinion was instructive in two respects. First, it explained that Article 2 of the constitution requires, in the court's view, that "a legislative act may not be in contradiction with the Islamic *shari'a* principles that are definitive in certainty as to the source from which they derive and as to their meaning, and that those principles alone are not subject to discretionary interpretation," while "this is not so in relation to other rules where there is no such certainty."[18] The *khul'* law is this type of law, requiring interpretation because it "lacks detailed rules," and so legislation may enact what it sees fit in this regard. Because the law did not, therefore, violate *shari'a*, it did not violate the constitution. In reaching this conclusion, the court did not restrict the sphere of Islamic law; quite the reverse, it engaged in an analysis of the *shari'a* bases of *khul'* in the Qur'an and sunna (Prophetic precedent) and made it clear that laws must conform to *shari'a* as an necessary condition of their constitutionality.

Arabi argues persuasively that the Egyptian court has developed a judicial approach that has provided a progressive outcome – greater divorce rights for women – by both upholding the role of *shari'a* in legislation and rejecting the history of Islamic jurisprudence in favor of a return to the foundational sources of the Qur'an and sunna.[19] The approach, in other words, is conservative, but the results may be surprising. While the Jordanian constitutional context is somewhat different, having no prescription as to the pre-eminence of *shari'a*, the borrowing that exists among systems, as demonstrated in the close similarity of text and timing, makes developments in *khul'* and other *shari'a* jurisprudence relevant beyond the Egyptian system. There is no guarantee that this recent conservative doctrinal approach will always operate to the benefit of equality or individual rights and liberties, but it is clear that the simple juxtaposition of "Islam's official role in legislation" and "greater rights for women" is not simple at all but quite complex.

This brings us back to the question of the role that *shari'a* plays in supporting or limiting traditional practices that have disadvantaged women. As I suggest at the outset of this study, women's rights have found both support and harm

17 Constitution of the Arab Republic of Egypt, Article 2 (as amended, 1980).

18 See "Egypt" country report in Eugene Cotran and Martin Lau (eds), *Yearbook of Islamic and Middle Eastern Law* 2002–2003 (The Hague: Kluwer Law International). Emphasis added.

19 Arabi, 2001.

within each of the state's strands of legitimacy, traditionalist and liberal; the two preceding chapters demonstrate that nonreligious law is as significantly gendered as is religious law. It is useful here to return to the question of how religious law has been brought into the family law of the modern state and with what effect. The personal status codes of the Arab states are often portrayed and understood as simple codifications of "the *shari'a*," but this is merely a useful simplifying myth. As was discussed in Chapter 3, not only has there never been a single body of *shari'a*, the process of codification itself required the selection of particular rules from a wide range of sources and varying legal interpretations and practices in the history of Islamic law. In a way, the process of codification did what had historically been done, which was to choose particular rules suiting contemporary needs and to combine the provisions of more than one school in compiling the codes. Historians have pointed out that while particularly schools of Islamic law predominated in different geographic regions, the schools all coexisted to some degree and were simultaneously accessible to people seeking legal rulings.[20] Forum-shopping, where possible, meant that individuals could apply to the courts and jurists they believed were likeliest to provide them a favorable ruling in the matter at hand. The compilation and eventual modification of the modern codes has likewise tended to reflect a predominant school – the Hanafi, in the case of Jordan and other former Ottoman lands – but to select the most desired rules within it and to supplement these with rules from other schools to fill in gaps or allow for alteration. For example, the Hanafi school is considered by some to be the most progressive in regard to women's status, but its rules on divorce are quite restrictive, allowing divorce to be initiated by women under very few circumstances. Thus, the Egyptian code incorporated reforms, in 1920 and 1929, adducing Maliki divorce rules to the Hanafi-based family law corpus, in order to provide somewhat easier access to divorce for women by broadening the scope of circumstances understood as "harmful" to the wife.[21]

Once compiled, however, the modern personal status codes are unlike classical Islamic law, both in their fairly rigid specifications and in their exclusivity. The selection of the rules may have been, if not catholic, at least somewhat broad in reach, but now that the rules are codified, they constrain the practice of the courts by making alternative rules effectively unavailable to judges and alternative courts unavailable to litigants. This limitation has been particularly the case in family law; Lynn Welchman has made the interesting observation that the Jordanian Personal Status Law requires judges to resort to the predominant opinions of the Hanafi school in matters for which the law has no specific instruction, while the Civil

20 Stowasser and Abul-Magd (2004), 168 point out that in Egypt, Jordan, Syria and Palestine in the Ottoman era, Shafi'i and Maliki courts operated as well as the Hanafi-based courts of the state, and litigants could choose among them.

21 Arabi, 2001.

Code, by contrast, instructs judges to make decisions in such matters "according to the Islamic *fiqh* (jurisprudence) most suited to the terms of this law."[22]

Khul' in Practice

The addition of *khul'* to the personal status law has unarguably improved women's legal options in relation to divorce, and it has proved a popular option since becoming available in 2001; as many as 80 percent of cases filed by women in family court in 2006 were reported to be *khul'* requests. [23] However, it has not put divorce within equal reach of all spouses. Men still have significantly easier access to divorce than do women, and most divorces are initiated by husbands rather than wives.[24] Poor women in particular may find it impossible to take advantage of *khul'* because of the financial burdens involved. This may explain why, of the 1,635 *khul'* cases before the Jordanian courts in 2007, nearly half (785) were dropped before adjudication and fewer than a third (468) were adjudicated (the remainder were continuing).[25]

There is no equivalent of marital property in Muslim personal status law; spouses own property (both real and personal) only individually. The wife may possess in her own right property that was hers before the marriage, that she inherited during the marriage or that she purchased with her own money; all other property acquired during the marriage belongs to the husband and is not divisible in the manner of joint assets upon a divorce. Wives also have the sole right to their

22 Lynn Welchman, "The Development of Islamic Family Law in the Legal System of Jordan," *International and Comparative Law Quarterly* 37:4 (1988): 868–886, 885.

23 "*Khul'* represents 80 percent of cases pending before the Jordanian courts," *Ad-Dustour* (in Arabic), December 23, 2006. The article also claims incorrectly that Jordan was the first Arab country to apply *khul'*.

24 It is somewhat difficult to track total divorce numbers even through official records; the figures provided by the Qadi al-Qudah (Islamic chief justice's office) do not agree with those provided by the Department of Statistics, and the former distinguishes between "divorce" (*talaq*) and "separation" (*tafriq*) in its records although most cases under the heading of *tafriq* would be counted as divorces in ordinary parlance. A significant number of cases registered as divorces are filed after the marriage contract has been agreed but before consummation of the marriage and cohabitation; while these are technically divorces in the *shari'a* courts, they are more analogous to ending an engagement than to divorce in the West. According to the 2003 annual report of the Islamic chief justice, 1,466 of 1,898 *talaq* cases fell into this category ("*qabl ad-dukhul,*" or before consummation); if these cases are taken out of consideration, the total number of divorces would be significantly lower. See "*al-Taqrir al-sanawi* 2003," Department of the (Islamic) Chief Justice (*Da'irat Qadi al-Qudah*), Hashemite Kingdom of Jordan, at www.sjd.gov.jo/annual_report2003.html.

25 "Rise in the number of women requesting *khul'* in Jordan," *Laha* (in Arabic), November 3, 2008, at www.lahaonline.com.

own income, if they work outside the home, and are not legally responsible for using this income for family expenses, although most do.

Historically, this regulation of the wife's property compares favorably with the old Western legal practice of coverture, in which all property owned by the wife before marriage or acquired by her during marriage became the sole legal property of the husband. Muslim women have never suffered this disadvantage in law (although their ability to manage and benefit from their property has often been constrained in practice). However, the wife's right to her own property – and to the sole use of her own income if she works outside the home – during the marriage is scant protection in the event of a divorce. In many, if not most, cases the husband is still the sole income provider for the family, and the wife will have very little property or income of her own. Even her use of her own income, if any, for household expenses is not taken into consideration for property division in the case of divorce; as such contributions from the wife's income are not required, they are treated as voluntary gifts rather than establishing a financial interest in what, elsewhere, would be marital or communal property.

In this context, it is clear that divorce of any kind will likely present serious financial burdens for the wife. *Khul'* divorces, in which the wife must renounce both her *mahr* and her right to maintenance, are even more costly to the wife and thus are accessible only to women of means or those with families who are able and willing to support them after a divorce. An author writing on *khul'* in Egypt points out that "for the majority of the population the sum required to release herself from an intolerable marriage may be equal to or more than everything a woman owns."[26] Thus, although the *khul'* provisions recently added to a number of Arab legal systems represent an improvement of women's relative position with regard to divorce, some rights groups still condemn the legal treatment of divorce as inherently unfair and burdensome to women.[27]

Conclusion

Despite having the power to do so, the Jordanian state and its constituent elements have not demonstrated much willingness to alter traditional power structures – whether religious or not – where they affect gender roles. Other traditional structures, such as the Tribal Courts, have been abolished as the state's need for

26 Dawoud S. El-Alami, "Can the Islamic Device of *Khul'* Provide a Remedy for non-Muslim Women in Egypt?" *Yearbook of Islamic and Middle Eastern Law* 2002–2003, 122–125.

27 For example, Human Rights Watch points out that Egyptian courts are notoriously cumbersome and slow, which puts women at an even greater disadvantage as they must resort to the courts for any type of divorce while men can divorce by oral repudiation. "Divorced from Justice: Women's Unequal Access to Divorce," 2004, http://www.hrw.org/en/reports/2004/11/30/divorced-justice.

them declined.[28] But gender issues remain a basis for claims of traditional cultural authenticity, and where traditional structures have a religious component, as in the body of family law, they are doubly difficult to challenge. This is one of the constraining effects of reliance on traditional sources of state legitimation; the close alliance between religion and conservative tradition makes it politically impossible to remove religion from the areas of law in which it has been enshrined. Most people probably do not want family law completely secularized, in any case, and the *shari'a* itself has proven as amenable as, for example, the secular criminal code to interpretations and applications that produce at least marginal improvements in women's positions. But while it has become increasingly possible to tinker on the margins of personal status law, extensive reforms remain unlikely. Notably, even where radical changes have been introduced, as with Tunisia's ban on polygamy, these changes are publicly justified as conforming to a correct or more authentic interpretation of *shari'a*, not as a necessary or justifiable abandonment of it.

Thus it is difficult to judge how progressive reforms to the personal status law really are. Increasingly, the state appears to be trying to ride two horses at once in its use of law to serve its legitimation needs as efforts to rectify sex-based inequalities to satisfy domestic demands (and international legal obligations) inevitably require challenge to, if not the role of *shari'a* itself, at least the dominant traditional understandings of *shari'a* in Jordanian society. At many points the government's rhetoric about equality and women's advancement comes into direct conflict with existing legal practice, and although legal practice would seem to be well within the control of the authoritarian state, negotiation is nonetheless necessary in order to preserve the state's careful balance of legitimacy.

28 Tribal law was formally abolished in June 1976.

Chapter 7

Protected Spaces: The Presence of Women in the Institutions of State Power

Assessments of women's status and rights have often focused on the presence or absence of women in the key institutions of public life. The proportion of parliamentary seats held by women, for example, is often taken as a measure of the degree of the political inclusion of women. Other frequently-cited indicators for gauging women's (and girls') presence in public life are the proportion of female students in primary, secondary and tertiary education and the proportion of the labor force that is female. None of these indicators alone is a valid measurement of the status of women, of course, as they capture only narrow slices of the various aspects of public life. But women's public presence does tell us something about their social status and their degree of freedom and opportunity. Useful aggregate indicators have been developed to facilitate cross-national comparison, such as the Gender Empowerment Measure (GEM) and the Gender-Linked Development Index (GDI). These measures are of great use in comparative analysis, but they do not (and were not designed to) explain the political and social forces that shape women's roles in public life. In order to better understand the reasons for the particular state of affairs regarding women's presence in public life, this chapter examines two spheres in which the state has made explicit choices about the inclusion of women: the national parliament and the armed forces. In both cases, policy choices have significantly improved women's presence in institutions traditionally virtually closed to them – and in both cases, an effective increase in women's equality has been achieved through the use of the tools and the language of special circumstances.

The presence of women in any aspect of public life is the product of a host of factors – educational opportunities, family structures, public attitudes, individual choices, economic constraints and many others. Because this study is about state legitimacy, the choices of the state (and its various agents) are of primary interest; the state has, by definition, a primary role in shaping the membership of its own institutions, and the choices it makes in this regard have important implications for women's roles in public life. In acting – or failing – to improve women's membership in its own institutions, the state is both responding to external demands and constructing its own position with regard to the requirements of democracy and tradition – the elements of Jordanian state legitimacy that we have seen at work in many areas of law and policy in the preceding chapters.

The Women's Quota in Parliament

Women have long been included in Jordanian electoral politics as voters; the right to vote in national elections was secured in 1974, and voter turnout has been quite high among women in the post-1989 era. The Elections Law of 1986 carefully defined "Jordanian" as "every person, male or female, who has Jordanian nationality."[1] The language of this law is an explicit declaration of the electoral inclusion of women, since the plural "Jordanians" (*'urduniyyun*) and singular "Jordanian" (*'urduni*) are elsewhere generally held to include women despite their masculine grammatical gender, unless otherwise specified or made clear by context.[2]

Despite their presence as voters, however, women have been notably absent as candidates and elected officials. Elections for the lower house of Parliament have been held five times since the resumption of parliamentary life in 1989. Despite increasing numbers of women candidates, by 2003 only one woman, Toujan al-Faisal, had ever won a seat in regular elections. Faisal's win in 1993 was hailed as a positive sign for the viability of women candidates, but the election returns of 1997 dashed these hopes; not only was Faisal not returned to her seat, none of the 17 female candidates were elected that year, leaving no women in the lower house.[3] It was increasingly clear to women's organizations that policy intervention would be necessary to overcome the many obstacles to the participation of women in parliamentary life. By the late 1990s, the leading women's organizations were united in their demand for a quota for women in the lower house. While the government originally rejected the notion of a women's quota outright, it eventually conceded, and the 2003 elections were the first in which women were guaranteed seats in the lower house.

The Call for a Quota: Complexities of the Jordanian Electoral System

The creation of reserved seats for women was meant to solve not only a problem of attitudinal barriers to women's parliamentary inclusion but also to address the

1 "*Kul shakhs thakar aw 'untha yahmalu al-jinsiyya al-'urduniyya bimuqtada ahkam al-qanun al-jinsiyya al-'urdiniyya.*" Article 2, Law of Elections to the House of Representatives, No. 22 for 1986.

2 For example, in the Nationality Law's declaration that the children of a Jordanian (*'urduni*) are Jordanians, the grammatical masculine is also the legal meaning, in that only male citizens pass Jordanian nationality to their children. See Chapter 5.

3 One woman, Nuha Maaytah, received a seat in the lower house in March of 2001 as the result of an internal house by-election to fill a seat vacated by the death of a member. Maaytah defeated several male candidates to win the seat after four rounds of voting. However, as the king dissolved Parliament three months later, her presence in the legislature was very brief. Maaytah lost her seat in the 2003 elections.

structural problems presented by Jordan's electoral system design. In order to understand the context in which quotas were a favored strategy, we must begin with the electoral system itself.

Jordanian parliamentary life, and the electoral system in particular, have long been managed by the executive to facilitate political stability and support from the monarchy's traditional allies. At times, this management has been very heavy-handed, as with the suspension of Parliament and application of martial law. Even after the resumption of parliamentary life, the executive has continued to dominate the legislature, using tactics such as banning opposition members from running in elections and limiting critical speech. Toujan Faisal, for example, was convicted of speech crimes relating to her criticism of government corruption and was subsequently banned from candidacy in 2003 and 2007.

Perhaps the most effective tactic, however, has been the deliberate construction of a parliamentary sphere that accords well with regime priorities. Until 1993, parliamentary elections were based on plurality voting in multiple-member districts of varying magnitude,[4] and voters could vote for as many candidates as there were seats in the district. For example, in a district allotted three seats, voters got three votes, and the three candidates with the highest vote totals won the seats. The variation in district size and magnitude is not random; rural areas are deliberately overrepresented in Parliament. Currently, rural areas have one legislator for every 2,000 citizens, while urban districts have one for every 95,000.[5] Nine seats of the 110 in the lower house are reserved for Christians and three for Circassians/Chechens.[6]

In 1993, the government "reformed" the elections law, instituting a system the regime persists in calling "one person, one vote," a name apparently chosen more for marketing appeal than for descriptive accuracy. In ordinary political parlance, "one person, one vote" refers to the principle that all voters are equal, with no individual's voice carrying more weight than another's. In the Jordanian context, however, "one person, one vote" means that each voter in a district may vote for only one candidate, no matter how many seats are contested in that district – in political science terms, a single nontransferable vote (SNTV) system.

The switch to the SNTV system has been unpopular and was, rightly, widely regarded as an attempt by the government to influence the outcome of elections by managing the process of elections. It had become clear that the Islamist party, the Islamic Action Front (IAF), was the most powerful, most capable and best-organized party in Jordanian political life by the 1990s; its electoral success made it a source of regime opposition that could not be ignored. It could, however, be

4 District magnitude is the number of seats assigned to each district.

5 Thanassis Cambanis, "Jordan, Fearing Islamists, Tightens Grip on Elections," *New York Times*, November 11, 2007.

6 These seats are assigned to particular districts having higher populations of these minorities. Voting is not done on a sectarian basis; any voter in the district can vote for any candidate, whether Christian, Muslim or Circassian/Chechen.

thwarted, through a rather clever redesign of the elections law. In the absence of viable and relevant political parties, most people chose candidates based on family connections – the so-called "tribal vote." But if a voter also found other candidates appealing, he or she could, before the 1993 changes, cast the first vote for a family member and other votes on the basis of personal preference. This meant that the political parties could attract votes without asking people to choose between their traditional family loyalties and their political views.

"One person, one vote" changed this, with highly predictable results. Voters could no longer select more than one candidate, but the other factors shaping electoral choices – particularly family loyalty, the importance of personal ties for obtaining public services and the absence of a coherent party system – remained the same. Faced with a ballot that allowed only one choice, many voters continued to give that first (and now only) vote to a family or tribal figure. This simultaneously reduced the electoral support for the IAF and other potential opposition actors and entrenched the power of the sector of society that has long been a bulwark of support for the monarchy.

All of the parties stood to lose by this system, liberals as well as Islamists. In the wake of their serious losses in 1993, the IAF and other parties boycotted the 1997 elections in protest. Criticism of the 1993 SNTV system continues from all points on the political spectrum, but the regime has held fast, refusing to alter a system that so reliably serves the purposes of stability and regime support.

In the context of an electoral system that underrepresents urban areas (where most women's activists and their supporters are found) and encourages voting based on traditional power relationships, women candidates have found it particularly difficult to reach office through ordinary electoral competition. Even where individual candidates obtained substantial support, they rarely won seats. The 1997 parliamentary elections provide an instructive example of the vagaries of the Jordanian electoral system. In that election, under the SNTV rules in place since 1993, 80 seats were contested. Seventeen women stood for election, and none won a seat, – but not necessarily because they received fewer votes than the winners. The two best-performing women candidates were Toujan Faisal (the only female incumbent) and activist Emily Nafa'a. Both stood in the wealthy urban Third District of Amman, which had five seats (three designated as Muslim, one Circassian/Chechen, one Christian). Faisal stood for the Circassian/Chechen seat and Nafa'a for the Christian seat. Faisal received 4,227 votes, but lost to Nayef Mawla, who received 5,213.[7] Nafa'a received 2,292 votes, losing to Khalil Haddadin's 3,134. However, of the three Muslim seats in Amman 3, two were won with vote totals far below those of Faisal and Nafa'a: Ra'ad Bakri and Lutfi Barghouti received only 1,306 and 1,044 votes, respectively.

Clearly, Faisal's and Nafa'a's losses were due to the greater popularity of their direct opponents but equally to the oddities of electoral system design that made

7 Election data are available at www.jordanembassyus.org/resultsof%20elections.htm, "Results of Jordan's Parliamentary Elections, November 4, 1997."

it possible for candidates to win seats with relatively few votes in many cases. This held true across the country; Faisal lost her seat despite having won more votes than 49 of the 80 candidates who won seats (and tied with another). Nafa'a, similarly, received more votes than eight of the winners. Outcomes like these are attributable to far more than simply attitudes about female candidates; district magnitude, district size, minority quotas and SNTV balloting rival actual voter preferences in producing winners and losers from among the pool of candidates.

No women gained office in the 1997 parliamentary elections. Under these circumstances, the leading women's organizations in Jordan concluded that for all practical purposes, a quota was "the only way for women to reach the Parliament in the year 2001."[8] However, the government disagreed; while a few women had been included among the members of the appointed Senate for several years, the government was unwilling to establish a quota for women in the lower house. The Speaker of the House of Representatives, Abdul Hadi Majali, endorsed the idea of women's participation in Parliament but called a quota impractical and suggested that women should, instead, work harder at mobilizing support.[9] Others condemned a quota as unfair or undemocratic. While a principled opposition to quotas is understandable – even some women's activists have criticized the notion on egalitarian grounds – the government was in no position to dismiss the concept outright because of the existing quotas for Christians and Circassians/Chechens. Neither of these quotas has been very controversial, even though they actually overrepresent both groups in the parliament, relative to their proportion of the general population.[10] Women's organizations were asking not for overrepresentation, or even parity; the initial quota proposal was for 20 percent of seats to be designated for women members.

After several years of consistent refusal, by 2002 the government had decided to give in. As part of the "Jordan First" development program announced by King Abdullah, five committees were created to address specific challenges facing the Jordanian political order, one of which was charged with making recommendations regarding a parliamentary quota for women. The women's quota committee eventually recommended the adoption of a quota in the lower house of eight reserved seats; the government agreed to reserve only six, alongside other changes increasing the size of the lower house from 80 seats to 110.

The women's quota is, in the Jordanian electoral context, not an innovation but a continuation of the instrumental use of system design in ways meant to bolster the regime's position. The regime's support for a quota came about in the context of

8 Salwa Nasser of the Jordanian National Committee for Women, quoted in "Women appeal to House speaker for help in securing women's quota," *Jordan Times*, July 26, 1999.

9 Quoted ibid.

10 Of the 110 seats in the lower house, currently nine (8 percent) are reserved for Christians and three (2.7 percent) for Circassians or Chechens. Christians make up at most 4 percent of the population, and Circassians about 1 percent.

increasing demands and remarkable consensus among the women's organizations – and at a time when the king and his government were promising progress on a number of issues relevant to women's status and welfare. The temporary laws of 2001 addressing honor killings and divorce were part of this agenda, and the quota was another effort by the regime to make demonstrable, but not radical, gains for Jordanian women.

How the Quota Works

The quota reserves six seats in the 110-seat lower house (about 5.5 percent) for women. Female candidates may theoretically win any number of seats outright in ordinary electoral competition; the six quota seats are in addition to any other seats won. The quota seats are assigned to the six women candidates who receive the highest percentage of the vote in their districts and are filled without regard to religion, ethnicity or district distribution. Women do not campaign specifically for the quota seats; rather, they campaign in the ordinary fashion for seats in their districts and must meet all the regular candidacy requirements. The quota provision comes into the electoral process only after the balloting is completed and votes are counted.

Criticisms of the Women's Quota

One frequently-offered argument against the women's quota is that it is unconstitutional. This line of reasoning cites the Jordanian constitution's statement of nondiscrimination: "Jordanians shall be equal before the law. There shall be no discrimination between them as regards their rights and duties on the grounds of race, language or religion."[11] This argument has been put forward primarily by conservatives, such as Hayat Museimi, the IAF candidate mentioned above. Dr. Museimi has described the quota system as "unfair" and "unconstitutional"[12] although she held a quota seat in the 2003 parliament and ran again (but did not win) in 2007.

The constitutional argument is, however, weak at best. The constitution does not identify gender as a protected class or as a basis on which discrimination is prohibited or equality guaranteed. While the constitution does not exclude gender as a basis of equality, neither does it promise it, so it is somewhat puzzling that commentators, including activists, officials and occasionally academics, so frequently cite a constitutional guarantee of gender equality, as one simply does not exist as a matter of constitutional text, practice or tradition.

Even if the constitution did guarantee gender equality, however, the quota might still pass muster as an acceptable remedial strategy to achieve that equality, as it is

11 Constitution of the Hashemite Kingdom of Jordan (1952), Article 6 (1).

12 Quoted in Ahmad Khatib, "Record number of women running in Jordan polls," *Agence France Presse*, November 20, 2007.

meant as a temporary measure to ameliorate both past and present discrimination against women. Especially in light of the Christian and Circassian/Chechen quotas mentioned above, it seems that protected inclusion on the basis of group identity is, at the very least, tolerable within the constitutional order. In any case, the women's quota is very unlikely to fall to a constitutional challenge so long as there exist so many Jordanian laws and policies which draw sex-based distinctions that are actually discriminatory in purpose, rather than ameliorative, such as the Nationality Law.

Another complaint about the quota is that its design has produced two related and possibly unintended outcomes: it disadvantages urban women, and it has tended to favor conservatives. Filling the quota seats on the basis of percentages rather than numbers of votes favors women running in small districts with few competitors. These tend to be the rural districts; urban districts are much more heavily contested, so total votes are split among more candidates. In both 2003 and 2007, the quota seats were won by women from outside the capital who, for the most part, had no experience in the women's organizations and little sympathy for many of the goals of the women's movement.

Women's activists have pointed out that the skewed distribution of seats is excluding the most experienced female politicians, who live and work in the capital, from Parliament. So far, however, the government has shown no willingness to reform the quota design. Then Interior Minister Qaftan Majali took a favorable view of the outcome, saying that "we need to give women in remote and less fortunate areas a chance to come to the city and experience life."[13]

The possibilities presented by the quota have not been lost on the tribes or the Islamists. Although both sectors of society are conservative with regard to gender issues, they have recognized in the women's quota an opportunity to serve their interests through new means. By nominating women candidates they improve their electoral odds, and, likewise, women candidates nominated by their tribes or the IAF have a secure pool of electoral support on which to draw. Five of the women elected to the quota seats in 2003 were described as "tribal" or Islamist candidates, including the IAF's candidate, Dr. Hayat al-Museimi, three women from the very conservative southern towns of Tafila and Kerak and a tribal candidate from the north. These women often voted against the amendments to legislation, such as the honor crimes and divorce measures. Adab Saoud of Tafila, for example, complained that the government's proposed amendments failed to "develop women's causes in a way to safeguard their Islamic and Arab identity" and that increased divorce rights for women would harm families and be used frivolously.[14] Dr. Museimi of the IAF offered a similar rationale for voting against

13 Quoted in Rana Husseini, "Quota system leaves bad taste in mouths of capital candidates," *Jordan Times*, July 15, 2003.

14 Quoted in Hala Boncompagni, "Jordanian women campaign for rights revoked by parliament," *Agence France Presse*, August 25, 2003.

the measure to tighten penalties for honor killings, saying that the amendment "encouraged family disintegration."[15]

Tribalism is considered by many to be, in the words of one activist, "the greatest obstacle towards women's emancipation."[16] A woman candidate for a municipal council seat exemplified this when she said, in explaining why she had not voted for herself, "I would not break my commitment to the tribe. We are a tribal community and the priority is for electing a man."[17] (Ironically, she won her seat without a single vote because of the new municipal council quota for women). But tribalism is clearly a double-edged sword; while it generally seeks to limit women's rights and restrict them to subordinate and traditionalist roles, the quota gives even these conservative actors an interest in supporting women for public office. The support of the tribe can be a very empowering factor for women candidates.

Is the Quota Good for Women?

The implementation of the quota in 2003 has secured women a presence in the lower house that they would certainly otherwise have lacked; of the 54 women candidates running that year, none won a seat outside the quota framework. However, in 2007, one woman, Falak Jamaani, was re-elected; she was seated through the quota in 2003 but won her Madaba district seat outright, against some 15 male competitors, in 2007. Another candidate, Nariman Rousan of Irbid, came within 14 votes of winning her seat outright but lost and was seated through the quota provision instead.[18] These two candidates had both served in the 2003 parliament; their success in 2007 is likely attributable to the advantages of incumbency as well as to their demonstration of their skills while in office. There are currently seven women in the lower house, just over 6 percent of the membership, the highest in Jordan's history.

Although it has faced some controversy, the quota is fairly well supported among Jordanians; a recent survey found that 74 percent of respondents felt there should be a quota in the lower house, with similar proportions supporting quotas at the municipal and Senate levels.[19] Approximately two-thirds favored doubling the size of the quota, while just over a quarter wanted the quota cancelled entirely.

---

15 Quoted in Jamal Halaby, "Women's Rights Plan Rejected in Jordan," *Associated Press*, August 5, 2003.

16 Ellen Khouri, quoted in Sahar Aloul, "House rejects khuloe law by a narrow margin," *Jordan Times*, June 28, 2004.

17 Fardous al-Khaldi, quoted in "New female council member wins seat with zero votes," *Jordan Times*, August 3, 2007.

18 Rana Husseini, "Women activists see Jamaani's win good sign," *Jordan Times*, November 22, 2007.

19 "Poll: Democratic Transformation and Political Reform in Jordan," Jordan Center for Social Research, September 2005.

In seeking to improve women's political standing through quotas, Jordan is far from alone. According to the IDEAS quota database, there are currently 99 countries in the world using some form of gender quota for parliamentary representation.[20] Gender quotas are somewhat rarer in the Arab world, however, which partly accounts for the region's especially low levels of women in legislatures. Iraq's most recent constitution provides for women to make up 25 percent of the national parliament (by regulating the composition of party lists); Tunisia, Morocco and the Occupied Palestinian Territories likewise have party-list-based quotas, in the Palestinian case supplemented by additional provisions regarding local council representation. Egypt initiated a quota (reserved seats) in 1979 but discontinued it in 1986. By comparison, the Jordanian quota is fairly modest in scope and effect. Activists have recently called for the number of reserved seats to be doubled, so that one could be assigned to each of the country's governorates, but the government has so far refused, leaving the number at six.

The design of the quota could certainly be improved if the government were interested in correcting the distributional anomalies of the current quota. The quota itself, however, although intended as a temporary tactic, is probably going to stay in place for the foreseeable future. In 2005, the government added a quota at the municipal level and went even further than the parliamentary quota by requiring that 20 percent of municipal council seats go to women. This quota, too, suffers from some oddities in its implementation – such as the candidate mentioned above who won her seat with zero votes because the seat had to be filled by a woman – but it is generally seen as an appropriate move to increase women's participation at the local level, in the interests of development as much as rights.

Quotas will not alter Jordanian political reality or attitudes immediately, of course. The problems that plague women candidates are very much the problems that plague Jordanian politics as a whole: corruption, traditional hierarchies of family power, the need to rely on family loyalty to obtain public services. Women voters turn out in large numbers, in fact at higher rates than men,[21] but they are not particularly likely to support women candidates, in part because of the recognition that male candidates are usually better connected and thus more able to deliver services.

An anecdote from the 1997 elections demonstrates this conundrum. I was observing activities at a polling station in a wealthy Amman district and fell into conversation with some teenage girls. They were holding campaign signs and were obviously enthusiastic about the election in general and one of the candidates, who was their relative, in particular. I asked them what they thought of the female candidates running in that election, and they were eager to praise them as strong, intelligent and well qualified. The girls were slightly too young to

20 http://www.quotaproject.org/country.cfm.

21 National Democratic Institute for International Affairs, "Middle East and North Africa: NDI's Program with Women Candidates in Jordan's June 2003 Parliamentary Election," July 2003, at www.ndi.org/worldwide/mena/jordan/jordan_women_pf.asp.

be voters themselves, but I asked if they would have voted for a woman candidate had they been eligible. "No, of course not!" came the immediate answer. Why not? "Because [candidate X] is our uncle!" This is an often-heard assessment of women candidates: they may be admirably well-educated, experienced, persuasive and capable, but "being a good candidate" is a far cry from "being a candidate I'll choose." So long as family obligations and connections are more important than political conviction, only candidates with traditional social bases of support are likely to be elected. This may be changing slowly, but it continues to be a factor in elections.[22]

The quota can change many things, primarily women's input into national legislation and women's visibility as political leaders, but it cannot directly change voter preferences unless other elements of the system also change. The creation of "protected space" for women in Parliament is a useful tool for promoting change, but it is a partial and limited measure at best.

Women in the Armed Forces

Another arena in which women have achieved greater opportunities and greater equality through the use of a protected space is in the Jordanian military. Unlike in some countries, the issue of women's military service has not been a particularly controversial issue in Jordan and is not one of the priorities for the women's movement. Militaries everywhere are fairly conservative and male-dominated institutions, and the Jordanian military has long been at the core of the state's support; in his 1997 speech from the throne, King Hussein lauded the military for its "great national awareness, true belonging, and unshaken loyalty" and called it the "finest example of Arab morality and the refined Jordanian character."[23] The military's membership is heavily drawn from the East Bank Jordanian tribes, and it is widely considered a bastion of traditional power. It is not, therefore, the likeliest arena for significant social change. However, the last decade has seen important progress in the incorporation of women into the military in an increasing range of professional roles.

In 1995, the Jordanian military inaugurated a formal program, then known as the Directorate of Women's Affairs, for the development of women's roles and status as military members.[24] The origin, goals and methods of this program provide an interesting example of the interplay between cultural forces and political

---

22 Rana Husseini, "Family ties dominate women's choice, but new tone sensed," *Jordan Times*, November 21, 2007.

23 Speech from the Throne, Opening of the Thirteenth Parliament, Amman, November 29, 1997. Available at www.kinghussein.gov.jo/97_nov29.html.

24 Unless otherwise cited, information on the establishment and early operations of the DWA was collected in interviews with DWA personnel in Jordan in 1998. I am grateful for the generous assistance provided by the Directorate.

development. Although the Jordanian military is now professional (rather than conscript-based) and formally divorced from political contestation (its members cannot vote, for example), its role within the Jordanian state is such that military developments carry direct and indirect political implications. Thus the change and expansion of women's military roles reveals a great deal about the types of state power, the relevance of cultural mores to state decision making, and the tactics that are used to pursue progressive (or conservative) agendas successfully.

The policies of the Jordanian military with regard to women's roles reveals above all the ability of certain elements of the state to operate in partial isolation from society. To a certain extent, the development of what is now called the Directorate of Military Women's Affairs (DMWA) has been an internal military matter, and the competing interests shaping the program have been traditional military authority and the agenda of the royal family. However, at the same time, even in such an isolated (or purely state) realm as the military, the state and its agents do not ignore, and cannot afford to ignore, the cultural context in which their agendas are contested. Thus, the DMWA takes traditional mores into account when formulating its proposed changes, and those opposed to such changes are able to bring pressure from non-military sources. In this way, the various state agents contest with one another over competing agendas, with all of them conscious of, and to a greater or lesser degree able to make use of, the sociocultural context in which the military is situated.

Women have worked in or with the Jordanian military in some capacity since the 1950s, when women teachers were employed in military schools. In 1962, the Princess Muna College of Nursing was established, and its first graduates were commissioned as second lieutenants in the Royal Medical Corps. Women were also employed as civilians in administrative jobs. This history follows the common pattern of women's military service in many countries, in that women served in traditional caregiver and administrative occupations that are considered auxiliary services to the military itself. This state of affairs began to change with the establishment of the DWA in 1995, a development instigated and managed by Princess ʻAisha bint al-Hussein, at that time a lieutenant colonel in the Jordan Armed Forces (and, as her name indicates, the daughter of King Hussein and the sister of the current king, Abdullah II).

The development of the Directorate reveals the various types of power that have been brought to bear inside the state and points to how those (sometimes competing) sources of authority can be selectively employed. It originated in a petition in the early 1990s to King Hussein by Princess ʻAisha and her cousin, Princess Basma.[25] At the king's behest, and with high-level military acquiescence, a research office was created in 1993, later upgraded to the Directorate and given

25 This is Basma bint Ali bin Nayef, first cousin to ʻAisha bint al-Hussein, not the Princess Basma often connected with women's rights organizations, who is a generation older and the sister of the late King Hussein.

a staff. Royal support was essential in establishing the program despite a certain amount of opposition from within the military.

However, having used royal authority to initiate the program, the leaders have shifted, in a sense, to military authority. This facilitates the incorporation of women into the military on equal terms, rather than as a special case. Operating on a basis of professional military competence, rather than personal status, is absolutely essential to the mission of the DMWA (see below). Such military authority is not a fiction; it has been carefully earned by the directorate's leaders. For example, now-Brigadier General 'Aisha is a graduate of the British military academy Sandhurst, as is her brother King Abdullah. She has also completed Special Forces parachute courses, earning her jump wings, and taken first place in weapons competitions in the Jordanian Royal Guard Course. Possessing earned military competence enables her to claim the authority of a military professional; this type of authority seems to replace or occasionally supplement her royal authority.[26] This ability to shift among types of authority makes Brig. Gen. 'Aisha particularly able to operate within a state structure that possesses diverse agendas and power centers and is a large component of the success of her directorate.

The DMWA's approach to developing women's military roles has several notable characteristics that explain, to a great degree, its successful operation to date. The language of rights and equality is not used, direct challenges to traditional roles are not offered, and the whole program is guided by a notable degree of pragmatic gradualism. This strategy has helped the DMWA to avoid opposition where possible and to meet it successfully when it does arise. Their mission statement concerns improving the skills and professionalism of women already in the military; another apparent goal, that of expanding women's duties within the military, is not explicitly stated. In interviews, officers repeatedly stressed that neither they nor the majority of military women want the same jobs and roles as men. This is no doubt reassuring to those elements in the military who still entertain doubts as to the presence of women among the forces.

The Directorate has managed opposition to its work by carefully demonstrating competence, implementing changes slowly and in small steps and making certain tactical arrangements, such as the design of women's uniforms, which remove bases upon which they could be criticized. For example, women who wish to wear the hijab have a uniform option that permits them to do so by wearing a long skirt and jacket and an army-issued headscarf. At the same time, the DMWA has quietly accomplished a great deal in terms of changing women's images. Since the late 1990s, women's training has covered all the same topics as that given to men; initially women were taught infantry tactics only in a classroom setting, on

26 It must be noted that many royal family members, from Jordan and elsewhere, have received military training (often at Sandhurst) and hold nominal or real military positions. However, the military training and employment of royal women is something of a novelty, and they had to prove their competence "in spite of" their gender rather than being accepted automatically.

the grounds that they could not be assigned to jobs requiring those skills. As of 2006, however, "all specialized training programs for women will be identical to their male counterparts."[27] All military women receive weapons training. Upon the graduation of the first unit of policewomen several years ago, a public ceremony was held to mark the occasion, in which the women demonstrated their sharpshooting skills and King Hussein was present to indicate his support for the new unit. However, these policewomen have not been incorporated into all regular duties; they are specially tasked with matters relating to the discipline of military women. Again we see a careful balance being struck to allow progressive change without presenting a serious challenge to existing practices.

The DMWA has also proven a useful platform for programs that reach beyond the military itself. Brigadier General ʻAisha has long been an advocate of improved health services for women and has incorporated many health initiatives into the directorate's work. Women in the Jordanian military have some of the best maternity leave provisions in the country, with a guarantee of three months of paid leave. The directorate has also sponsored public health awareness events, breast and cervical cancer screening programs and the establishment of a public hospital in the impoverished southern region, all of which benefit civilians as well as members of the military.

All of the above practices take place in a context of the recognized importance of being "culturally appropriate." The DMWA places a strong emphasis on demonstrating competence to win respect rather than demanding changes on the basis of rights claims. As a result, although the agenda of the DMWA is, in the larger analysis, a radical one, the methods and goals are such that their program looks quite moderate and is even able to incorporate traditionalism where that is of tactical value (as in neutralizing opposition). That the military itself must take such cultural considerations into account, despite its aforementioned isolation from social pressure, is not surprising. Indeed, as the Jordanian military has a special role in representing the traditional, tribal elements of state support, cultural concerns about gender are quite likely to permeate such a setting. Opposition (albeit limited) to the DMWA from outside the military reveals the importance of gender as a contestational element representing "authentic" or "Islamic" culture; on non-gender-related issues, the military is generally immune to such opposition.

The success of the DMWA's strategies and tactics are borne out by increasing numbers of women who seek to join the military. The military now has more female applicants than it can accommodate, and entrance requires sitting competitive examinations.[28] In the military, women receive the same pay as men and are subject to the same promotions schedule, meaning that the professional opportunities and benefits are much greater than those found in many other sectors of the workforce.

27 "National Report: Jordan Armed Forces 2006," on file with NATO's International Military Staff section, at www.nato.int/ims/2006/win/pdf/jordan_brief.pdf.

28 "National Report: Jordan Armed Forces 2006."

In 2006, the DMWA began a program designed to promote women's integration into a larger range of military jobs. This program received its impetus from the 2005 suicide bombings in Amman, in which at least one woman attacker had participated; this provided a clear security-based rationale for including women in counterterrorism and intelligence forces. The DMWA has begun overseeing the training of women as members of the Special Security Missions Company and ultimately plans to establish a regional training center for military women, with the twin purpose of providing direct training to women soldiers and advising other countries on successful integration of women into their armed forces.[29] The success of Jordan's gradualist and highly competence-based strategy for incorporating women into the military is expected to be a useful model for other militaries.

The Directorate of Military Women's Affairs continues to expand women's professional military roles. This type of progressive state policy is, however, limited in its potential to affect the political order. The opportunities offered by the program incorporating women into the Jordanian military are not easily replicable in other areas of the state. The military is a unique environment in many ways; its special characteristics, and particularly the role of royal authority, were able to produce changes through means that could not be applied elsewhere. Nonetheless, the effects of this program create new opportunities for women and challenge some fairly fundamental beliefs about gender roles.

In its gradualist and moderate approach and its concern for cultural appropriateness, the DMWA shares some tactical similarities with the women's movement, as the next chapter will show. The unit's success, however, is only partly attributable to their careful approach; clearly, it also relies on the operation of royal power and the absence of public conflict over the issue. If military women were demanding combat roles on an equal footing with men, the outcome would likely have been different, and if the royal family had not supported women's military service, Jordan would have no women soldiers at all. Thus, while the DMWA is a development entirely outside the context of the women's movement, it follows a similar pattern: royal endorsement, minimization of challenges to traditional practices and gradualism. It has been a successful formula for women's military service; the next chapter will analyze whether it has worked as well in other aspects of public life.

Conclusion

While earlier chapters have identified serious limitations in the state's protection of women's rights and status in Jordan, policies such as the quota for women and the incorporation of women into the military suggest a much more progressive state approach to women's roles. In both cases, the state's policies have opened up significant new opportunities to women in the public sphere, with very little

29 "National Report."

disruption of existing traditional powers, an approach that could be characterized as either subversive or conservative but which is most notable for its pragmatism. This careful dance of traditional power hierarchies with progressive roles is replicated throughout the Jordanian political context, as earlier chapters have shown. While the monarchy cannot call the tune, it is clearly the partner that leads the dance; indeed, it is a small irony of Jordanian politics that monarchical power, not usually considered a progressive force in political science, has been the best safeguard of women's rights. However, while the royal-liberal strand of legitimacy is generally compatible with the achievement of changes in women's status, the political relevance of traditionalist claims cannot be overlooked. The state's need for cultural legitimacy is at present a leading determinant of the extent to which challenges to traditional social practice are effective. This will remain the case so long as gender roles are considered an essential element of cultural authenticity – and so long as the state finds it necessary to base its legitimacy upon the demands of sectors of society that value the preservation of traditional social practices.

PART III
Developing Institutions, Maintaining Legacy

Chapter 8
The Women's Movement

The achievements and limitations of the women's movement are determined by dominant political forces rather than by radical challenges to the existing order. Political activism on behalf of women's interests in Jordan is led by a few prominent NGOs and quasi-governmental organizations, whose efforts on behalf of women's rights have been associated with many of the significant legal changes of the last dozen years. While these organizations do not always present a united front, and while their particular agendas may vary somewhat, they are sufficiently similar in their goals and their activities that they can be loosely designated the "women's movement."[1]

The movement's primary contribution to political contestation lies in its efforts to strengthen the royal-liberal element of the political hegemony. Most of the organizational leaders of the movement are well-educated urban women, and the large quasi-state organizations enjoy royal patronage. However, it is important to note that not all politically active women are associated with these women's organizations or endorse their goals. The Islamic Action Front has fielded women candidates for public office, and as the previous chapter noted, women elected to Parliament under the quota are often conservatives who have no connection to the women's movement. However, most political activism by women occurs within a set of well-known organizations dominated by the Jordanian National Commission for Women (JNCW), the Jordanian National Forum for Women (JNFW) and private groups such as the Jordanian Women's Union (JWU) and the Sisterhood Is Global Institute (SIGI-Jordan).

These organizations, and the women's movement generally, are characterized by a moderate, incrementalist approach that achieves small and steady gains over time but does not make radical demands or challenges to the political order. This moderation has led to some criticism of the women's movement as too bourgeois or too state-controlled to achieve significant change. Yet, if the movement were to adopt radical demands and tactics, its effectiveness would certainly be reduced, its organizations disbanded and its members silenced. The moderation of the women's

---

1 Both this general political orientation and the groups themselves are commonly called "women's" rather than "feminist," in the press and in their own discourse, so that is the term I will use here. The subject of this chapter is limited to the women's groups with a primarily political agenda, which excludes the many charity organizations whose membership is largely female but whose work is focused on material assistance to the poor rather than on political or social change with regard to gender issues.

movement has, as in so many other contexts in the Jordanian political system, been a necessary condition for its success.

Organizations

Jordanian women's organizations are not a new phenomenon, having existed for several decades. Women's groups were politically active as early as the 1940s, and their agendas, particularly during the politically-liberalized 1950s, were remarkably similar to those of the current organizations: improving women's political inclusion (particularly securing voting rights for women, a feat nearly achieved in 1956 before the imposition of martial law), amending the Personal Status Law and promoting equality in employment and education.[2] However, like other organizations, the women's groups found themselves at the mercy of the increasingly authoritarian state, and organizational life was limited from the mid-1950s to the late 1980s. The resumption of parliamentary elections in 1989 and the subsequent re-emergence of political parties sparked a new era for the women's movement, and many of the groups currently operating have emerged since that time.

Quasi-Governmental Organizations

The Jordanian National Committee for Women

The largest women's organizations in Jordan are usually called NGOs, but they are, strictly speaking, not nongovernmental but rather quasi-governmental. The most prominent of the women's organizations, the Jordanian National Commission for Women, was actually a creation of the Cabinet in 1992 and is chaired by Princess Basma bint Talal, the sister of the late King Hussein and aunt of the current king. Its original task was to create a "national strategy" for women in Jordan, a duty that has since expanded to include providing legislative and policy recommendations to the government. The JNCW also serves as the government's representative in a number of forums; for example, it provides Jordan's periodic reports to the U.N. on the country's progress in implementing the CEDAW treaty requirements. The group's board of directors includes the ministers of Justice, Planning and Social Development, representatives of the ministries of Labour, Municipal and Rural Affairs and Education and representatives from the legal committees of both houses of Parliament, as well as members from most of the quasi-governmental

2 For the history of the women's movement in Jordan, see the work of Laurie Brand, particularly her *Women, the State and Political Liberalization: Middle Eastern and North African Experiences* (New York: Columbia University Press, 1998).

women's and development organizations.[3] Clearly, the government has significant input into the agenda and work of the JNCW.

The JNCW's official status has ensured a place for women's interests (as officially defined) in legislation and policymaking. The Cabinet has declared that the JNCW is "to be consulted by all official parties before any related actions or decisions are taken."[4] The Legal Committee of the JNCW is of particular importance in this regard, as it is the body that examines the Prime Ministry's agenda for parliamentary sessions, reviews proposed legislation and suggests amendments. This consultation does not, of course, guarantee that the JNCW's priorities will be met by the government; the recommendation of an electoral quota, described in Chapter 7, was rejected by the government for several years before it was finally adopted.

In its function as an umbrella organization for the women's movement, the JNCW has organized an NGO Coordinating Committee whose "purpose is to coordinate the activities of the various organizations dealing with women's issues in order to avoid duplication."[5] This committee is also charged with "evaluating and providing feed-back on all the activities carried out by the different organizations." The JNCW does not have policy control over other organizations, but the group's pre-eminent role is widely acknowledged; one journalist described the women's movement as "spearheaded and initiated by the [JNCW]."[6]

The JNCW's recent programs have included an updating of the National Strategy for Women, begun in a series of workshops in 2000. The process was an extended one, involving any number of meetings and public discussion forums and including both the various women's organizations and, to some degree, public input. The bureaucracy associated with such a production can be cumbersome; one newspaper report on the progress of the National Strategy in 2004 mentioned that the JNCW was "in the process of creating a committee to take part in the preparatory meetings for [an upcoming] conference."[7] It is little wonder the revised National Strategy took several years to produce. The updated strategy was finally completed and endorsed by the government in 2006. Like the first National Strategy, the statement is intended to serve as a coherent and public agenda for the

---

3 Including the General Federation of Jordanian Women, the Jordanian National Forum for Women, the Jordanian Women's Union, the Jordanian Hashemite Fund for Human Development, the Queen Zain al-Sharaf Institute for Development and the Noor al-Hussein Foundation, among others. For a complete list of JNCW board members, see www.jncw.jo/docs/4.doc.

4 www.jncw.jo/chronology.html.

5 www.jncw.jo/docs/9.doc.

6 Rana Husseini, "Activists hopeful demands will be met," *Jordan Times*, March 3, 2008.

7 "Women academics and professionals discuss Jordan's national strategy for women," *Jordan Times*, March 25, 2004.

women's movement, but it is never clear how much of a direct effect such strategy declarations have on actual policymaking.

The organization's other activities may have more immediate and concrete effect. For example, the group has recently begun work on a "frequently asked questions" document as part of a campaign to promote awareness of the legal rights of women and children.[8] With the assistance of the Women's Studies Centre at the University of Jordan, the JNCW selected the 100 most important questions from a longer list distributed to several hundred people, both men and women. They found that the most important issues identified by participants were related to labor, retirement and social security provisions, as well as personal status issues concerning divorce.

The JNCW, currently led by lawyer and prominent women's activist Asma Khader, works on a wide range of issues, both legislative and social. The Legal Committee has contributed to the amendment of a number of discriminatory laws on labor regulations, social security and income tax, as well as the penal code, the personal status code and the civil status code.[9] These amendments have provided a number of important gains to women, such as paid maternity leave, better pension provisions, better access to divorce and improved (although not equal) rights to family books, an important identity document discussed further below.

On the social front, the group's activities have included awareness-raising events and policy advocacy as well as practical efforts to support women's greater public roles. The JNCW has established the Women's Knowledge Network, designed as a means for women in local government to share their experiences with one another, thus promoting solidarity and developing professional skills.[10] Around 250 women serve on municipal councils, thanks in large part to the quota that sets aside 20 percent of council seats for women. Early views of women's involvement in local government have been favorable, and the women's movement has come to regard local participation as a valuable means for improving women's status. Women working in their local communities are now popularly cited as an important factor in national development, and the portrayal of women in local politics as engaged in a kind of "caregiving" on a community basis has probably contributed to the social acceptability of this political role.

The group also sponsored an event on women's economic empowerment held to mark International Women's Day in 2008, at which the organization and the Minister of Labour both endorsed the idea of a government "motherhood fund" to

8 Rana Husseini, "Campaign seeks to increase women's awareness about their legal rights," *Jordan Times*, July 1, 2008.

9 For a list of legislative amendments associated with the JNCW, see www.jncw.jo/docs/3.doc.

10 "Knowledge network seeks to empower female municipal council members," *Jordan Times*, October 28, 2008.

help cover the costs of maternity leave for employed women.[11] The need for such a fund reflects both the strength and the limitations of the women's movement; after working for the enactment of the law providing maternity leave in 1996,[12] the women's movement found that businesses regarded the cost of the maternity leave provision as a deterrent to hiring young women. Because no law prohibits sex discrimination in hiring, the maternity leave provision might actually harm women's employability. The "motherhood fund" is meant to redress this by sharing the cost of maternity leave among employees and businesses, in much the same way that other taxes are collected.

It should be noted that the government minister speaking at the event was encouraging the women's movement to advocate a specific policy for the government's consideration; it might seem that if the ministry, or the government in general, favored such a policy, it could simply adopt it, but this kind of exhortation to the women's movement is in fact not unusual. Ministers often meet with women's organizations and encourage them publicly to engage in specific advocacy activities. For example, before the 2007 elections, when the women's movement had been disappointed by the government's decision not to amend the electoral law to increase the women's quota in Parliament, a minister speaking to several women's organizations assembled at the JNCW's offices urged them to "continue to hold dialogue with the government on the quota system. The door is not closed yet and there is a possibility to reach a solution that would be in the nation's interest."[13] The quota remains unchanged as of 2008, but the prospect of its expansion in the future requires that the demand be put forward for the government to answer; this is an important function of the women's organizations from the state's point of view.

I recently asked a JNCW legal programs coordinator, Ra'edah Freahat, what the organization's most important issues were, and she readily rank-ordered them with work-related issues at the top of the list, followed by personal status issues and then criminal law issues such as honor crimes, rape and domestic violence.[14] This reflects the views that emerge from surveys and grass-roots organizing work over the past decade. While issues such as inequalities in the Nationality Law are important in the organization's view, too, they do not affect as many women on a daily basis. Although the JNCW is sometimes criticized as elitist in its orientation, its work does take into account the problems that are important to ordinary women.

The JNCW is an excellent example of the character of the Jordanian women's movement. It exists because the state chose to create it, and while its advocacy of

---

11 Rana Husseini, "Women's movement urged to push for motherhood fund," *Jordan Times*, March 10, 2008.

12 Labour Law No. 8 for the year 1996.

13 Minister for Prime Ministry Affairs Muhyiddine Touq, quoted in Rana Husseini, "Touq reviews CEDAW with women's groups," *Jordan Times*, August 28, 2007.

14 Interview, Amman, July 1, 2008.

greater equality for women is sincere and often effective, where the organization finds itself at odds with the state's own agenda, it acts as, at most, a loyal opposition. Even its efforts at grassroots inclusion tend to be, as Laurie Brand wrote about the 1993 drafting of the original National Strategy for Women, "carefully orchestrated from above."[15] Nonetheless, this careful orchestration produces results that might not be possible otherwise. The JNCW is careful not to bite the hand that feeds it, but it has become over its life more a well-trained tiger than a sleepy pussycat. As a result, the regime finds that it must at least give the appearance of taking the women's movement seriously.

The Jordanian National Forum for Women

The Jordanian National Forum for Women (JNFW) came into existence after the Beijing conference in 1995 although it had been in the planning stages for some time. Like the JNCW, the JNFW is a quasi-governmental organization, and the two organizations share many agenda items and activities, although the JNFW is conceived as a grassroots organization, with individual members around the country, rather than an umbrella organization bringing together other groups. Princess Basma plays an important role in the leadership of this group, too, serving as the head of the JNFW's higher council.

The JNFW works with the government, other civil society organizations, and international bodies in advocacy, training programs and awareness-raising projects. For example, the JNFW and UNIFEM co-sponsored an event entitled "Jordanian Women's Priorities" in June 2007, designed to build on the outcome of the king's 2006 "We are All Jordan" campaign to produce a consensus on priorities for national development. Princess Basma declared the "We are All Jordan" campaign an "umbrella" under which "we can overcome challenges and ensure an atmosphere of fairness, forgiveness and equality in Jordan."[16] JNFW Secretary General May Abul Samen pointed out that the campaign had not identified any women's issues in its 15 priorities, but this has not deterred the group from situating itself within the government's reform agenda; Princess Basma and the Secretary General characterized the work of the JNFW as a "national duty" and a "pledge to our country." This approach complements another, which is to stress that increasing women's political participation and social status is in the national interest. This latter approach is not unique to the JNFW or the quasi-governmental organizations but is widely followed throughout the women's movement, as with regard to the issue of women's municipal council service, mentioned above.

15 "Women and the Struggle for Political Opening," in Eleanor Abdella Doumato and Marsha Pripstein Posusney, (eds), *Women and Globalization in the Arab Middle East* (Boulder, CO: Lynne Rienner Publishers, 2003), 160.

16 Rana Husseini, "Activists focus on women's priorities," *Jordan Times*, June 5, 2007.

Nongovernmental Organizations

For nongovernmental organizations, in particular, such as the JWU and SIGI/Jordan, the liberalizations of the political sphere since 1989 have been vital to their ability to operate. These groups are much more under the control of the Ministry of Social Development than the quasi-governmental organizations such as the JNCW and must receive permission for fundraising and submit to oversight of their membership and activities. Despite these limitations, these organizations have played an important role in the activities of the women's movement.

The Jordanian Women's Union

One of the most notable non-state women's organizations is the Jordanian Women's Union, currently led by Amneh al-Zo'bi. The JWU dates in its current form from the early 1990s, but its roots extend to the 1970s and a predecessor organization called the Women's Federation of Jordan (WFJ).[17] The WFJ was a successful group that held conferences, conducted research, and ultimately attracted around 3,000 members before it was shut down by the government in the early 1980s, the era when state domination of the women's movement took off.[18] The JWU was resurrected from the old WFJ structure in 1990 and has since been an active group with a wide range of programs. The JWU's agenda is similar to that of the other major women's organizations: to end discrimination against women, to improve their social status, to facilitate women's organization and political participation, to raise awareness of women's issues and to encourage the implementation of laws and treaties that improve women's rights. The JWU agenda also includes some specific items not generally addressed by the other groups, such as "helping women to benefit from the family planning program" and "supporting the Palestinian women and their national rights."[19] The group now has offices around the kingdom and a membership of around 10,000; membership is open to any adult woman for an annual fee of JD 2 (about US$2.82). The JWU is internally democratic in its leadership selection and maintains a number of committees on various topics from children's rights to violence against women to poverty alleviation.

The JWU is particularly noteworthy for its efforts to combat violence against women. The group was one of the earliest organizations in Jordan to begin addressing this issue publicly. In 1996, the group established the first hotline for abused women, operating in Amman, Madaba and the Baqaa refugee camp. With a dozen or more calls per day, the hotline has provided confidential legal advice and psychological counseling to several thousand women to date.[20] The JWU

17 Some of the JWU's own materials trace its origins to an organization that existed from 1945–1957; see http://www.jwu.itgo.com/bg.htm.

18 Brand (1998), 124–127.

19 See www.jwu.itgo.com/tao.htm.

20 www.jwu.itgo.com/hotline.htm.

recognizes that the hotline's reach is limited not only geographically but also due to the fact that many poor women do not have access to telephones. Nonetheless, the hotline has been an important service in the group's efforts against domestic violence. The group also established the first shelter in the country for abused women (see below).

Like other organizations, the JWU partners with various groups to conduct joint programs and also attracts funding from external donors. For example, the group's shelter for abused women was originally established with the assistance of Canadian and Spanish funding. The (U.S.) National Endowment for Democracy has also funded some of the JWU's programs since 1994; since 2000, the group has received several NED grants to fund legal literacy and human rights training programs, volunteer development and to extend its hotline service to Zarqa, a large town near the capital.[21]

The JWU is a well-respected organization that has received recognition both in Jordan and abroad for its promotion of women's rights. In 2003, the group received the U.N. High Commissioner for Refugees' Award for the Promotion of Gender Equality and the Empowerment of Refugee Women. The JWU is independent, having no royal patron, and is generally on the left of the political spectrum, but it operates well within the mainstream of the women's movement, partnering with the other major women's organizations on many projects.

Sisterhood Is Global Institute, Jordan

The Sisterhood Is Global Institute was founded in 1984 by women's rights advocates from several dozen countries; founding members included Simone de Beauvoir, Egyptian feminist Nawal al-Saadawi, and Moroccan feminist Fatima Mernissi. The Jordan chapter was established in 1998 by Asma Khader, who had previously led the JWU (1993–1997) and who currently heads the JNCW. Although the group is a nongovernmental rather than a quasi-governmental organization, it has clear, if informal, ties to the royal family; Princess Basma was on hand at its opening, and Ms. Khader served as a government spokesperson after her directorship of SIGI.

SIGI's primary focus is on women's legal and political rights. As a chapter of a larger transnational group, SIGI/Jordan is able to make use of its parent group's training resources, primarily a collection of specialized materials that were developed for use in the Muslim world, and which SIGI/Jordan has further adapted to the local Jordanian context. For example, two of SIGI/J's major programs have been its human rights education workshops and its program on Combating Violence against Women and Girls; the former program uses an Arabic version of the SIGI manual "Claiming our Rights," and the latter has adapted the Arabic version of the "Safe and Secure" training manual. SIGI/Jordan collaborates

21 All NED grant information is available at www.ned.org.

with the Women's Learning Partnership in many of its activities; its external ties have been an important resource for the group.

Like the Jordanian Women's Union, the group has made use of external funding from NGOs, in SIGI's cases to offer a number of workshops on citizens' rights. Recent priorities for the group have included equal rights for women in the nationality law and a reduction in the number of girls who marry at early ages.[22] SIGI also sought a law against domestic violence, a priority supported by other organizations and finally taken up by the government in legislation in 2008.[23] SIGI has also held a number of conferences and joined with other groups in lobbying for the permanent passage of the 2001 amendments affecting divorce and honor killings.

Royal Patronage

Laurie Brand calls the quasi-governmental organizations with royal patronage not NGOs but RONGOs.[24] RONGOs (pun probably intended) make a rather complicated contribution to civil society; they are organized, and act, as NGOs, but they are clearly allied with the government, particularly the monarchy. They exist, in an important sense, because the royal family wishes them to exist, and they work to pursue the agenda of the monarchy. In terms of the development of a free and pluralist civil society, this type of quasi-state organization is not ideal, as it cooperates with authoritarian power rather than limiting it. On the other hand, no one impugns Princess Basma's, Queen Noor's or Queen Rania's commitment to improving women's rights, and it is undeniable that royal patronage empowers these organizations as well as circumscribes them. Until the political system undergoes real democratization, with the concomitant secure protections for free speech, free organization, open political competition and tolerance of opposition, the women's movement may consider itself reasonably well-served by the friendship of the royal family.

The effect of royal patronage extends beyond the RONGOs themselves. Many activities of the women's movement are the product of collaboration among several groups. A series of events under the title "Action Not Words: Dialogue and Participation in Decision Making," were held in 2003 to encourage dialogue between members of the lower house and women's representatives on the issue of divorce law reform; the program was a joint product of the JNCW, the JNFW, the General Federation of Jordanian Women and the JWU. Likewise, the Equal Rights Campaign of 2008 has been sponsored by a coalition including the JNFW,

22 SIGI/Jordan materials provided by the organization in September 2004; on file with author.

23 Protection from Family Violence Law, No. 6 for the year 2008, available (in Arabic) at www.lob.gov.jo ui/laws/search_no.jsp?no=6&year=2008.

24 Brand, *Women, the State and Political Liberalization*, 171.

the Jordanian Hashemite Fund for Human Development, which has a women's empowerment program, the Queen Zein al-Sharaf Institute, the Performing Arts Centre and Freedom House, making the campaign a partnership of RONGOs and domestic and international NGOs. The royally-sponsored set of organizations often collaborates in this way, and their greater power makes them a useful partner for private organizations in joint undertakings.

Legislative and Policy Priorities of the Women's Movement

While the attention of external observers often focuses on topics such as honor killings, Jordanians' own assessment of the priorities for women's rights are often more focused on economic and daily-life issues. While honor crimes, nationality and divorce have been important political issues in Jordan, and have received commensurate attention from the women's movement, a number of other issues have also been the focus of reform and policy-making efforts. These include women's access to passports and family books, the labor law and social security and the creation of a women's shelter.

Family Books

The Jordanian government has long used a form of identity document known as the family book (*daftar 'a'ileh*). As the name indicates, these books are issued to families rather than individuals; the holder of the book is the "head of household" (*rab al-'a'ileh*), by definition a man, and there are separate pages in the book for his wife[25] and each of their children. The family book is used as an identity document for enrolling children in school and obtaining government services, such as food assistance or health care. Children, including adult children of both sexes, remain in their father's family book until they are married; married men receive their own family books, and married women are recorded in the family books of their husbands.

While the government now issues individual identity cards to all adult citizens, the family book is still required for many purposes. The potential practical problems are obvious; a woman whose husband will not give her the family book cannot conduct government-related business such as applying for a passport or for health care. This is especially problematic for widows and divorced women. A woman who has lost her husband would revert to the family book of her father (or senior male relative, if the father is deceased); children remain in their father's family book in the case of divorce or are transferred to the family book of the father's nearest male relative in case of death. This means, for example, that a divorced woman might have physical custody of her young children, but her ex-husband

25 Men married to more than one woman are reportedly issued separate family books for each family.

controls the family book that she must show in order to register the children for school.

In practice, some accommodation could be made for widows in special circumstances who had no male relatives. Officials would sometimes issue a family book to a widow, but they would mark out the designation "head of household" on the first page and write in "widow." Divorced women generally had no recourse at all to family books of their own. The practical problems arising from this led the government to include changes to the rules for family books in its 2001 legislative reforms; the reforms allow not only widows and divorced women but also Jordanian women married to foreigners to receive their own family books.[26] Most women, however, remain in the subordinate position indicated by their husbands' official designation as "head of household" in the family book. Like the nationality law, this practice indicates that female citizens have a different relationship to the state, one mediated through their connection to male citizens.

Passports

Another documentary problem unique to female citizens is found in the passports law. The form on which one applies for a first-time passport is different for men and women; the women's form long in use required a signature at the bottom in the space designated for the "husband or guardian" (*al-zawj/al-wali*), and without this signature no passport would be issued. Efforts to allow adult women to obtain passports without a husband's or relative's signature began in the 1990s; a law to this effect was defeated in 1994.[27] The measure was later reported to have been passed in July 1998, needing only royal endorsement to bring it into force,[28] but the change was apparently never made. It is not clear what derailed the reform. Certainly some religious conservatives opposed the measure, such as the mufti of the Armed Forces who said it would lead to women traveling without their husbands' permission and would "increase the number of divorces in our society [and] cause an embarrassing danger" and "lead to the corruption of society through women."[29] Other conservative forces endorsed the change, however, including the Islamic Action Front, one of whose members stated that it "does not contradict sharia."[30] The women's movement, not surprisingly, welcomed the move as necessary and in conformity with international rights requirements; however, in

26 Reported by the JNCW in "Amendments to Legislation," www.jncw.jo/docs/3.doc.

27 Brand (1998), 136–137.

28 "Endorsement of controversial amendment on women's right to passports expected 'soon'," *Jordan Times,* August 30, 1998.

29 Mahmoud Shouiat, quoted ibid.

30 Magda Ashour, "Feminists, IAF welcome new draft law on women's right to passport," *Jordan Times*, June 22, 1998.

practice the requirement of a husband's or guardian's permission continued in force.[31]

In 2002, the government announced – again – that the law had been changed, as part of the set of changes made in Parliament's absence, and this time the announcement appears to have taken tangible form in the law. The text of the 2003 passports law contains no gender-specific requirements,[32] but it does allow the Minister of the Interior to establish passport-related procedures, which may themselves treat women and men differently, as it turns out. Furthermore, this law was passed as "temporary legislation," and Parliament originally rejected the amendment when it reconvened in 2003.

The Civil Status and Passports Department continues as of 2008 to publish passport application instructions and passport forms that effectively require women to demonstrate their husbands' consent to obtain a passport. In the "Procedures for issuing a first-time passport," item eight says that if the applicant is a woman married to a Jordanian or non-Jordanian, the family book must be shown as part of the application requirements.[33] Item nine requires that single, widowed or divorced women attest that they are unmarried at the time of application. Clearly the purpose is to ensure that married women have their husbands' consent. Passport application forms available on line through the CSPD and various Jordanian embassy websites, even those dated after the legislative changes, are still gender-specific, with different information required from men and women. The U.S. Department of State's annual human rights report for Jordan likewise confirms that "[t]he law states that women have the right to obtain passports without the written permission of their husbands, although in practice the husband's permission is often required."[34] While the recent legal changes may improve women's access to passports in the long run, the problem now appears to be that law means one thing in writing and another in practice.

The Labour Law and the Social Security Law

The Labour Law was amended in 1996 to provide several new protections for employed women.[35] One of the most important provisions was the entitlement

31 In 1999, many people believed that the law had been changed, based on news reports, but then stories began circulating that officials were still requiring women applicants to show a husband's or father's permission to get a passport. I asked two unmarried Jordanian women to go to the passport office on separate occasions and obtain the application forms. In both case they were told that the signature of permission was still required. One woman pointed out that the law had allegedly been changed, but was told to get a signature nonetheless.

32 Available (in Arabic) at www.lob.gov.jo/ui/laws/search_no.jsp?no=5&year=2003.

33 This document is available (in Arabic) at www.cspd.gov.jo/FT.HTM.

34 U.S. Department of State Country Report on Human Rights (Jordan), 2007, at www.state.gov/g/drl/rls/hrrpt/2007/100598.htm, March 11, 2008.

35 Labour Law No. 8 for 1996, summarized at www.jncw.org.jo/docs/3.doc.

of "female salaried employees" to ten weeks of paid maternity leave as well as time during the workday to breastfeed infants. The law also limits the ability of employers to fire pregnant women and allows women to take up to a one-year leave of absence for childcare purposes, with the right of returning to her job after the leave. As there are very few legal protections against gender discrimination and few accommodations for working mothers, these provisions are an important step toward facilitating women's participation in the workforce. A more dubious provision of the Labour Law, however, is the protectionist Article 69, which allows the Minister of Labour to "determine those activities and the hours in which women are prohibited from working," on the basis of women's "health and safety." This is comparable to the regulation of child labor in that it governs not work environments but workers presumed to be uniquely vulnerable.

Women employees are actually at an advantage on the basis of gender in regard to the Social Security Law.[36] Men must complete 18 years of employment before they are eligible for a pension, while women need only complete 15 years. Women may retire with a pension at age 45, earlier than men, and may opt to have their pension paid out in one lump sum under certain conditions. However, while a man's pension is inheritable by his widow, children and other dependents upon his death, a woman's pension is not inheritable by her husband "unless he is totally disabled and has no income of his own." This reflects the view that husbands, as heads of household, support wives, but wives do not support their husbands except in unusual circumstances.

The Establishment of a Shelter for Domestic Violence Victims

One of the problems in dealing with domestic violence in Jordan was that until 1999, there was not a single shelter for abused women in the country. Two shelters were planned in the late 1990s by the Ministry of Social Development and the Jordanian Women's Union, respectively. Despite the presumably greater resources, both political and monetary, of the government ministry, it was the JWU's shelter that opened first. This is an excellent example of the constraints faced by the state with regard to gender issues, in this case because of internal divisions among various actors. The government could have opened a shelter, of course, without public consultation. However, some conservative opposition to the idea of a shelter emerged within the government itself, on the grounds that it would contribute to family breakup by permitting public interference in private family matters and encouraging women to leave their homes.

Although the Ministry had secured funding for the shelter from UNIFEM by 1998, the shelter did not come into existence until early 2007. In the interim, the government repeatedly announced that the shelter was on the point of opening: in 2001, it was "within three months" of opening, the next year "within six months"

36 Social Security Law No. 19 for 2001, summarized at www.jncw.org.jo/docs/3.doc.

and in 2003 and 2004 "within one month."[37] Reports on the various ministries and groups involved with the shelter project varied over the years, and ultimately the original project was somewhat scaled back; the shelter is now a "family reconciliation house" that will offer services to men as well as women. In defending the idea of the shelter, an official from the Ministry of Social Development promised that "our main concern at the ministry is to preserve family unity, strengthen social relationships, and ensure that families are productive under any circumstances."[38] From protecting abused women to preserving family unity is an important rhetorical leap, whatever its effect on the policies of the shelter may be. (The use of the shelter for protective custody is addressed in the next chapter).

The shelter run by the JWU, by contrast, has been a smaller, less public, and in some ways more promising project. The JWU shelter was developed as part of the group's work in combating domestic violence, and it began operating in 1999. The facility was originally able to take in only a few women at a time, but it now serves hundreds of women every year, allowing them to stay at the shelter for up to three months.[39] The JWU has also provided services to refugee women, including Iraqis, who are victims of domestic violence. The JWU also provides a child-friendly space in which divorced parents can meet for visitation with their children.

Both of these shelters assist women who are victims of violence, and both provide family-related services, but their approach to the family is somewhat different. While the Ministry's shelter focuses on "family unity" and reconciliation, the JWU's focuses on practical services that help women protect themselves and care for their children in cases of divorce as well as physical abuse. There is no doubt that in Jordan, as in the United States and elsewhere, demonstrating an affiliation with "family values" is a good political tactic as well as a meaningful framework for many people's lives; however, assessments of what is good for families may vary widely across different political actors. The state takes care to satisfy its conservative and traditional bases of support, but the JWU has no such constraint, which can sometimes be an advantage.

The Convention on the Elimination of All Forms of Discrimination Against Women

Another recent development with regard to women's legal rights is Jordan's renewed declaration of its commitment to the U.N. Convention on the Elimination

---

37 Rana Husseini, "Abused women to have safe haven within three months" (April 26, 2001), "Ministry announces first women's shelter to open in 6 months" (September 4, 2002), "Family Reconciliation House to open soon" (December 7, 2003) and "Family Reconciliation House to open soon" (June 9, 2004); all stories are from the *Jordan Times*.

38 Rana Husseini, "Family Reconciliation House to open soon," *Jordan Times*, December 7, 2003.

39 IRIN (Integrated Regional Information Networks), U.N. Office for the Coordination of Humanitarian Affairs, "Jordan: Iraqi domestic violence victims find shelter," March 8, 2004.

of All Forms of Discrimination against Women (CEDAW). Jordan was an early signatory to the treaty, in 1980, and ratified it on January 7, 1992. This ratification created an international legal obligation to adhere to the terms of the treaty, but the effects of this adherence were somewhat limited by Jordan's expressed reservations with regard to parts of the document, generally those relating to equality in marriage and equal nationality rights.[40] CEDAW's effect on domestic policies is unclear; the process of implementation of the treaty obligations has been slow, but the presumed willingness of the government to take on the legal duties indicated support in at least some sectors for the changes required. In the Jordanian legal system, international legal obligations take precedence over Jordanian law, and thus claims could, in theory, be made in Jordanian courts to demand the implementation of these laws even where they conflict with domestic law. No formal challenge to a law has ever been brought on this basis, however.

In 2007, the government published the text of CEDAW in the Official Gazette, which makes it not only an international legal obligation but an operative part of domestic law. Whether this will serve as a catalyst for greater legal reform or for court challenges to government policy is unclear; the effect may be primarily symbolic. However, Islamists decried the move, with a legal scholar of the Islamic Action Front describing the treaty as "one of the most dangerous agreements that affects the rights of citizens as well as the nation's identity and values."[41] He condemned CEDAW as an effort to "steer people away from religion" and "destro[y] the Muslim family."

Women's rights activists, on the other hand, were predictably pleased by the further incorporation of CEDAW. The treaty's incorporation into domestic law had not been a top priority for the women's movement, as Jordan's obligations under the treaty existed whether it had the status of domestic law or not. However, the regime's decision to publish CEDAW in the Official Gazette is seen as an indication that women's rights are being elevated to a higher priority.

Conclusion

It is not surprising that the women's movement has had a close relationship with the state, even to the extent of state sponsorship of the major women's organizations. The Jordanian political system remains an authoritarian one, and civil society is in many ways more corporatist than pluralist; state domination is not unique to the women's movement but is a general characteristic of political contestation in Jordan. Consequently, women's organizations find it necessary to be moderate

40 Jordan's reservations concern Article 9 paragraph 2, Article 15 paragraph 4 and Article 16 paragraph 1, items c, d and g. These provisions are therefore not included in Jordan's obligations under the treaty.

41 Ibrahim Zeid Kilani, quoted in "Islamists slam women's rights convention," *Agence France Presse* in the *Jordan Times*, August 6, 2007.

in their demands and gradualist in their approach. Not only do they rely on state sponsorship in many cases, they are also more vulnerable than other kinds of organizations to criticisms on grounds of traditional culture. Royal patronage may therefore be a useful hedge against both state and traditional power.

As another means of defusing conservative criticism, the women's movement's moderate approach has included consistent efforts to demonstrate their respect for religion. The first National Strategy for Women began with an article declaring that it was based on the Constitution, the National Charter and "further founded on the principles of Islamic Jurisprudence, the values of Arab and Muslim society, and the principles of human rights," and the legislative objectives of the strategy included "legislation which ensures that women can exercise their political, economic, social and cultural rights as enshrined in Islamic Jurisprudence."[42] The demonstration of respect for religion also sometimes includes the tactic of seeking religious approval for the movement's goals – an approach used, for example, on the issue of honor killings (see Chapter 4). The 2008 equal rights campaign, meant to achieve the final passage of the 2001 reforms (regarding divorce, honor crimes, etc.) and to build on these changes, explicitly sought "to win the support of clerics and imams, encouraging them to raise the issue of equal rights in their Friday sermons and to address misconceptions surrounding women's empowerment, the Personal Status Law and Islam."[43] This is a widely-approved strategy often encouraged by policymakers, as it would reduce the regime's potential political costs of acceding to the demands of women's organizations where those are opposed by conservatives. The effect of engaging in religious dialogue can work both ways, of course; a minister who recently encouraged the women's movement to engage in such dialogue said that this practice would help them to "stay on the right track and achieve more gains." The "right track" is clear; it is the avenue of progress that opens up when the goals of the women's movement are seen as consonant with, or, even better, required by, the dictates of religion and a respect for tradition.

The power of the state, and more particularly of the royal family, will continue to dominate the political activities of the women's movement for the foreseeable future. The progress (or lack) of democratization in Jordan will be of vital importance for the women's movement, as it would open up new avenues of participation and public voice. It is a small irony of Jordanian politics that monarchical power, not usually considered a progressive force in political science, has been the best safeguard of women's rights. While this strand is generally compatible with the achievement of changes in women's status, the political relevance of traditionalist claims cannot be overlooked. The state's needs for cultural legitimacy are at present a leading determinant of the extent to which challenges to traditional

42 National Strategy for Women, section 1, paragraph 1, and section 2(a), paragraph 3. www.jncw.org.jo/ docs/11/doc.

43 Taylor Luck, "New campaign to raise awareness on women's rights," *Jordan Times*, February 21, 2008.

social practice are effective. This will remain the case so long as gender roles are considered essential to cultural authenticity, and so long as the state finds it necessary to base its legitimacy upon the demands of sectors of society that value the preservation of traditional social practices. Much of what Jordanian women can hope to accomplish in the future thus rests upon circumstances beyond the control of the women's movement. Even so, the ability of the women's movement to achieve gains for women, along with increasing rates of higher education and political activity among women, make it increasingly likely that the fulfillment of the constitutional promise that "Jordanians shall be equal before the law" will be claimed by more and more Jordanians.

Chapter 9

Government Institutions and Policy Frameworks

Over the past several years, a variety of important new institutions and procedures have greatly improved the state's handling of crimes against women, among other matters. The creation of a government-run shelter has meant that girls and women who are likely victims of honor-related murders are no longer sent to the women's prison at Juweideh for "protective custody." Judges are receiving training in human rights and women's rights. Specialized police institutions are increasingly capable of dealing with domestic violence.

These developments have emerged from an effective collaboration among Jordanian liberals (both inside and outside the public sector), the state and foreign organizations willing to provide funding and training. While sometimes less visible, these changes are as important as the debates over amendments to the laws discussed in earlier chapters. The practical landscape of the law has been altered in ways that both improve women's legal protections in the immediate term and will likely serve as a basis for progress in the longer term. These changes are not, for the most part, radical; there is no equal rights amendment, no dramatic shift in sentencing patterns, no about-face in the attitudes of judges in honor crimes cases. But continual small-scale progress in a number of arenas has amounted to a great deal of progress overall. As a result of some of these innovations, Jordan is increasingly becoming a model for similar developments in other Arab countries.

But while the progress is significant, it is also likely to be constrained in the long run by an approach that situates policies affecting women within a family framework. The rhetoric of the family permeates many policy arenas, and while this is useful in promoting women's interests in a way that forestalls some conservative challenges, it also tacitly accepts the view that women's wellbeing is important for instrumental reasons, not because of the rights of women themselves. Violence against women is addressed on the grounds that the harm it does to women is bad for their families; women's nationality rights are understood as a means of preventing harm to their children; even women's electoral representation is often presented as a means of fostering national development rather than women's own interests. This approach is an effective one but only up to a point because it comes with built-in limitations. Even in the areas where the greatest progress is made, we see a continuation of the careful balancing of progressive and traditionalist claims that reflects the state's dual strands of legitimacy.

The Family Protection Department of the Public Security Directorate

A significant problem in dealing with violence against women, from rape to domestic abuse to honor killings, has been the widespread perception that the police do not take such crimes seriously, that the police are a bastion of conservative and traditional attitudes, thus unlikely to deal sympathetically with women victims in crimes involving sexual or familial issues.[1] As in many countries, women are often reluctant to report domestic abuse to the police out of a belief that the police will not help them (and some women believe that abusive behavior is acceptable), and in fact women who do report such crimes have sometimes found that the police are reluctant to intervene in a "personal matter." In some cases, the police reportedly simply phone the woman's husband or father and ask him to retrieve her from the police station, thus releasing her back into the custody of the person against whom she made the complaint.[2] A 2007 study found that abused women who go to the police are commonly "ridiculed and met with indifference."[3] The situation is similarly deplorable with regard to honor crimes; reports are common of police stations treating confessed honor killers as heroes who carried out a disagreeable but worthy task. According to one officer, most police officers tend to see the victim as the offender, and behave accordingly.[4]

In this context, one of the most notable practical developments of recent years has been the creation of the Public Security Department's Family Protection Department (FPD). The department has now been in operation for a decade and has been one of the best-developed government efforts to address the problem of violence against women.

The initial political impetus for the project came not from the police themselves, nor from other executive agencies or programs seeking to address sex crimes or domestic violence. Instead, the policy was shaped, originally, by personal political connections; it has since become much more institutionalized, but as in the case of

---

1 This depends, to some degree, on the context and social status of the victim. A young American woman who was the victim of a street crime in Amman in the late 1990s reported the crime to her local police station, greatly upset. The station's officers, upon learning that she was in Jordan to study traditional dance forms, quickly gathered together to perform an impromptu *dabka* (traditional dance) to cheer her up. During my own research and travels in Jordan, I have never encountered a police officer who was other than helpful, friendly and professional. On the other hand, I have never had to report a sex crime or family violence, and one's nationality and class also matter; Jordanian and Palestinian friends had low expectations of the police, but the wealthier among them were more confident of good treatment.

2 Interview with Umm Safyan, social worker, Pontifical Mission for Palestine medical clinic, Zarqa, Jordan, May 1999.

3 Cited in Dalya Dajani, "Stakeholders call for regional cooperation to protect victims of domestic abuse," *Jordan Times*, October 21, 2008.

4 Lt. Taghreed Abu-Sarhan, Family Protection Unit, November 1998.

women in the military (see Chapter 7), the personal support of powerful individuals was a chief factor in sparking change in the first place.

The creation of what was originally called the "family protection unit" originated in a crime committed in Jordan in 1996, when a British-Iraqi woman was raped and subsequently treated badly by the Jordanian police officers investigating her complaint. A British newspaper reported the incident, and the story caught the attention of Patricia Salti, a woman of originally British nationality who worked on the staff of (then-Crown) Prince Hassan.[5] Mrs. Salti pursued the issue and arranged, with the support of the prince and others, a training relationship between the British Embassy and the Jordanian police. Two officers (one male and one female) were sent from the United Kingdom to teach a short course to 21 Jordanian officers (both male and female) on sex crimes and child abuse. The British police explained the Family Protection Units that exist in British police forces, and Mrs. Salti secured the support of Prince Hassan for the establishment of such a unit in Jordan.

The Jordanian unit opened on February 7, 1998.[6] It was incorporated into the national police force, the Public Security Directorate, and staffed by regular police officers, male and female, who had received special training on techniques for dealing with sex crimes and cases of abuse. Originally the unit had only one office, in an upper-middle-class neighborhood of Amman; this limited both its visibility and women's access to it as a practical matter. However, all police stations in Amman were required to refer sex assault and child abuse cases to this unit, so the effect of the Family Protection Unit always extended, at least potentially, beyond its original location.

The unit has grown significantly since its creation and is now the Family Protection Department, housed in a dedicated building in western Amman. New Family Protection offices have been opened around the kingdom, in Irbid, Karak, Aqaba, Madaba, Balqa and Zarqa, and four more such units are planned for the future. The unit's original personnel were a commander and second-in-command, with a staff of three female and five male officers in addition to three lower-ranking personnel. As of 2008, there are 300 officers assigned to the unit, in approximately equal numbers of male and female officers.[7] The department dealt with 3,000 cases in 2007, most of which were in Amman; demand for the department's services is so great in the capital that they hope to open another two offices there. The department investigates sexual assaults, child abuse and other crimes of violence against women and children.

5 This account of the unit's establishment was given to me by Mrs Salti in an interview, May 1999. Its main points were confirmed in an interview with officers of the unit.

6 Information on the operation and staffing of the unit was provided by FPU officers in interviews in 1998, 1999 and 2008.

7 It is interesting to note that the FPD was the first police unit in which female officers could work as investigators. Elsewhere, they have been confined to clerical and, in recent years, traffic duties.

In addition to the police personnel assigned to the department, social workers are provided by the Ministry of Social Development. A forensic physician from the national Institute for Forensic Medicine is also attached to the department; he conducts physical exams and autopsies. The department seeks to integrate services to crime victims, drawing not only on police powers of investigation but also on social, medical, legal and conflict-resolution services. As the department has grown, so has its authority; the FPD can now mediate domestic disputes in order to resolve conflicts in a way that protects the parties without going to court or filing criminal charges.[8] Most of the cases that come to the department are now resolved in this manner; an FPD officer contacts a judge about a case; they meet to discuss it, often with the family members concerned, and seek to reach a solution without going to court because "family unity is an important priority."[9] The mediation option does not apply to crimes of obligatory reporting, such as rape, but it is apparently often used in domestic violence situations, in which it is the victim's decision to go to court or not.

At its creation in the late 1990s, the Family Protection Unit was originally instructed to deal with domestic violence complaints. However, the influx of such complaints was so overwhelming that the unit's staff were unable to deal with them; they also felt that they lacked effective training on this issue. The director of Public Security instructed the unit to stop taking domestic violence cases; local police offices remained the only place to report such crimes, but few women choose to do so. The FPU hoped to take domestic violence cases into its purview again in the future, but it was a particularly thorny issue. Until 2007 there were no shelters to which women could be referred, and women often fear reprisals from their families if it becomes known that they have complained to the police. However, the establishment of a government-run shelter in February of 2007 made it possible for the department to deal with domestic violence cases again. The shelter, run by the Ministry of Social Development in a secret location, can accommodate up to 60 women for periods as long as six months; the director of the FPD described it as "very useful" and professionally run. There is also a shelter for children.

The existence of the government's shelter has given the police a new option in protecting women from violence. In past years, as discussed in Chapter 4, women who were believed to be at risk of murder by their families were sent to the women's prison at Juweideh where they were held in "protective custody" indefinitely until, in the government's view, they could safely be released to the custody of a male relative. With the opening of the shelter, the Family Protection Department no longer sends women to Juweideh for protective custody.[10]

---

8 Interview with Col. Mohammad al-Zu'bi, Family Protection Department, Amman, June 2008.

9 Judge Dr. Mohammad al-Tarawneh, interview, Amman, July 2008.

10 Interview with Col. Mohammad al-Zu'bi, Family Protection Department, June 2008.

In addition to criminal investigation, Family Protection officers also engage in a great deal of public outreach, conducting lectures and talking to schoolchildren about violence in the family. This outreach, combined with the growth in the department's size and the opening of new offices, has probably contributed to increased reporting of domestic violence and sex crimes that would, in the past, have remained hidden. Police assistance has been made even more accessible by the establishment of a hotline, 111, through which victims and others can seek the assistance of family protection officers.

The FPD now conducts much of its own training domestically, with support from the British and Danish governments. Officers are still sent abroad for additional training and to engage in exchanges with their colleagues in other countries including the United States, the United Kingdom and Denmark. By the end of 2008, the department plans to have its own dedicated center for training new officers and providing professional development for existing officers. The orientation of the FPD continues to be toward professional development that takes promising ideas from other systems and uses them as applicable in the Jordanian context.

The FPD's approach to training and to cross-profession integration has proven effective, and the department has now trained officers from a number of other countries, including Syria, Sudan, Lebanon, the United Arab Emirates and Qatar. The Jordanian strategy of dealing with sex crimes and domestic violence in the "family protection" rubric is becoming a model for the development of similar institutional approaches and professional practices elsewhere in the region.

This unit is one of the most promising and well-organized government strategies for dealing with violence against women. While activists and others have well-founded complaints about police attitudes toward rape, honor killing and other crimes, the officers of this unit are clearly sensitive to these issues and trained to deal with them. Their attitudes toward victims of such crimes seem to be sympathetic and professional; having met some of the unit's officers, it appears to me that female crime victims now have a means of receiving fair treatment from the police. The officers themselves said even in the early days of the unit that they believed their presence and training was having a gradual sensitizing effect on the police department as a whole although it is unlikely that radical attitudinal changes will take place in the near future.

Judicial Reform and Development

The judiciary has been a high priority in the reforms of the last decade. The primary concern has been with "rule of law" issues such as judicial independence and the operational capabilities of the courts as necessary conditions for economic development. If the courts are incapable of resolving disputes efficiently, and if the outcome of judicial proceedings depends on personal connections and power, potential investors are unlikely to regard Jordan favorably as a place to do business.

Attracting foreign investment is a priority in the current wisdom on economic development, and thus the motives for reforming the judiciary are at least as much economic as law- or rights-related. In September 1999, a few months after King Abdullah II's ascension to the throne, I had the opportunity to ask the king about judicial reforms, having in mind judicial independence and attitudes as they affected trials. He replied that judicial reform was a top priority in his plans but went on to characterize its importance entirely in terms of economic development. As it turns out, several years on, the two concerns go hand in hand; improving the overall professional standards of the judiciary has benefits in many areas of politics and economics.

While judicial reform may have begun largely out of economic motivations, many of the programs have focused on improving individual rights protections. In its 2007 annual report, the Judicial Council identified a number of workshops, co-sponsored by the Council and attended by its judges, including two on family violence and one on human rights and fair trials.[11] The Council has also collaborated on the development of a comprehensive collection of legislation and regulations relating to family issues, designed to be used by researches, policymakers and professionals and a pamphlet entitled "Know Your Rights," intended to "inform people of their constitutional rights."[12]

One of the most important venues for judicial reform has been the Judicial Institute, established in 1988, which trains all judges in Jordan. In addition to initial training of new judges, the Judicial Institute provides continuing education programs and workshops to judges throughout their careers, including opportunities to study abroad. In recent years, the Institute has added training programs on human and women's rights and children and the law, often with the assistance of external grant providers such as the U.S. Agency for International Development, which in 2007 provided US$14 million for political development, $2.5 million of which was designated for judicial training programs.[13] UNICEF and UNIFEM have reportedly also provided resources for the development of judicial training materials.[14] These developments have led to the creation of a new manual for judges on domestic violence, providing a guide to the correct procedures in such cases.

The availability of foreign funds has also been crucial to the refurbishment of court facilities, including a recent upgrade of the main court building in Amman to provide touchscreen video interfaces in courtrooms and public spaces as well as improved computer networking to facilitate court officials' access to case information. The improvements in technology are not merely a matter of

---

11 Judicial Council, *al-Taqrir al-sanawi 'an 'umaal al-mahakim li-'aam 2007* [Annual Report, 2007], 30–31. http://jc.jo/files/docs/ Report2007.pdf. Translation mine.

12 Ibid., 31.

13 Hani Hazaimeh, "US provides $14 million for judicial sector," *Jordan Times*, September 20, 2007.

14 Judge Dr Mohammad al-Tarawneh, interview, Amman, July 2, 2008.

convenience; the recent installation of video equipment in special rooms allows children and sex crime victims to testify without having to appear in an open courtroom in the presence of the defendant, which should increase the successful prosecution of such cases by facilitating victim cooperation.

Another development in court practice has been the increasing availability of judicially-overseen alternative dispute resolution (ADR) methods, as a result of the Mediation Law of 2006. The use of ADR is, in part, an effort to ease the backlog of cases facing the courts, as well as a means of streamlining dispute resolution. Parties in cases settled by mediation report a 98 percent satisfaction rate with the process.[15] As an example of the success of the new ADR mechanisms, I was told of a case involving a foreign company doing business in Jordan, which became embroiled in a dispute that would ordinarily have gone to the courts. Through the use of ADR mechanisms, the dispute was resolved within a month, where the courts would have taken many times longer. The company was pleased and declared its willingness to invest further in Jordan.[16] This outcome reflects one of the purposes of the law, which like other judicial reforms is intended to "create an attractive investment climate."[17]

Another development effort in the judiciary focuses on increasing the number of women judges. Jordan currently has some 700 judges in the state courts and another 150 in the *shari'a* courts. Of these, only 36 are women, but that number is expected to increase in the coming years. The government has set targets for women's inclusion in the judiciary; at the training level, a quota of 15 percent has been approved to ensure women's participation in the Judicial Institute's programs.[18] The Judicial Institute has found, however, that this quota may be unnecessary, as 40 percent of recent enrollees are female, well beyond the minimum stipulated by the quota.[19] However, the government acknowledges that "the problem of bias against one sex remains widespread. There was a clear preference [in a 2005 survey] for male judges over female judges."[20]

While the training of judges, the operation of the courts and efforts at public outreach have undergone significant improvements, there remain important problems in the judiciary. The EU points out in a recent report that "none of the core issues hindering the independence of the judiciary – such as its total financial

15 Mediation Law No. 12 of 2006, passed as part of the Judicial Upgrading Strategy for 2004–2009. Linda Hindi, "Overburdened courts welcome mediation programme," *Jordan Times*, December 18, 2007.

16 Judge Tarawneh, interview, Amman, July 2008.

17 Hindi, "Overburdened courts welcome mediation programme."

18 Khalid Neimat, "Ministry launches fund to prepare highly qualified future judges," *Jordan Times*, November 19, 2007.

19 Ibid.

20 Judicial Council, *al-Taqrir al-sanawi 'an 'umaal al-mahakim fil-mamlakah al-urduniyya al-hashemiyya lil-'aam 2005* [Annual Report on the Activities of the Courts in the Hashemite Kingdom of Jordan, 2005], 61. Available at www.moj.gov.jo/tabid/127/Default.aspx. Translation mine.

and administrative dependence on the Ministry of Justice – have been addressed,"[21] and the ability of the security courts, whose proceedings are secret, to punish civilians for criticism of the government remains apparently unchecked as well.

The National Council on Family Affairs

Developments such as the creation of the FPD and the improvements in judicial training and court resources have required both political will and material support; the importance of foreign partners in providing resources is undeniable, but equally important has been the development of a policy framework that has not only facilitated meaningful institutional development but has coordinated the work of disparate agencies more effectively than is the norm.

In 2001, the Jordanian government established a quasi-nongovernmental organization, the National Council on Family Affairs, to serve as a coordinating body for the work of several government agencies and ministries in the area of "family protection." The Council's membership incorporates government ministers and agency directors, participating ex officio, and civil society organizations in the field of human rights. The NCFA sponsors workshops to develop policy and familiarize employees of diverse ministries with the regulations and procedures that are being developed, and it also conducts and publishes its own research into subjects such as violence against women and children. The NCFA is also an "advocacy body" tasked with mobilizing support for policies and securing funding.[22]

As is obvious from its name, the NCFA operates within the family protection rhetoric currently guiding Jordanian social policy. The organization's description of its work points out that it "regards the family as one unit" and specifies that one of its aims "is to curb domestic violence and secure a stable environment for all family members in line with the religious directives, the cultural heritage and the basic human rights principles."[23] This citing of religion and tradition alongside rights claims is the same careful choice of language and strategy that we have seen from other actors. It should not be dismissed as merely a tactic for thwarting conservative opposition, however, but as a statement that no choice need be made between religion on the one hand and human rights on the other. This does not necessarily suggest that rights are to be limited by what religion requires but rather that religious arguments against human rights are potentially suspect and misguided. This has so far proven a sensible strategy.

21 Commission of the European Communities, Commission Staff Working Document, Accompanying the Communication from the Commission to the Council and the European Parliament 'Implementation of the European Neighbourhood Policy in 2007,' *Progress Report Jordan*, Brussels, 2008,3.

22 See NCFA website at www.ncfa.org.jo.

23 www.ncfa.org.jo.

Effectiveness of the Family Protection Framework

Opposition to all of these reforms has been somewhat muted. Occasional objections have been raised by social and religious conservatives, as in the example of Islamist opposition to CEDAW because, among other things, it would give women and men equal rights over their children. Such opposition has been effective elsewhere in derailing the amendments to the divorce and honor crimes laws but has had little effect on the reforms described above. There are two likely reasons for this: the support of the royal-liberal strand of Jordanian political authority, as evidenced by Queen Rania's involvement with many of these initiatives (in the same way that Princess Basma has been closely associated with the work of the women's organizations) and, perhaps even more importantly, the use of the "family protection" vocabulary.

The reforms dealing with women's rights and sex crimes have been part and parcel of "family-oriented" reforms that are also seen as (and deliberately marketed as) protections for children. While public opinion is divided on honor killings and other crimes against women, there is, of course, no support for child abuse, and thus the strategy of combining the two under the "family" rubric is a sensible one. For example, the video-testimony technology is meant to provide a way for children to testify against those who have harmed them, just as it does in American courtrooms. But it can also be used to obtain testimony from rape victims, who would be unwilling to testify in an open courtroom. This benefits the victim by shielding her from further mental anguish, and it benefits society by making it possible to prosecute more rapists, as fewer cases will dissolve over the reluctance of the victim to give detailed testimony.

The rhetoric of family protection is a way to pursue improvements in women's living situations and legal protections without using women's rights language and thus is likelier to avoid opposition from conservatives. The success of the family protection approach in the Jordanian case is borne out by the policy changes achieved by the institutions described above and also by the selection of the Family Protection Program's Project Management Team for the United Nations Prize in the Field of Human Rights in 2003. The U.N. commended the Jordanian program for helping to "lift the taboo on the subject of domestic violence and promote open debate on issues of human rights, equity and gender."[24]

However, while the emphasis on family unity and protection is useful in policy terms, it may come at a price for individual women. A recent NCFA study of public attitudes found that "most of the respondents stated that a wife should tolerate acts of violence for the sake of the wellbeing of her family and children."[25] These attitudes are not necessarily shared by policymakers, of course, but they

---

24 Quoted in Barbara Borst, "UN announces human rights awards," *Associated Press*, December 2, 2003.

25 Family Violence Study report available at www.ncfa.org.jo, under "Research and Data Resource."

are potentially reinforced by policies that couch women's protection in terms of family unity. The view that abuse can be solved by "reconciling" the family members involved can be taken to suggest that both parties are at fault in causing the abuse – a small step from old-fashioned outright victim blaming.

This view even permeates the Ministry of Social Development's women's shelter, which is called the "Family Reconciliation Centre." The shelter's director reported that the FRC dealt with 251 cases of domestic abuse in its first year of operation, and that "23 per cent of these cases were the result of the mother's weak character in her family."[26] There is no doubt that the center does valuable work in providing services to abused women and genuinely seeks to protect them from further abuse. However, the framework of family protection contains obvious limitations that may ultimately reinforce the social attitudes that underlie the problem of violence against women.

Another interesting element of the "family" rhetoric is its political history; rather than an ancient and unchanging concept integral to local culture, the concept of the family, currently so useful in the state's policies protecting women, has a curiously state-based lineage. Stowasser and Abul-Magd point out that

> the notion of 'family' first appeared in the Arab-Islamic discourse on marriage and divorce during the second half of the nineteenth century. Its initiators were mainly Egyptian reformist and/or nationalist intellectuals…who had encountered European culture and adopted Western (French or British) definitions of family and the family's role in the modern nation-state. The European model emphasized 'family stability' and limited divorce rights, largely on the basis of Christian doctrine, in order to solidify citizen relations for the ultimate purpose of state control and planning in the political and economic realms.[27]

This historical development of the concept of the family is perhaps somewhat ironic, in light of its current incarnation as the "fundamental unit of society" and the encapsulation of all valuable tradition. However, the state's deployment of family rhetoric demonstrates again the degree to which tradition is malleable for political purposes.

Foreign Influences and Domestic Politics

An element that stands out in several of the programs described here is the external factor. The use of foreign funding, from direct government assistance or foreign NGOs, is certainly not unique to Jordan. The question of how far it shapes policy choices is an open one; my own sense of the matter is that foreign funding is

26 Amal Azzam, quoted in Rana Husseini, "Family Reconciliation Centre gives solace to abused victims," *Jordan Times*, January 4, 2008.

27 Stowasser and Abul-Magd (2004), 168.

welcomed when it enables local actors to do what they had wanted to do anyway. Foreign partners themselves are often sensitive to the need to avoid the appearance of domination or cultural imperialism in helping to address domestic problems. For example, the British Council, which is closely involved with the Family Protection Project, acknowledges that "at first there was distrust about the role of the U.K. in matters so central to the social fabric of Jordan" and that "[i]t was important that the project did not cause a backlash."[28] This led them to seek the involvement of the powerful Ministry of Islamic Affairs to train religious counselors in their program, a sensible choice both tactically and substantively.

Perhaps more important than the source of funds is the "borrowing" that arises from the examination of foreign institutions, policies and methods. From the military to the judiciary to the police, Jordanian leaders have been enthusiastic about looking around them for ideas that can be applied within, and tailored to, the domestic context. While some conservatives criticize this approach as damaging to Jordan's own culture, policymakers seem to regard it as a means of developing the most effective policies possible. One consequence of this approach is that in several issue areas, Jordan itself is now in a position to serve as a model, and even a training ground, for other developing countries. The Directorate of Military Women's Affairs and the Family Protection Department have concrete plans to establish such training centers in the near future. This energetic use of foreign exchange relationships has been one of the key factors in policy innovation in the last several years. In the words of a judge involved in the family protection developments, "I am like a bee taking pollen from different flowers to bring to my own garden to make honey."[29]

More Slogans than Change?

The last five years have witnessed three major national reform programs initiated by the regime. In 2003, the "Jordan First" campaign brought together representatives from multiple sectors of public life to identify priorities for political reform. There was some controversy over the name, which was taken by some to imply privileging East Bank Jordanians over Palestinians and by others to imply isolation from regional neighbors at the time of the Iraq war. However, this program may have been the most effective of the three, producing a document containing concrete and specific recommendations such as the reform of the nationality law to allow female citizens to pass their nationality on to their children. Not all of the recommendations of the Jordan First program have been achieved, but some are still being pursued.

In 2005, the king inaugurated the "National Agenda" program, designed to bring conservative and reformist figures together to agree on major issues. Only

28 British Council Development Services, "Family Protection Project, Jordan," 2003, at www.britishcouncil.org/development-family-protection-project-jordan.pdf.

29 Judge Tarawneh, interview, Amman, July 2008.

around two dozen participants were involved, but the process was reportedly highly conflictual and unproductive. The next year, the regime tried again, with the "We are all Jordan" program, but altered its strategy and invited several hundred participants, from all branches of government, civil society and academics. This forum has produced a set of recommendations and an advisory committee meant to shepherd these recommendations into policy and legislation.

Despite some question as to the effectiveness of these reform programs, their mere existence is indicative of an important political choice; the monarch wields sufficient power in the Jordanian system that public consultation is not, strictly speaking, necessary to the formulation of public policy. Even legislative power is sharply circumscribed, and the judiciary has not become as independent as most observers would wish. Why, then, should the king pursue public campaigns designed to solicit – or at least to give the credible appearance of soliciting – input from a range of actors in the public sphere? These programs are very different from actually empowering such actors, of course, which would require the liberalizing of political party, election and speech regulations. Nonetheless, the reform programs indicate a need to appeal to the public on the basis not only of traditional authority but of some degree of popular inclusion. This approach accords well with the Jordanian regime's longstanding practice of stressing national unity in political development and combining both traditionalist and democratic (or at least inclusionary) appeal.

The recent institutional and policy developments in the "family protection" framework reflect the same approach, which is no doubt one of the reasons for their success. The state is walking a careful path, tending to the concerns of conservatives on one side by presenting reforms as designed to strengthen families and tending to the concerns of progressives by providing better protections, and more justice, to victims of sex crimes, domestic violence and honor killings. These reforms generally bolster the "royal-liberal" strand of state legitimacy, but they are carefully managed in a way that avoids undermining the traditionalist aspect of legitimacy. Queen Rania captured this approach by suggesting, in her capacity as NCFA president, that "[i]t would be wise to employ a new formula, combining traditional as well as innovative solutions and practices, that will ensure that the family unit – with all its individual members – continues to be nurtured and preserved, serving as the unshakeable foundation of any healthy and stable society."[30] So long as the state can select the elements of tradition and liberal rights claims that it wishes to satisfy, and plausibly claim to satisfy both, the family protection strategy will provide a secure, but circumscribed, basis for political development.

30 Quoted at NCFA website, www.ncfa.org.jo.

Chapter 10
Conclusions

The findings of this study offer new insights into the legitimacy issues that shape Jordanian political development both for good and for ill. The extent to which the state should enshrine tradition in law and politics, the question of which traditions merit such enshrinement, the extension of rights and the morality of society are all issues integral to the establishment of a stable political system that satisfies demands of both authenticity and justice.

The relevance of the study, however, extends well beyond the Jordanian case. The essential issue in the case examined here is one that is fundamental to the study of politics: what makes a good political system? There is probably nearly universal agreement that political systems should reflect the will of the people they govern, they should be "moral," (although of course the definition of morality will vary enormously over time, place, segment of society, etc.), they should be indigenous rather than externally imposed (in U.N. language, respecting the inherent right of peoples to self-determination) and they should have technical competence in all the administrative tasks of government. Where contestation arises is over the meanings of terms like "the will of the people," "moral" and "indigenous."

This, in terms of the study of legitimacy and development, is where politics becomes interesting because the outcome of this type of contestation will shape not only policy choices and the distribution of power among political actors but the fundamental character of the system itself. Each of these issues, popular will, morality and indigenousness or authenticity, is at the heart of legitimacy issues in Jordanian politics. The Jordanian government claims to represent the general will not by democratic responsiveness but by shared identity and having the nation's best interests at heart. In this case, and indeed in any post-colonial context, a significant amount of political competition takes place around the issue of which interests and values constitute "indigenous" ones; thus, the debate on honor crimes features two opposing sides arguing about whether the law should be eradicated (because it is foreign in origin) or the practice itself should be preserved (because it is a traditional means of ensuring morality).

The requirements of morality also feature significantly in the legitimation issues in Jordan, often in connection to the question of cultural authenticity. Political actors with a traditionalist agenda often claim the mantle of Islam for themselves, thus linking religious morality with cultural tradition, which are logically contrasted with immorality and imported foreign values, respectively. Progressives are more likely to argue against this linkage of tradition with religion, decrying certain practices as traditional but un-Islamic, and to argue that democracy and "modern" politics require a greater protection of rights against outdated practices that are no longer suited to the society. They are arguing about their own interests, certainly, but also about the attributes that a just society and a good political system should exhibit.

Politics is not simply about the pursuit of power, the amassing of advantages and resources for oneself or one's own interests. It is also, and perhaps even more, about the establishment of systems that make sense to people in the way they order society, systems that reflect what people believe and the ways in which they live their lives. This is not to suggest that any system reflects all of its citizens' beliefs or interests, or indeed that any system even succeeds in establishing equal citizenship, in the fullest sense, among all those it governs. Rather, politics at the system level has an inherent requirement of legitimacy, that it be recognized as valid by the people. The "consent of the governed," in the Declaration of Independence's happy phrase, need not be actively solicited, but its absence or even erosion will seriously hamper the stability of the state and will bring into political contestation elements of shared sociocultural meaning that the state has the power to destroy but not to create.

In one sense, then, the Jordanian political system is no different from any other, as it partakes of this basic question of the good political life. In some systems the issue is already largely settled, while in Jordan and elsewhere in the developing world, the nature of the system is, to a greater or lesser degree, an open question. The Jordanian case is significantly different, therefore, from those for which Habermas's theory was intended; it is a developing system both politically and economically. The legitimation issues that I argue are key to the course of Jordanian political development arise precisely because the relationship between the state and the society is still being formulated, but they are analytically similar to the legitimation issues that arise in developed countries according to Habermas's model.

At the most practical level, this study tells us something about the prospects for democracy and the expansion of rights in the Jordanian case. The system remains an authoritarian one, and while progress toward greater democracy and better rights protections has not been absent in recent decades, neither has it been a simple linear trend of improvement over time. A number of factors shape both the political environment and choices made within it. The post-September 11 context has bolstered authoritarian regimes as a bulwark against terrorism, and it has also increased popular dissatisfaction on a number of fronts. In this context, it is not surprising that democracy and rights have been occasionally derailed. By the same token, Jordan's longstanding approach to legitimacy, weaving together the disparate strands of traditionalism and democratic development, serves it particularly well in the present context and is unlikely to be undermined by regional and international events. This legitimation strategy has certainly limited the quality and degree of political contestation and equality of rights, but it has equally served as the means for achieving limited gains in these areas, rather than none at all.

At a second level, I would argue that the study of legitimacy in developing, post-colonial systems warrants further attention for scholars, as it may be a key to explaining democratic (and undemocratic) development in many cases. Most broadly, the findings of this study suggest a need for a more broadly comparative consideration of the force of tradition in contemporary politics, especially where tradition is linked to religion. From the rise of the Christian right in the United States to Hindu nationalism in India, the mobilization of citizens on the basis of a perceived need to protect meaningful sociocultural elements (faith, language, family structures) from the predations of an insufficiently-moral or insufficiently-authentic state is a notable phenomenon. Considering it in the light of legitimation issues and system development should suggest parallels between the politics of development in rich and poor countries, and democratic and non-democratic systems, that can help us better understand not only conditions and policies in a variety of settings, but politics as a common human enterprise.

The Pursuit of Legitimacy

This study demonstrates that while tradition is an important factor in Jordanian political contestation, the course of Jordanian political development should not be characterized as merely the product of a continuing struggle between tradition and modernity. The preceding chapters have shown that many Jordanian laws and policies – regarding honor crimes, nationality, passports and other issues – have the political effect of distancing female citizens from the normal regulatory operations of the state by making them a special category in the relations between state and citizen. Other laws, such as the Personal Status laws, distance women's legal status from the realm of straightforward political demands, placing them within the usefully and deceptively simple constructs of the family and religion, rather than the political order.

On their face, these laws and policies appear to be merely various ways in which the state endorses traditional practices and so fails to act as a fully "modern" political order. However, the state's endorsement of such practices is neither automatic nor uniform over all areas of social tradition. Rather, the state and other actors are making conscious political choices about shared identity (what does it mean to be Jordanian?) and values (the preservation of a moral and/or authentic society). These choices are best understood not as reflexive traditionalism but as attempts to satisfy legitimation needs by managing sociocultural elements, using their social meaningfulness to bolster the connection between citizens and state. As this approach to legitimacy is equally salient in the study of advanced capitalist states, for which the theory was originally intended, its applicability here demonstrates that something more interesting than a simple clash of tradition and modernity is taking place.

The Jordanian state's approach to citizenship, its understanding of individuals' relation to the state, results in the mediation of women's relations with the state through social traditions of male authority over women. This is not a simple reflection of predominant social realities in the political realm; the state does not, after all, replicate or endorse all forms of traditional social hierarchy in its administrative functions. The authority of fathers over sons or tribe leaders over other members, for example, does not formally enter into men's interactions with the state. When a man applies for a passport, no one asks him if his father approves or if his tribe's leader has given permission. Men are individual citizens before the state, while women are regarded as representatives of "cultural tradition," serving as what Mary Ann Tétreault called the "last Bedouins."[1]

Thus gender issues are an important means by which the state seeks to preserve or enhance its legitimacy. However, as the research discussed above indicates, this does not mean that the state engages only in "traditionalist" legitimation through gender issues. Another source of legitimacy is found in the wielding of "forward-thinking, democratic" values. This is one basis for the regime's opposition to honor crimes and domestic violence. Advocacy of women's rights is therefore sometimes couched in terms of compatibility with Islamic teaching or local custom, at other times presented as necessary for the Jordan of the twenty-first century or for the future of democracy and, particularly in the skillful hands of the late King Hussein, sometimes tied to both claims simultaneously.[2] The type of appeal varies, of course, by issue and intended audience, and the state is neither a staunch opponent of women's rights nor a promoter of gender egalitarianism.

The primary goal of the study was to demonstrate this integral importance of sociocultural elements to the maintenance of state legitimacy and to investigate the implications of this for the nature of the developing political system. However, the findings described above also contribute to an understanding of the difference between "tradition" and "tradition-as-politics." The latter phenomenon, whose effects on Jordanian politics are investigated here, is a reification of tradition, in order to make it a basis for political authority and a guide to policy. It posits "tradition" as a fixed and demarcated cultural entity. This is a political position, rather than a scholarly one; where scholars uncritically accept it as synonymous and coterminous with tradition itself, they introduce a politically important epistemological flaw into their work.

The packaging of "tradition" for the purposes of politics is not, however, merely a cynical or disingenuous use of chosen elements of culture in order to promote particular interests. Rather, tradition-as-politics arises out of the way in which we understand traditions; they are elements of social practice that have

---

1 Mary Ann Tétreault, "A State of Two Minds: State Cultures, Women, and Politics in Kuwait," *International Journal of Middle East Studies*, vol. 33, No. 2 (May 2001): 213–216.

2 An excellent example is King Hussein's speech from the throne at the opening of Parliament in 1997. The speech was notable for his condemnation of violence against women, which he denounced as harmful to national development, "an inhuman violation of their basic rights" and unbefitting "our Arab and Islamic society: the society of solidarity." An official English translation of the speech is available at http://www.kinghussein.gov.jo/speeches_letters.html.

continuity over time, and while they are not truly static, we think of them that way because the element of continuity is central to the meaning of tradition. It is this "naturalness" of tradition that makes it desirable as an element in the state's attempts to legitimate itself by borrowing the mantle of meaningful sociocultural elements. The difference between tradition and tradition-as-politics thus goes directly to the issues of legitimacy raised in Habermas's theory.

The Jordanian state's management of sociocultural elements for purposes of legitimacy has the unintended but unavoidable consequences predicted by the theory. It politicizes these formerly "natural" social practices and values, bringing them into the realm of political contestation and demands on the state. The preservation of social practices like paternal and spousal authority over women is consequently not incorporated into state practices without comment but instead gives rise to a lively debate on the proper role of tradition – what actually constitutes "tradition," and the requirements of a political system that is democratizing, or that is Jordanian or that governs a Muslim society. All of these issues are contested rather than consensual despite the state's continual exhortations for national unity, consensus and harmony. The outcome of this contestation and the state's management of it will shape the course of Jordanian political development for the foreseeable future.

Political Prospects for Jordan

So far, this politicization of cultural elements has shaped the legitimacy issues of the Jordanian state without yet producing a "legitimation crisis." Habermas predicted the collapse of the system not as an immediate consequence of legitimation problems but "when the consensual foundations of normative structures are so much impaired that the society becomes anomic."[3] The state's ability to manipulate two strands of hegemonic discourse, the royal-liberal and the "traditional," serve to ground its legitimacy at more than one point in the sociocultural realm. The current legitimacy politics is not about the absence of consensus but, rather, its mobilization around two different poles of legitimacy. The partisans of each position are not alienated, even from the other camp, and may even use the language and tactics of the other discourse to broaden their own appeal. Legitimation crisis in Jordan is not inevitable, and political development has more than one possible course.

However, if the legitimacy of the Jordanian state, and more broadly of the political system and its constituent actors, becomes entirely a matter of success in a battle for cultural legitimacy, then those who define "authentic tradition" will have much more power than others to shape the prospects for democratization. The significance of the politics of legitimacy as played out in issues of gender and

3 Jürgen Habermas, *Legitimation Crisis* (Beacon Press: Boston, 1973) 3.

law is not only about the content of policies and competition of interests but about the power to determine the nature of the political system itself.

The Jordanian system contains the elements upon which to build a democratic system respectful of individual rights and equality before the law; it also has the potential to revert to more coercive authoritarianism, either secular or religio-traditional. In its favor, lively contestation exists over the cultural-legal issues considered by this study likely to be partially determinative of the course of political development, and the very fact of this contestation draws more participants into political life and contributes to the development and representation of a wider variety of interests.

Potential Avenues of Future Research

The Jordanian case offers several lessons about the role of legitimacy in political development. In terms of general theory, rather than regarding democratization as a product of economic development, elite bargaining strategies or some combination of the two, this case suggests that a great deal of contestation is likely to take place over the definition of tradition and the means by which it is to be compatible with other goods like individual freedom, civil rights, and equality before the law. The study of the role of tradition in politics could benefit, therefore, from a reinvigoration; it would, I argue, be more useful to consider tradition one of the variables in legitimacy and thus relevant to general political development rather than to maintain the old dichotomy which has more political force than scholarly value.

The relationship between traditions and legitimacy for state stability and regime type is significant – and not merely because democracy in which rights and participation are limited by traditional social hierarchies is little democracy at all. The contestation over which conception of rights and freedoms should serve as the foundation of the political order is more than merely a negotiation of the "rules of the game." Rather, it is a determinative element in the character of the system itself; the nature of the system will be a product of the legitimacy upon which it rests.

This study is predicated upon the understanding of law as not merely a coercive state tool but both a reflection of social values and a shaper of them. This is the source of its political power and the reason that law is an important arena for the pursuit of political legitimacy. A comprehensive comparative study of law and legitimacy in other Arab countries would be valuable in refining the theory offered here; subsequently, a cross-regional comparison could contribute to the further development of general theory on the politics of law in developing systems and on the incorporation of cultural elements into political legitimacy strategies. This area of research is one of the most promising avenues for increasing our understanding of democracy and its prospects in many types of systems.

I would further suggest that the findings of this study demonstrate the relevance of gender issues to the central questions of political development. Despite decades of interesting and thorough research on gender issues in the Middle East and elsewhere, the field is still considered by many to represent a "special interest" subcategory of politics, in a way that research on other social elements such as class, race and religion is not. This study shows that gender issues, from both traditionalist and reformist perspectives, are connected to the central values in society and politics and can, especially in a developing system, have enormous symbolic and functional significance across a wide variety of political issues.

The importance of culture to political development is not, at the most important level, located in questions such as the compatibility of women's rights and tradition or Islam and democracy, although these are interesting issues in themselves. It is about the creation and operation of political systems that are meaningful to their citizens, that reflect what people understand and value. This political system must be comprehensible to and considered appropriate by its people, and the state must, for its own preservation, work to achieve this legitimacy. The state has a great deal of power to affect the environment in which legitimacy is pursued and contested, both through authoritarian controls common in the developing world and through every state's preeminence in the field of law, wherein social values are given political recognition and coercive power. However, the state cannot create legitimacy out of whole cloth. It must rely on the sociocultural realm for the substance of what is meaningful; this draws the state into a relationship with its society, although not of course with every member or interest within it. The choices made with respect to legitimation, the selection of cultural elements as sources and symbols, are fundamental to politics, particularly in cases wherein the foundations and attributes of the political system are still largely an open question. This relationship of state and society through legitimation is fundamentally important in shaping the nature of the political system; the elevation of legitimacy to a position of greater attention in research and theory-building will serve to improve our understanding of the processes and outcomes of the building of political systems.

Bibliography

____ (1952), *La Nationalité Egyptienne, le Service Militaire, et le Statut des Etrangers – textes législatif et réglementaires* (Alexandria (Egypt): Journal du Commerce et de la Marine).

____ (1983), *Tashria'at al-jinsiyya al-'arabiyya al-suriyya* (Damascus: Khalid bin Walid Press).

____ (1997), "Results of Jordan's Parliamentary Elections, November 4, 1997." <www.jordanembassyus.org/resultsof%20elections.htm>.

____ (2006), "National Report: Jordan Armed Forces 2006," on file with NATO's International Military Staff section <http://www.nato.int/ims/2006/win/pdf/jordan_brief.pdf>.

'Abd al-Fattah, Nabil (1999), "The Anarchy of Egyptian Legal System: Wearing Away the Legal and Political Modernity," in Dupret, Berger and al-Zwaini (eds).

Abu Hassan, Reem and Lynn Welchman (2005), "Changing the Rules? Developments on 'crimes of honour' in Jordan," in Welchman and Hossain (eds).

Abu Odeh, Lama (1996), "Crimes of Honour and the Construction of Gender in Arab Societies," in Mai Yamani (ed.).

____ (1997), "Comparatively Speaking: the 'Honor' of the 'East' and the 'Passion' of the 'West,'" *Utah Law Review* 1997:2, 287–307.

____ (2004), "The Politics of (Mis)recognition: Islamic Law Pedagogy in American Academia," *American Journal of Comparative Law* 52:4, 789–824.

Adams, Charles J. (1983), "Mawdudi and the Islamic State," in John Esposito (ed.), *Voices of Resurgent Islam* (Oxford University Press: New York).

Ahmed, Leila (1992), *Women and Gender in Islam: Historical Roots of a Modern Debate* (New Haven: Yale University Press).

el-Alami, Dawoud S. (2003), "Can the Islamic Device of *Khul'* Provide a Remedy for non-Muslim Women in Egypt?" *Yearbook of Islamic and Middle Eastern Law 2002-2003*, 122–125.

al-Atiyyat, Ibtisam, Musa Shteiwi and Suleiman Sweiss (2005), "Building Democracy in Jordan: Women's Political Participation, Political Party Life, and Democratic Elections," International IDEA (Institute for Democracy and Electoral Assistance) and Arab NGO Network for Development. <http://www.idea.int/publications/dem_jordan/upload/Jordan_country_report_English.pdf>.

Amawi, Abla (2000), "Gender and Citizenship in Jordan," in Joseph (ed.).

____ (2001), *Against All Odds: Jordanian Women, Elections, and Political Empowerment* (Amman: Al-Kutba Institute for Human Development and Konrad Adenauer Foundation).

Amnesty International (2004), Amnesty International Report 2004 – Jordan , 26 May 2004. UNHCR Refworld. <http://www.unhcr.org/refworld/docid/40b5a1f88.html>. Last accessed 18 December 2008.

Anderson, J.N.D. (1952), "Recent Developments in *Shari'a* Law VIII: The Jordanian Law of Family Rights, 1951," *The Muslim World* 42:3, 190–206.

Antoun, Richard (1972), *Arab Village: a Social Structural Study of a Transjordanian Peasant Community* (Bloomington: Indiana University Press).

____ (2000), "Civil Society, Tribal Process, and Change in Jordan: an Anthropological View," *International Journal of Middle East Studies* 32:4, 441–463.

Arabi, Oussama (2001), "The Dawning of the Third Millennium on *Shari'a*: Egypt's Law No. 1 of 2000, or Women May Divorce at Will," *Arab Law Quarterly* 16:1, 2–21.

Arebi, Saddeka (1994), *Women and Words in Saudi Arabia: the Politics of Literary Discourse* (New York: Columbia University Press).

Arnold, Kathryn Christine (2001), "Are the Perpetrators of Honor Killings Getting Away With Murder? Article 340 of the Jordanian Penal Code Analyzed Under the Convention on the Elimination of All Forms of Discrimination Against Women," *American University International Law Review* 16:5, 1343–1409.

Ayubi, Nazih (1995), *Over-stating the Arab State: Politics and Society in the Middle East* (New York: I.B. Tauris).

Bälz, Kilian (1999), "The Secular Reconstruction of Islamic Law: the Egyptian Supreme Constitutional Court and the 'Battle over the Veil' in State-Run Schools," in Dupret, Berger and al-Zwaini (eds).

Bechor, Guy (2007), *The Sanhuri Code, and the Emergence of Modern Arab Civil Law (1932 to 1949)* (Leiden: Brill, 2007).

Benthall, Jonathan (2001), "A Comment on Richard T. Antoun, 'Civil Society, Tribal Process, and Change in Jordan: an Anthropological View,'" *International Journal of Middle East Studies* 33:4, 668–670.

Bill, James A. and Springborg, Robert (1994), *Politics in the Middle East*, 4th edition (New York: HarperCollins).

Blackstone, Sir William, *Commentaries on the Laws of England*. The Avalon Project at Yale Law School <http://www.yale.edu/lawweb/avalon/blackstone/blacksto.htm>.

Botman, Selma (1999), *Engendering Citizenship in Egypt* (New York: Columbia University Press).

Braizat, Faris (2007), "Democracy in Jordan 2007," Public Opinion Poll Unit, Center for Strategic Studies, University of Jordan <http://www.jcss.org/UploadPolling/258.pdf>.

Brand, Laurie (1994), *Jordan's Inter-Arab Relations: the Political Economy of Alliance Making* (New York: Columbia University Press).

____ (1995), "Palestinians and Jordanians: a Crisis of Identity," *Journal of Palestine Studies* 24:4, 46–61.

____ (1998), *Women, the State, and Political Liberalization: Middle Eastern and North African Experiences* (New York: Columbia University Press).

____ (1998), "Women and the State in Jordan: Inclusion or Exclusion?" in Haddad and Esposito (eds).

____ (2003), "Women and the Struggle for Political Opening," in Doumato and Posusney (eds).

Bratton, Michael and van de Walle, Nicolas (1994), "Neopatrimonial Regimes and Political Transitions in Africa," *World Politics* 46:4, 453–489.

British Council Development Services (2003), "Family Protection Project, Jordan" <http://www.britishcouncil.org/development-family-protection-project-jordan.pdf>.

Brown, Nathan J. (1996), "Women and Law in the Arab World," unpublished paper. Cited with permission of author.

____ (1997), *The Rule of Law in the Arab World* (Cambridge: Cambridge University Press).

____ (1998), "Judicial Review and the Arab World," *Journal of Democracy* 9:4, 85–99.

____ (1998), "The Emerging Islamic Constitutionalism," paper presented to Middle East Studies Association, December, 1998. Used with permission.

Brownlee, Jason (2002), "...And Yet They Persist: Explaining Survival and Transition in Neopatrimonial Regimes," *Studies in Comparative International Development* 37:3, 35–64.

Brynen, Rex (1992), "Economic Crisis and Post-Rentier Democratization in the Arab World: the Case of Jordan," *Canadian Journal of Political Science* 25:1, 69–97.

____ (1995), "The Neopatrimonial Dimension of Palestinian Politics," *Journal of Palestine Studies* 25:1, 23–36.

Brynen, Rex, Baghat Korany and Paul Noble (eds) (1995), *Political Liberalization and Democratization in the Middle East, Volume 1: Theoretical Perspectives* (Boulder: Lynne Rienner Publishers).

Bunch, Charlotte (1997), "The Intolerable Status Quo: Violence Against Women and Girls," in *The Progress of Nations*, 1997. UNICEF. <http://www.unicef.org/pon97/women1.htm>.

Butenschun, Nils August, Uri Davis, and Manuel Sarkis Hassassian (eds) (2000), *Citizenship and the State in the Middle East: Approaches and Applications* (Syracuse: Syracuse University Press).

Carroll, Lucy (1996), "Qur'an 2 229: 'A Charter Granted to the Wife'? Judicial *Khul'* in Pakistan," *Islamic Law and Society* 3:1, 91–126.

Central Bank of Jordan (2007), Annual Report 2007 <http://www.cbj.gov.jo> (homepage).

Cheriet, Bouthaina (1996), "Gender, Civil Society and Citizenship in Algeria," *Middle East Report* January–March, 22–26.

Civil Status and Passports Department, Ministry of Interior. Hashemite Kingdom of Jordan "Issuing a First-Time Passport" <http://www.cspd.gov.jo/FT.HTM>. Last accessed 22 December 2008.

Clapham, Christopher (1985), *Third World Politics: an Introduction* (Madison, WI: University of Wisconsin Press).

Clark, Janine (2006), "The Conditions of Islamist Moderation: Unpacking Cross-Ideological Cooperation in Jordan," *International Journal of Middle East Studies* 38:4, 539–560.

Commission of the European Communities (2008), "Progress Report Jordan," Commission Staff Working Document, Accompanying the Communication from the Commission to the Council and the European Parliament 'Implementation of the European Neighbourhood Policy in 2007.' 3 April 2008. Available at <http://ec.europa.eu/world/enp/pdf/progress2008/sec08_396_en.pdf>.

Cotran, Eugene and Mallat, Chibli (eds) (1996), *Yearbook of Islamic and Middle Eastern Law*, vol. 3 (1996–1997) (London: Kluwer Law International).

Cotran, Eugene and Lau, Martin (eds) (2003), "Egypt" country report in *Yearbook of Islamic and Middle Eastern Law*, vol. 9 (2002–2003) (The Hague: Kluwer Law International).

Coulson, Noel J. (1968), "Islamic Law," in Derrett (ed.).

____ (1969), *Conflicts and Tensions in Islamic Jurisprudence* (Chicago: University of Chicago Press).

Crick, Bernard (1992), *In Defense of Politics*, 4th edition (Chicago: University of Chicago Press).

Davis, Uri (1995), "*Jinsiyya* versus *Muwatana*: the Question of Citizenship and the State in the Middle East: the Cases of Israel, Jordan and Palestine," *Arab Studies Quarterly* 17:1 and 2, 19–50.

____ (2000) "State, Nation, and People," in Butenschun et al. (eds).

Department of Statistics, Hashemite Kingdom of Jordan (1996), *Statistical Yearbook* (Amman: n.p.).

Department of Statistics and Ministry of Health, Hashemite Kingdom of Jordan. (1992), Jordan Population and Family Health Survey, 1990. Amman, Department of Statistics, Ministry of Health, in cooperation with Demographic and Health Surveys, IRD/Macro International, Inc.

Department of the (Islamic) Chief Justice (*Da'irat Qadi al-Qudah*), Hashemite Kingdom of Jordan, "*al-Taqrir al-sanawi* 2003" <www.sjd.gov.jo/annual_report2003.html>.

Derrett, J.D.M. (ed.) (1968), *An Introduction to Legal Systems* (London: Sweet and Maxwell).

Directorate of Military Women's Affairs. Jordanian Armed Forces (2003), "Presentation to Defense Department Advisory Committee on Women in the Services," <http://www.dtic.mil/dacowits/briefings/Presentation_WM.dmwa.ppt>.

Doumato, Eleanor Abdella and Posusney, Marsha Pripstein (eds) (2003), *Women and Globalization in the Arab Middle East* (Boulder: Lynne Rienner Publishers).

Duncan, Graeme (ed.) (1989), *Democracy and the Capitalist State* (Cambridge: Cambridge University Press).

Dupret, Baudouin, Berger, Maurits and al-Zwaini, Laila (eds) (1999), *Legal Pluralism in the Arab World* (Boston: Kluwer Law International).

Eickelman, Dale F. and Piscatori, James (2004), *Muslim Politics* (Princeton: Princeton University Press).

Esposito, John L. and Natana J. DeLong-Bas (2001), *Women in Muslim Family Law*, 2nd Edition (Syracuse: Syracuse University Press).

Fadel, Mohammad (2000), "Islamic Law Sources Against Honor Crimes," written for the Islamic Supreme Council of America, 2000 <http://www.islamicsupremecouncil.org>. (no longer available).

FAFO, Department of Statistics (Jordan) and United Nations Population Fund. (2007), "Iraqis in Jordan: their Number and Characteristics," <www.fafo.no/ais/middeast/jordan/IJ.pdf>.

Faqir, Fadia (1997), "Engendering Democracy and Islam in the Arab World," *Third World Quarterly* 18:1, 165–174.

Foucault, Michel (1980), *Power/Knowledge: Selected Interviews and Other Writings, 1972-1977*, Colin Gordon (ed.) (New York: Pantheon Books).

Friedrich, Carl Joachim (1963), *The Philosophy of Law in Historical Perspective*, 2nd edition (Chicago: University of Chicago Press).

Frohmann, Lisa (1997), "Convictability and Discordant Locales: Reproducing Race, Class, and Gender Ideologies in Prosecutorial Decisionmaking," *Law and Society Review* 31:3, 531–555.

Gellner, Ernest (1992), *Postmodernism, Reason and Religion* (London: Routledge).

General Federation of Jordanian Women (1997), "Women's Agenda for the Next Parliamentary Period 1997-2001," in al Kutba Institute and Konrad Adenauer Foundation, "Jordanian Women's Guide to Participation in Public and Political Life."

Gerber, Haim (1994), *State, Society, and Law in Islam: Ottoman Law in Comparative Perspective* (Albany: State University of New York Press).

Ghazi bin Muhammad (Prince) (1999), *The Tribes of Jordan at the Beginning of the Twenty-first Century* (Jordan: Jami'ia turath al-urdun al-baqi).

Gibson, James L. (1989), "Understandings of Justice: Institutional Legitimacy, Procedural Justice, and Political Tolerance," *Law and Society Review* 23:3, 469–496.

Goldberg, Ellis, Resat Kasaba and Joel S. Migdal (eds) (1993), *Rules and Rights in the Middle East: Democracy, Law and Society* (Seattle: University of Washington Press).

Government of Egypt (n.d.), "Facilities Offered by the Ministry of Interior to Egyptian Nationals Living Abroad." <http://www.emigration.gov.eg/GovernmentalServices/ Interior.aspx>. Last accessed 18 December 2008.

Gramsci, Antonio (1971), *Selections from the Prison Notebooks*, Quintin Hoare and Geoffrey Nowell Smith (eds and trans) (New York: International Publishers).

Griffiths, John (1999), Preface essay, in Dupret et al. (eds).

Habermas, Jürgen (1973), *Legitimation Crisis*, Thomas McCarthy (trans) (Boston: Beacon Press).

Haddad, Yvonne Yazbeck (1985), "Islam, Women and Revolution in Twentieth-Century Arab Thought," in Haddad and Findly (eds).

Haddad, Yvonne Yazbeck and Findly, Ellison Banks (eds) (1985), *Women, Religion and Social Change* (Albany: State University of New York).

Haddad, Yvonne Yazbeck and Esposito, John L. (eds) (1998), *Islam, Gender, and Social Change* (New York: Oxford University Press).

Halsa, Adeeb Salaama (1997), *Asas al-tashri'ia wal-nizam al-qada'ii fil-mamlaka al- urduniyya al-hashemiyya* (Amman: n.p.).

Hadawi, Hassan (1994), *Al-jinsiyya wa ahkamuha fil-qanun al-urduni*. (Amman: Dar Majdlawi).

al-Hakim, Tawfik (1987), *Maze of Justice: Diary of a Country Prosecutor* (1947) Abba Eban (trans) (Austin: University of Texas Press).

Hamzeh, A. Nizar (1994), "Qatar: the Duality of the Legal System," *Middle Eastern Studies* 30:1, 79–90.

Hanssen-Bauer, Jon, Pedersen, Jon and Tiltnes, Åge A. (eds). (1998), *Jordanian Society: Living Conditions in the Hashemite Kingdom of Jordan. Report #253* (Oslo: Fafo Institute for Applied Social Science).

Hardacre, Helen (1993), "The Impact of Fundamentalism on Women, the Family and Interpersonal Relations," in Marty and Appleby (eds).

Harik, Ilya (1994), "Pluralism in the Arab World," *Journal of Democracy*, 5:3, 43–56.

Hatem, Mervat (1995), "Political Liberalization, Gender, and the State," in Brynen et al. (eds).

Hélie-Lucas, Marie-Aimée (1994), "The Preferential Symbol for Islamic Identity: Women in Muslim Personal Laws," in Moghadam (ed.).

Hourani, Hani and Abu-Rumman, Hussein (eds) (1996), *The Democratic Process in Jordan. Deliberations of the Conference on the Democratic Process in Jordan – Realities and Prospects, Amman, 31 May–4 June, 1994*. Al-Urdun al-Jadid Research Center. George A. Musleh, trans. (Amman: Sindbad Publishing House).

Hudson, Michael (1977), *Arab Politics and the Search for Legitimacy* (New Haven: Yale University Press).

____ (1995), "The Political Culture Approach to Arab Democratization: the Case for Bringing it Back In, Carefully," in Brynen et al. (eds).

Human Rights Watch (1995), *The Human Rights Watch Global Report on Women's Human Rights* (New York: Human Rights Watch).

____ (2004), "Divorced from Justice: Women's Unequal Access to Divorce In Egypt," 30 November 2004. <http://www.hrw.org/en/reports/2004/11/30/divorced-justice>. Last accessed 18 December 2008.

Huntington, Samuel (1996), *The Clash of Civilizations and the Remaking of World Order* (New York: Simon & Schuster).

Inter-American Commission on Human Rights (1999), Third Report on the Situation of Human Rights in Colombia. <http://www.cidh.org/women/chapter-12.htm>.

_____ (2000), Second Report on the Situation of Human Rights in Peru. <http://www.cidh.org/women/chapter7.htm>.

_____ (2001), Fifth Report on the Situation of Human Rights in Guatemala, document OEA/Ser.L/V/II.III. <http://www.cidh.oas.org/countryrep/Guate01eng/TOC.htm>.

International IDEA and Stockholm University (n.d.), Global Database of Quotas for Women. <http://www.quotaproject.org/country.cfm>.

IRIN (Integrated Regional Information Networks), UN Office for the Coordination of Humanitarian Affairs (2004), "Jordan: Iraqi domestic violence victims find shelter," 8 March. < http://www.irinnews.org/report.aspx?reportid=23635>.

Islamic Resistance Movement (Hamas) (1993), Charter. Muhammad Maqdsi, trans. *Journal of Palestine Studies* (22:4) 122–134.

Jabbour, Muhammad (2000), *al-Jara'im al-waqi'ah 'ala al-ashkhas fi qanun al-'uqubat al-urdunii: dirasah muqaranah* (Amman: Dar al-thaqafah lil-nashr wa-al-tawzi').

Jaradat, Saleh Ahmad (1998), *Huquq al-muwatin al-urdunii*, 1st edition (Jordan: Matba'a al-Ruzna).

Jewett, Jennifer (1996), "The Recommendation of the International Conference on Population and Development: The Possibility of the Empowerment of Women in Egypt," *Cornell International Law Journal* 29:1, 191–223.

Jordan Center for Social Research (2005), "Poll: Democratic Transformation and Political Reform in Jordan," September 2005, available at <http://www.jordanembassyus.org/new/mep/poll/jcsr092005.htm>.

Jordanian National Committee for Women (n.d.) Selected documents <www.jncw.jo>.

Jordanian Women's Union <http://www.jwu.itgo.com>.

Joseph, Suad (1996), "Gender and Citizenship in Middle Eastern States," *Middle East Report*, January-March, 4–10.

Joseph, Suad (ed.) (2000), *Gender and Citizenship in the Middle East* (Syracuse: Syracuse University Press).

Judicial Council, Hashemite Kingdom of Jordan (2005), *al-Taqrir al-sanawi 'an 'umaal al-mahakim fil-mamlaka al-hashemiyya al-'urduniyya lil-'aam* 2005. <http://jc.jo/files/06042006final_Annual_Report_with_background.pdf>.

____ (2006), *al-Taqrir al-sanawi 'an 'umaal al-mahakim li-'aam* 2006 <http://jc.jo/files/docs/jc-report-2006.pdf>.

____ (2007), *al-Taqrir al-sanawi 'an 'umaal al-mahakim li-'aam* 2007 <http://jc.jo/files/docs/Report2007.pdf>.

Kandiyoti, Deniz (ed.) (1991), *Women, Islam and the State* (Philadelphia: Temple University Press).

Khoury, Nabil F. and Moghadam, Valentine M. (eds) (1995), *Gender and Development in the Arab World*. Published for the United Nations University, World Institute for Development Economics Research by Zed Books and United Nations University Press, Tokyo.

Kirschke, Linda (2007), "Semipresidentialism and the Perils of Power-Sharing in Neopatrimonial States," *Comparative Political Studies* 40:11, 1372–1394.

al Kutba Institute for Human Development and the Konrad Adenauer Foundation (1998), *Jordanian Women's Guide to Participation in Public and Political Life* Samira Kawar (trans) (Amman, Al-Kutba Institute for Human Development and Konrad Adenauer Foundation.)

Laitin, David (1986), *Hegemony and Culture: Politics and Religious Change among the Yoruba*. (Chicago: University of Chicago Press).

Lawrence, Philip K. (1989), "The State and Legitimation: the Work of Jurgen Habermas," in Duncan (ed.)

Layish, Aharon (1988), "Customary 'Khul'' as Reflected in the 'Sijill' of the Libyan '*Shari'a*' Courts," *Bulletin of the School of Oriental and African Studies*, University of London 51:3, 428–439.

Layne, Linda (1994), *Home and Homeland: the Dialogics of Tribal and National Identities in Jordan*. (Princeton: Princeton University Press).

Lazarus-Black, Mindie and Hirsch, Susan F. (1994), *Contested States: Law, Hegemony and Resistance* (London: Routledge).

Lerner, Daniel (1958), *The Passing of Traditional Society* (London: Collier-Macmillan Ltd.)

Liebesny, Herbert J. (1949), "Literature on the Law of the Middle East," *Middle East Journal* 3:4, 461–469.

____ (1983), "Judicial Systems in the Near and Middle East: Evolutionary Development and Islamic Revival," *Middle East Journal* 37:2, 202–217.

Lynch, Marc (1999), *State Interests and Public Spheres: the International Politics of Jordan's Identity* (New York: Columbia University Press).

Marty, Martin E. and Appleby, R. Scott (1993), *Fundamentalisms and Society: Reclaiming the Sciences, the Family, and Education. The Fundamentalism Project* (Chicago: University of Chicago Press).

Massad, Joseph (2001), *Colonial Effects: the Making of National Identity in Jordan* (New York: Columbia University Press).

Matoesian, Gergory M. (1993), *Reproducing Rape: Domination through Talk in the Courtroom* (Chicago: University of Chicago Press).

Mayer, Ann Elizabeth (1995), "Reform of Personal Status Laws in North Africa: a Problem of Islamic or Mediterranean Laws?" *Middle East Journal* 49:3, 432–446.

Merry, Sally Engle (1988), "Legal Pluralism," *Law and Society Review* 22:5, 869–896.

Merryman, John Henry (1985), *The Civil Law Tradition: an Introduction to the Legal Systems of Western Europe and Latin America*, 2nd edition (Stanford: Stanford University Press).

Miccio, G. Kristian (2000), "Notes from the Underground: Battered Women, the State, and Conceptions of Accountability," *Harvard Women's Law Journal* 23, 133–172.

Migdal, Joel (1988), *Strong Societies and Weak States: State-Society Relations and State Capabilities in the Third World* (Princeton: Princeton University Press).

Ministry of Justice, Hashemite Kingdom of Jordan (1997), *Judicial Institute of Jordan* (Amman: Ministry of Justice).

Mogannam, E. Theodore (1952), "Developments in the Legal System of Jordan," *Middle East Journal* 6:2, 194–206.

Moghadam, Valentine M. (1993), *Modernizing Women: Gender and Social Change in the Middle East* (Boulder: Lynne Rienner).

____ (1994), "Introduction: Women and Identity Politics in Theoretical and Comparative Perspective," in Moghadam (ed.).

Moghadam, Valentine M. (ed.) (1994), *Identity Politics and Women: Cultural Reassertions and Feminisms in International Perspective* (Boulder: Westview Press).

Moghadam, Valentine M. (1999), "Gender, National Identity and Citizenship: Reflections on the Middle East and North Africa," *Comparative Studies of South Asia, Africa and the Middle East* 19:1, 137–157.

Molyneux, Maxine (1995), "Women's Rights and Political Contingency: the Case of Yemen, 1990–1994," *Middle East Journal* 49:3, 418–431.

Namour, Muhammad Sa'eed (2004), *Dirasat fi fiqh al-qanun al-jina'iyy* (Amman: Dar al-thaqafa).

Nanes, Stephanie Eileen (2003), "Fighting Honor Crimes: Evidence of Civil Society in Jordan," *Middle East Journal* 57:1, 112–129.

Nasir, Jamal J. (1986), *The Islamic Law of Personal Status* (London: Graham and Trotman).

National Center for Human Rights (Jordan) (2006) Human Rights Status Report, 2005. Available through <http://www.nchr.org.jo> (homepage). Last accessed December 2008.

____ (2008) Human Rights Status Report, 2007. Available through <http://www.nchr.org.jo> (homepage).

National Council on Family Affairs (n.d.), Family Violence Study report. Available through <http://www.ncfa.org.jo> (homepage), under "Research and Data Resource."

National Democratic Institute for International Affairs (2003), "Middle East and North Africa: NDI's Program with Women Candidates in Jordan's June 2003 Parliamentary Election," July 2003. <http://www.ndi.org/worldwide/mena/jordan/jordan_women_pf.asp>.

Naveh, Immanuel (2001), "The Tort of Injury and Dissolution of Marriage at the Wife's Initiative in Egyptian Mahkamat al-Naqd Rulings," *Islamic Law and Society* 9:1, 16–41.

Norton, Augustus Richard (ed.) (1995), *Civil Society in the Middle East* (New York: E.J. Brill).

Nourse, Victoria F. (2002), "Law's Constitution: a Relational Critique," *Wisconsin Women's Law Journal* 17:1, 23–56.

Papanek, Hanna (1994), "The Ideal Woman and the Ideal Society: Control and Autonomy in the Construction of Identity," in Moghadam (ed.).

Parliament of the Hashemite Kingdom of Jordan (2006), "*al-Nas al-kamila li-wathiqa wa burnamij 'amal 'Kulna al-'Urdun'*," <http://parliament.jo/pdf/w4.doc>.

Putnam, Robert D. (1993), *Making Democracy Work: Civic Traditions in Modern Italy* (Princeton: Princeton University Press).

Quinney, Richard (1970), *The Social Reality of Crime* (New York: Little, Brown and Company).

Randall, Sara and Nawaf Khalaldeh (1998), "The Population of Jordan," in Jon Hanssen-Bauer, Jon Pedersen and Åge A. Tiltnes (eds), *Jordanian Society: Living Conditions in the Hashemite Kingdom of Jordan* (Oslo: Fafo Institute for Applied Social Science).

Randall, Vicky and Theobald, Robin (1998), *Political Change and Underdevelopment: a Critical Introduction to Third World Politics*, 2nd edition (Durham: Duke University Press).

Razzaz, Omar (1994), "Contestation and Mutual Adjustment: The Process of Controlling Land in Yajouz, Jordan," *Law and Society Review* 28:1, 7–39.

Rishmawi, Mona (1986), "The Legal Status of Palestinian Women in the Occupied Territories," in Toubia (ed.).

Robinson, Glenn (1997), "Can Islamists be Democrats? The Case of Jordan," *Middle East Journal* 51:3, 373–88.

____ (1998), "Defensive Democratization in Jordan," *International Journal of Middle East Studies* 30:3, 387–410.

Roskin, Michael G. and Coyle, James J. (2008), *Politics of the Middle East: Cultures and Conflicts*, 2nd edition (Saddle River, NJ: Prentice Hall).

Ruane, Rachel A. (2000), "Murder in the Name of Honor: Violence Against Women in Jordan and Pakistan," *Emory International Law Review* 14:3, 1523–1580.

Ruggi, Suzanne (1998) "Commodifying Honor in Female Sexuality: Honor Killings in Palestine," *Middle East Report* 12–15 (Spring).

Sabbagh, Suha (1996), *Arab Women: Between Defiance and Restraint* (New York: Olive Branch Press).

Said, Edward (1978), *Orientalism* (New York: Pantheon Books).

al-Sayyid, Mustapha Kamel (1995), "The Concept of Civil Society and the Arab World," in Brynen et al. (eds).

Schacht, Joseph (1964), *An Introduction to Islamic Law* (Oxford: Clarendon Press).

____ (1970), "Law and Justice," in Holt, Lambton and Lewis (eds), *Cambridge History of Islam*, vol. 2, part 8 (Cambridge: Cambridge University Press).

Schwedler, Jillian (ed.) (1995), *Toward Civil Society in the Middle East* (Boulder: Lynne Rienner).

Schwedler, Jillian (2001), "Islamic Identity: Myth, Menace, or Mobilizer?" *SAIS Review* 21:2, 1–17.

Sfeir, George N. (1998), "Basic Freedoms in a Fractured Legal Culture: Egypt and the case of Nasr Hamid Abu Zayd," *Middle East Journal* 52:3, 402–414.

____ (1997), *Modernization of the Law in Arab States* (San Francisco: Austin and Winfield Publishers).

____ (1988), "Source of Law and the Issue of Legitimacy and Rights," *Middle East Journal*, 42:3, 436–446.

Shakatreh, Hussein (1995), "Determinants of Female Labour-Force Participation in Jordan," in Khoury and Moghadam (eds).

Shami, Seteney (1990), *Women in Arab Society: Work Patterns and Gender Relations in Egypt, Jordan and Sudan* (Providence, R.I.: UNESCO).

Shehadeh, Lamia Rustum (1998), "The Legal Status of Married Women in Lebanon," *International Journal of Middle East Studies* 30:4, 501–519.

Shelley, Mary Lyndon (1989), *Feminism, Marriage and the Law in Victorian England* (Princeton: Princeton University Press).

Shryock, Andrew (1997), *Nationalism and the Genealogical Imagination: Oral History and Textual Authority in Tribal Jordan* (Berkeley: University of California Press).

Sonbol, Amira el-Azhary (1998), "Questioning Exceptionalism: *Shari'a* Law," *Arab Studies Journal* 6:1, 76–86.

Spatz, Melissa (1991), "A 'Lesser' Crime: A Comparative Case Study of Legal Defenses for Men Who Kill Their Wives," *Columbia Journal of Law and Social Problems* 24:4, 597–638.

Stowasser, Barbara Freyer and Abul-Magd, Zeinab (2004), "*Tahlil* Marriage in *Shari'a*, Legal Codes, and the Contemporary *Fatwa* Literature," in Stowasser and Haddad (eds).

Stowasser, Barbara Freyer and Haddad, Yvonne Yazbeck (eds) (2004), *Islamic Law and the Challenges of Modernity* (Walnut Creek, CA: Alta Mira Press).

Taraki, Lisa (1996), "Jordanian Islamists and the Agenda for Women: Between Discourse and Practice," *Middle East Studies* 32:1, 140–58.

Tetréault, Mary Ann (2000), "Gender, Citizenship, and State in the Middle East," in Butenschon et al. (eds).

____ (2001), "A State of Two Minds: State Cultures, Women, and Politics in Kuwait," *International Journal of Middle East Studies* 33:2, 203–220.

Tong, Rosemary (1989), *Feminist Thought: a Comprehensive Introduction* (Boulder: Westview Press).

Toubia, Nahid (ed.) (1986), *Women of the Arab World: the Coming Challenge* (London: Zed Books).

Tucker, Judith (ed.) (1993), *Arab Women: Old Boundaries, New Frontiers* (Bloomington: Indiana University Press).

Tucker, Judith (1998), *In the House of the Law: Gender and Islamic Law in Ottoman Syria and Palestine* (Berkeley: University of California Press).

United Nations. Convention on the Elimination of All Forms of Discrimination Against Women. Committee on the Elimination of All Forms of Discrimination Against Women. "Initial reports of States Parties: Jordan," (CEDAW/C/JOR/1) 10 November 1997. <http://daccessdds.un.org/doc/UNDOC/GEN/N97/325/54/PDF/N9732554.pdf?OpenElement>.

United Nations. Convention on the Elimination of All Forms of Discrimination Against Women. Committee on the Elimination of All Forms of Discrimination Against Women. "Second periodic reports of States parties: Jordan," (CEDAW/C/JOR/2) 26 October 1999. <http://daccessdds.un.org/doc/UNDOC/GEN/N00/223/96/PDF/N0022396.pdf?OpenElement>.

United Nations Development Programme (2008), Human Development Reports for 2007/2008. <http://hdr.undp.org/en/statistics/>.

United Nations Economic and Social Council (1995), Report on Crime Prevention and Criminal Justice, 8 June. <www.un.org/documents/ecosoc/docs/1995/e1995-78.htm>.

United States Agency for International Development. USAID in Jordan (2006), "Health." <http://jordan.usaid.gov/sectors.cfm?inSector=20> Last updated 12 June 2006.

United States Department of State. Bureau of Democracy, Human Rights and Labor (1999),Country Reports on Human Rights Practices for 1999. <http://www.state.gov/g/drl/rls/hrrpt/>.

_____ (2002),Country Reports on Human Rights Practices. <http://www.state.gov/g/drl/rls/hrrpt/>.

_____ (2003), Country Reports on Human Rights Practices. <http://www.state.gov/g/drl/rls/hrrpt/>.

_____ (2007), Country Reports on Human Rights Practices. <http://www.state.gov/g/drl/rls/hrrpt/>.

Warrick, Catherine (2005), "The Vanishing Victim: Criminal Law and Gender in Jordan," *Law & Society Review* 39:2, 315–348.

Weber, Max (1946), "Politics as a Vocation," in *From Max Weber: Essays in Sociology*, H.H. Gerth and C. Wright Mills (eds and trans) (New York: Oxford University Press).

Weinstein, Jeremy D. (1986), "Adultery, Law and the State: a History," *Hastings Law Journal* 38:1, 195–238.

Welchman, Lynn (1988), "The Development of Islamic Family Law in the Legal System of Jordan," *International and Comparative Law Quarterly* 37:4, 868–886.

____ (2007), *Women and Muslim Family Laws in Arab States* (Amsterdam: Amsterdam University Press).

Welchman, Lynn and Hossein, Sara (eds) (2005), *'Honour': Crimes, Paradigms, and Violence Against Women* (London: Zed Books).

WIDtech: A Women in Development Technical Assistance Project (1998), "Women and Development in Jordan: a review of current activities and future opportunities" (Washington, DC: n.p).

Yamani, Mai (ed.) (1996), *Feminism and Islam: Legal and Literary Perspectives* (New York: NYU Press).

Laws and Treaties

Jordanian Law

Constitution of Transjordan, 1947. Unofficial English translation, published in *Middle East Journal*, July 1947, 1:3.
Constitution of Jordan, 1952.
Law of Jordanian Nationality, No. 6 for the year 1954.
Penal Code, Law No. 16 for the year 1961.
Jordanian Civil Code of Muslim Jurisprudence, 1976.
Personal Status Law, No. 61 of 1976.
Law of Elections to the House of Representatives, No. 22 for 1986.
Article 9 of Temporary Law, No. 86 for the year 2001.
Law No. 82 for the year 2001, Amending the Personal Status Law (provisional).
Passports Law, No. 5 for the year 2003 (provisional).
Protection from Family Violence Law, No. 6 for the year 2008.
Other Arab law:
Ottoman Law of Nationality (1869).
Constitution of the Arab Republic of Egypt, as amended 1980.
Decret-Loi sur la Nationalité Egyptienne du 26 mai 1926
Decree-Law No. 19 of 1929 (Egyptian Nationality).
Penal Code (Egypt), Article 291 (Law No. 58 of 1937).
Loi n. 160 de 1950, relative a la nationalité égyptienne (as modified by Law No. 194 of 1951)
Law No. 26 of 1975 Concerning Egyptian Nationality.

International Law

Treaty of Lausanne (1923)
Agreement of 5 April 1954, Concerning some of the Rules of Nationality among the States of the Arab League
United Nations Convention on the Elimination of All Forms of Discrimination Against Women (1979)

Newspaper Articles

____ (1998), "Endorsement of controversial amendment on women's right to passports expected 'soon'," *Jordan Times*, 30 August.

____ (1999), "Egypt's president voids law setting free rapists who marry victim," *Associated Press*, 5 April.

____ (1999), "Legal loophole for rapists closed," *Cairo Times*, 28 April.

____ (1999), "Brother waits three years to cleanse family honor," *Arab Daily* (Jordan), 23 May.

____ (1999), "Government demands that veiled women show faces in upcoming municipal elections," *Jordan Times*, 12 July 12.

____ (1999), "Women appeal to House speaker for help in securing women's quota," *Jordan Times*, 26 July .

____ (2004), "Women academics and professionals discuss Jordan's national strategy for women," *Jordan Times*, 25 March.

____ (2006), "Gov't tasked with enacting 'We are All Jordan' recommendations," *Jordan Times*, 6 August.

____ (2007), "New female council member wins seat with zero votes," *Jordan Times*, 3 August.

____ (2007), "Islamists slam women's rights convention," *Agence France Presse* in the *Jordan Times*, 6 August.

____ (2007), "Justice ministry launches Ramadan radio campaign," *Jordan Times*, 16 September.

____ (2008), "Knowledge network seeks to empower female municipal council members," *Jordan Times*, 28 October.

____ (2008), "*Irtifa'a 'adaad al-nisa' al-talibat lil-khul' fil-'urdun*," *Laha*, 3 November, available through <http://www.lahaonline.com> (homepage).

Abu-Nasr, Donna (2000), "Family honor more important than life for some," *Associated Press*, 28 June.

Aloul, Sahar (2004), "House rejects khuloe law by a narrow margin," *Jordan Times*, 28 June.

Ashour, Magda (1998), "Feminists, IAF welcome new draft law on women's right to passport," *Jordan Times*, 22 June.

Ayyoub, Tareq (1998), "Ma'an riots continue; King warns Jordan will not tolerate instigation of violence," *Jordan Times*, 22 February.

____ (1998), "CBJ annual report details Jordan's '97 economic, financial performance," *Jordan Times*, 16 November.

Baghat, Hossam (2001), "Living on the Margins: a parliamentary proposal brings the long-ignored issue of citizenship to the fore," *Cairo Times*, 10–16 May.

Boncompagni, Hala (2003), "Jordanian women campaign for rights revoked by parliament," *Agence France Presse*, 25 August.

Borst, Barbara (2003), "UN announces human rights awards," *Associated Press*, 2 December.

Brooke, James (1981), "Machismo on Trial: the feminist backlash to Brazil's 'crimes of passion,'" *Washington Post*, 6 December.

Brooke, Jim (1991), "'Honor' Killing of Wives is Outlawed in Brazil," *New York Times*, 29 March.

Cambanis, Thanassis (2007), "Jordan, Fearing Islamists, Tightens Grip on Elections," *New York Times*, 11 November.

Ciriaci, Francesca and Ben Hussein, Mohammad (1999), "Rural residents show more enthusiasm than urban counterparts in elections," *Jordan Times*, 15–16 July.

Dajani, Dalya (2008), "Stakeholders call for regional cooperation to protect victims of domestic abuse," *Jordan Times*, 21 October.

Gavlak, Dale (2007), "Jordan appeals for help in dealing with Iraqi refugees," *Washington Post*, 27 July.

Halaby, Jamal (2003), "Women's rights plan rejected in Jordan," *Associated Press*, 5 August.

Hamdan, Dina (2000), "King expected to call extraordinary session," *Jordan Times*, 23 February.

Hazaimeh, Hani (2007), "US provides $14 million for judicial sector," *Jordan Times*, 20 September.

Hindi, Linda (2007), "Overburdened courts welcome mediation programme," *Jordan Times*, 18 December.

Husseini, Rana. (1998), "New penal code to be tougher on crimes against women, children – justice minister," *Jordan Times*, 18 February.

____ (1999a), "Man released after serving one year for murder of wife," *Jordan Times*, 21 March.

____ (1999b), "Criminal Court upholds 'fit of fury' arguments," *Jordan Times*, 25–26 March.

____ (1999c), "Two women killed in reported 'honour crimes'," *Jordan Times*, 14 April.

____ (1999d), "Governor reiterates demand that women uncover faces in tomorrow's municipal elections," *Jordan Times*, 13 July.

____ (1999e), "Justice ministry committee cancels article allowing for reduced penalty for honour crimes," *Jordan Times*, 22–23 July.

____ (1999f), "Courts sentence man to one year after killing sister with car, three men to five months after shooting," *Jordan Times*, 31 July.

____ (1999g), "Man kills married sister in Irbid," *Jordan Times*, 18 November.

____ (2000a), "Sabeel to publish survey on 'crimes of honour,'" *Jordan Times*, 22 February.

____ (2000b), "Al Sabeel survey weighs in against amending Article 340," *Jordan Times*, 23 February.

____ (2000c), "Boy, 13, claims honour crime in strangulation of sister, 14," *Jordan Times*, 24 February.

____ (2000d), "Opposition to Article 340 driven by 'Zionists, Western interests,' says Oweideh," *Jordan Times*, 25 February.

____ (2000e), "Lawyers, judges, intellectuals condemn national campaign against Article 340," *Jordan Times*, 10 March.

____ (2000f), "Deputy accuses West, Zionists of instigating campaign against 'honour crimes," *Jordan Times*, 20 May.

____ (2000g), "Married woman killed by brother in reported 'crime of honour,'" *Jordan Times*, 20 May.
____ (2001a), "Abused women to have safe haven within three months," *Jordan Times*, 26 April.
____ (2001b), "Deir Alla woman slain in suspected honor crime," *Jordan Times*, 4 November.
____ (2002a), "Women activists set their eyes on 2002 polls after positive legislative changes," *Jordan Times*, 3 January.
____ (2002b), "Murder charge reduced to misdemeanor in Azraq crime of honour case," *Jordan Times*, 12 June.
____ (2002c), "Ministry announces first women's shelter to open in 6 months," *Jordan Times*, 4 September.
____ (2002d), "'Crimes of Honour': One year in, amendments to Article 340 appear to have made little difference," *Jordan Times*, 22 December.
____ (2003a), "Quota system leaves bad taste in mouths of capital candidates," *Jordan Times*, 15 July.
____ (2003b), "Family Reconciliation House to open soon," *Jordan Times*, 7 December.
____ (2004a), "Family Reconciliation House to open soon," *Jordan Times*, 9 June.
____ (2004b), "Gov't working to eliminate legislative discrimination against women – Daoudiyeh," *Jordan Times*, 27 June.
____ (2004c), "Interior Ministry seeks cooperation to put an end to honour crimes," *Jordan Times*, 29 June.
____ (2004d), "Amendments to Penal Code proposed," *Jordan Times*, 7 July.
____ (2007a), "Activists focus on women's priorities," *Jordan Times*, 5 June.
____ (2007b), "Four charged with complicity in premeditated murder," *Jordan Times*, 20 August.
____ (2007c), "Touq reviews CEDAW with women's groups," *Jordan Times*, 28 August.
____ (2007d), "Judicial system to have face-lift by 2009 – minister," *Jordan Times*, 24 September.
____ (2007e), "Family ties dominate women's choice, but new tone sensed," *Jordan Times*, 21 November.
____ (2007f), "Women activists see Jamaani's win good sign," *Jordan Times*, 22 November.
____ (2007g), "Women seek equal rights under Citizenship Law," *Jordan Times*, 28 December.
____ (2008a), "Family Reconciliation Centre gives solace to abused victims," *Jordan Times*, 4 January.
____ (2008b), "25-year-old man handed 10-year term for rape, indecent exposure," *Jordan Times*, 4 February.
____ (2008c), "Man gets 15 years for abduction, rape," *Jordan Times*, 5 February.

____ (2008d), "Activists hopeful demands will be met," *Jordan Times*, 3 March.

____ (2008e), "Women's movement urged to push for motherhood fund," *Jordan Times*, 10 March.

____ (2008f), "Egyptian gets two months for murdering his Jordanian wife," *Jordan Times*, 4 April.

____ (2008g), "Man charged with killing daughter," *Jordan Times*, 11 April.

____ (2008h), "Man convicted of murdering daughter walks free," *Jordan Times*, 1 May.

____ (2008i), "Man charged with premeditated murder of his younger sister," *Jordan Times*, 11 May.

____ (2008j), "Campaign seeks to increase women's awareness about their legal rights," *Jordan Times*, 1 July.

____ (2008k), "19-year-old handed reduced sentence for murdering his sister," *Jordan Times*, 23 September.

____ (2008l), "Man charged in manslaughter of his niece," *Jordan Times*, 5 October.

____ (2008m), "40-year-old man sentenced to death for raping minor," *Jordan Times*, 30 October.

Husseini, Rana and Hamdan, Dina (2000), "Senate upholds decision on Article 340, reject gun draft law," *Jordan Times*, 22 February.

Jehl, Douglas (1999), "For Shame: a special report: Arab honor's price: a woman's blood," *New York Times*, 20 June.

Johnston, Cynthia (1999), "Egyptian law penalises children of foreign men," *Reuters*, *Jordan Times*, 22 May.

Khatatbeh, Kholoud (2006), "*al-Khu' yumathilu 80% qadayaa al-'urduniyyat al-manthura 'amam al-mahakim*," *Ad-Dustour* (Jordan), 23 December.

Khatib, Ahmad (2007), "Record number of women running in Jordan polls," *Agence France Presse*, 20 November.

Luck, Taylor (2008), "New campaign to raise awareness on women's rights," *Jordan Times*, 21 February.

MacFarquhar, Neil (2001), "Egyptian mothers fight for foreign offspring's rights," *New York Times* (online), 14 May.

Murad, Nermeen (2008), "Not a full Jordanian citizen," *Jordan Times*, 21 April.

Neimat, Khalid (2007), "Ministry launches fund to prepare highly qualified future judges," *Jordan Times*, 19 November.

el-Tablawy, Tarek (1999), "Egypt debates rape law," *Associated Press*, 6 April.

_____ (1997), "Bride pays with life for 'sullying' family honor in Egypt," *Associated Press*, 17 August.

Wazani, Noura (1999), "Article 340 of the Criminal Law is not fair to women," *Arab Daily* (Jordan), 23 May.

Yehia, Ranwa (1999), "Getting away with murder," *Daily Star* (Jordan), 27 August.

Other Materials

King Hussein (1997), "Speech from the Throne, Opening of the Thirteenth Parliament," 29 November 1997, http://www.kinghussein.gov.jo/speeches_letters.html.

United States Supreme Court Cases:

Miller v. Albright 523 U.S. 420 (1998).

Nguyen v. INS 533 U.S. 53 (2001).

Index